Universal Methods of Design

100 Ways to Research Complex Problems, Develop Innovative Ideas, and Design Effective Solutions

Bella Martin
Bruce Hanington

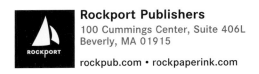

Rockport Publishers
100 Cummings Center, Suite 406L
Beverly, MA 01915

rockpub.com • rockpaperink.com

© 2012 Rockport Publishers
Text © 2012 Bruce Hanington and Bella Martin

First published in the United States of America in 2012 by
Rockport Publishers, a member of
Quayside Publishing Group
100 Cummings Center
Suite 406-L
Beverly, MA 01915-6101
Telephone: (978) 282-9590
Fax: (978) 283-2742
www.rockpub.com
www.rockpaperink.com

10 9 8 7 6 5 4 3 2

ISBN: 978-1-59253-756-3

Digital edition published in 2012
eISBN: 978-1-61058-199-8

Library of Congress Cataloging-in-Publication Data is available.

Design: Bella Martin
Cover Image: Bella Martin

Getty Images: page 187
Shutterstock.com: pages 15, 29, 85, 91, 103, 113, 115, 131, and 195

Printed in China

To Paul, my true north, and
my Belles, Victoria & Virginia.

Dedications

To my wife Lisa,
and my girls Nia and Emme,
who give my life balance and meaning,

And in memory of my mother, Elizabeth,
ever present.

Contents
& design phases ❶ ❷ ❸ ❹ ❺

"Supposing is good.
Finding out is better."
–Mark Twain

Introduction

Please note: this is not just a book about methods of design.

Yes, we know what the cover says. But the truth is, we believe that the power of the methods and techniques included in this book is that each provides an opportunity to structure conversations that can help us better understand and empathize with people, and as a result build more meaningful products.

When we set out to write this book, we admit that we began with the simple intention of aggregating 100 different ways to collect user-centered research data, synthesize and analyze information, and communicate results and design implications. But over the course of our writing process, we realized that integral to the methods and techniques are the conversations that they facilitate—conversations with stakeholders, team members, clients, and most importantly, with the people who will ultimately use designed products, systems, and services. We realized that these methods and techniques have a role to play in how the design community can establish expertise and build credibility, because they can help designers have the right conversations at the right time. Professional and academic excellence requires situating and articulating new knowledge in a timely and approachable manner. The 100 methods, techniques, and deliverables in this book have the potential to do just that.

In keeping with the work that we do, we have a simple, human-centered design intention in the presentation of this book. Methods and techniques are organized alphabetically for ongoing, quick reference. On each page spread, accessible, concise text descriptions of each method appear on the left page, accompanied by references for further reading that pay respect to the seminal works of those who have laid the foundations for us.

An info-graphic on the bottom left of each page characterizes the methods and techniques using several useful research facets. The *behavioral/attitudinal* facet suggests the type of content most appropriately targeted by the method. *Quantitative/qualitative* characterizes the form in which that content is typically collected and communicated. *Innovative/adapted/traditional* describes whether the method is original to design, adapted from other disciplines, or used traditionally across disciplines. *Exploratory/generative/evaluative* frames the methods by their primary purpose of early exploration, concept generation, or testing and evaluation. And finally, *participatory/observational/self-reporting/expert review/design process* describes the typical roles of the researcher and participant, with design process methods being those conducted by design teams as an integral part of an overall approach.

On the right facing page, images and case studies for each method are visually presented, most of these from actual projects contributed by our respected colleagues in design practice and research. Readers are directed to other related methods, and the relevant phases for design application are highlighted as numbered icons along the right side of the page, from phases numbered ❶ through ❺ .

Phase **❶** is Planning, Scoping, and Definition, where project parameters are explored and defined. Phase **❷**, Exploration, Synthesis, and Design Implications, is characterized by immersive research and design ethnography, leading to implications for design. Phase **❸** is Concept Generation and Early Prototype Iteration, involving participatory and generative design activities. Phase **❹** is Evaluation, Refinement, and Production, based on iterative testing and feedback. Phase **❺** is Launch and Monitor, the quality assurance testing of design to ensure readiness for market and public use, and ongoing review and analysis to course-correct when necessary. The table of contents displays an overview of methods in this context.

The work of design teams is not about expertise in any single type of method. It is also not about software, or the deliverables we develop. Our work is about knowing how to structure the conversations we need to inform the best design solutions for the work we do. Consider these 100 methods and techniques as a means to get to better design, rather than ends in and of themselves. Review them, try them, prioritize them, and sequence them based on the success criteria and focus of problems you want to solve. Treat them as conversations. We have.

01 A/B Testing

Use A/B testing to compare two versions of the same design to see which one performs statistically better against a predetermined goal.[1]

A/B testing is an optimization technique that allows you to compare two different versions of a design to see which one gets you closer to a business objective.[2] The tests are run by randomly assigning different people down two paths—the "A" test and the "B" test—until a statistically relevant sample size is reached. At the end of the test, you will be able to determine which design gets you closer to your goals.

Take, for instance, the challenge of increasing the number of people who sign up for a free trial of your online service. There could be many explanations why people aren't registering: Is the sign-up form too long? Are people worried about their privacy and what you will do with their data? Do they want to know about pricing information before they register? You can find out the answer to each of these questions by making small modifications to the interface, and then run an A/B test to see which version prompts more people to register. For instance, given the scenario above, you can design and run several tests that compare:

- different treatments of the page microcopy—the text that guides and reassures the user—regarding the terms of the service (tone, length, font size);
- the form elements (how many, layout, which are required); and
- different treatments of the button or call to action (page placement, size, color, labeling).

Even though there is a benefit to being able to measure *which* design generates better results, A/B testing won't help you understand *why* the design was preferred over the alternate. A/B testing is not a replacement for qualitative methods that can assess your customers' desires, attitudes, and needs, nor can it uncover larger problems like whether customers feel that they can trust your site or that it is credible.[3] To that end, A/B testing should always supplement qualitative methods that help you gain a deeper understanding of what really motivates your customers and what they really want.

1. A/B tests are adapted from the classic direct mail practice in which two different versions of the same mailing are sent out to different people in order to see which one gets the better response rates.

2. Nielsen, Jakob. "Putting A/B Testing in Its Place," 2005, http://www.useit.com

3. Kahavi, Ron, Randal M. Henne, and Dan Sommerfield. "Practical Guide to Controlled Experiments on the Web: Listen to Your Customer Not to the HiPPO." *Proceedings of the 13th ACM SIGKDD*, 2007.

Behavioral	Quantitative	Innovative	Exploratory	Participatory
Attitudinal	Qualitative	Adapted	Generative	Observational
		Traditional	Evaluative	Self reporting
				Expert review
				Design process

A/B TESTING: AN EBAY CASE STUDY

Experimentation with A/B testing can inform various hypotheses and product directions. It's important to experiment all the time and not just accept certain past observations as always holding true in the future. A set of experiments performed by eBay in 2010 on image size is a great example.

Over the course of several tests, eBay researchers generally observed that their buyers have a higher engagement when they can maximize the number of listings above the fold and minimize the need to scroll or paginate. Keeping this hypothesis in mind, the goal of the image size A/B test shown here sets out to prove that smaller images increased the number of listings on one page, and therefore would result in higher engagement.

To the researchers' surprise, the smaller image size test (Test B) did not perform as well as expected against the larger image size test (Test A). After more investigation and a follow-up experiment, the researchers learned that the reverse was actually occurring—that the buyers demonstrated higher engagement on the larger image sizes even when fewer items were able to fit on the first page. From the results of this experiment they quickly made the change to the larger image size across the site.

Courtesy of Robin Chiang, eBay, Inc.

Test A: *the larger image test*

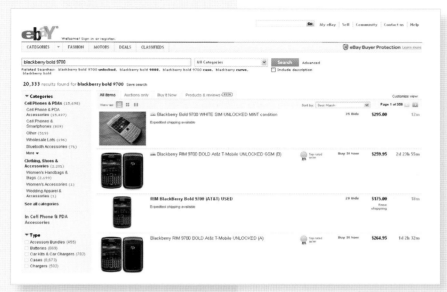

Test B: *the smaller image test*

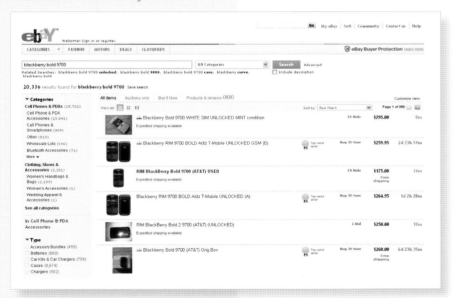

See also 38. Experiments • 51. Key Performance Indicators • 97. Web Analytics

Design Phase: ① ② ③ ④ ⑤

02 AEIOU

AEIOU is an organizational framework reminding the researcher to attend to, document, and code information under a guiding taxonomy of Activities, Environments, Interactions, Objects, and Users.[1]

Even when observations are only casually or semi-structured, it pays to have an organizational framework in mind, such that the researcher attends to key details. AEIOU is an easy mnemonic for guiding and coding observations. As a heuristic, or rule of thumb, the taxonomy defines each feature of the observation set as follows:

- **Activities** are goal-directed sets of actions. What are the pathways that people take toward the things they want to accomplish, including specific actions and processes?

- **Environments** include the entire arena in which activities take place. For example, what describes the atmosphere and function of the context, including individual and shared spaces?

- **Interactions** are between a person and someone or something else, and are the building blocks of activities. What is the nature of routine and special interactions between people, between people and objects in their environment, and across distances?

- **Objects** are the building blocks of the environment, key elements sometimes put to complex or even unintended uses, possibly changing their function, meaning, and context. For example, what are the objects and devices people have in their environments, and how do these relate to their activities?

- **Users** are the people whose behaviors, preferences, and needs are being observed. Who is present? What are their roles and relationships? What are their values and biases?

The elements of the framework are not independent, but are interrelated parts with critical interactions between each part. The AEIOU framework can be applied in any ethnographic or observational method, guiding familiar collection techniques including notes, photos, and interviews. AEIOU can be used to develop a worksheet for categorizing or coding observational notes as they occur, or as a set of broad categories under which several more specific subcategories or codes can be created. Although AEIOU offers preset categories for observation and coding, further analysis can be conducted.

1. The AEIOU framework is credited to Rick Robinson, Ilya Prokopoff, John Cain, and Julie Pokorny, then at the Doblin Group in Chicago, in 1991. Rick Robinson carried the framework to E-Lab LLC, where it appeared in company publicity materials in the late 1990s.

For a short description of the framework based on the work of Robinson et al. and the former E-Lab publicity materials, see http://www.ethnohub.com/faq/what-aeiou-framework

Further Reading

Wasson, Christina. "Ethnography in the Field of Design." *Human Organization* 59, no. 4 (2000): 377-388.

Behavioral	Quantitative	Innovative	Exploratory	Participatory
Attitudinal	Qualitative	Adapted	Generative	Observational
		Traditional	Evaluative	Self reporting
				Expert review
				Design process

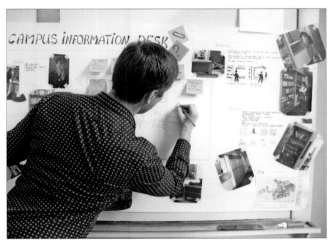

The AEIOU framework was used in a design thinking workshop to guide field observations and visualization techniques. Individual worksheets (above) for Activities, Environments, Interactions, Objects, and Users, were used to document research, and then converged onto a large team worksheet (left and below) for synthesis and design ideation.

See also 20. Contextual Inquiry • 42. Fly-on-the-Wall Observation • 57. Observation

03 Affinity Diagramming

Affinity diagramming is a process used to externalize and meaningfully cluster observations and insights from research, keeping design teams grounded in data as they design.

As long as research data is stored as tacit knowledge in people's minds or buried in interview transcripts, teams will experience difficulty synthesizing what has been observed and learned. Affinity diagramming helps designers capture research-backed insights, observations, concerns, or requirements on individual sticky notes, so that the design implication of each can be fully considered on its own. Notes are then clustered based on *affinity*, which form into research-based themes. Two common research variations of affinity diagramming include:

Affinity Diagramming for Contextual Inquiry:[1] Once researchers have conducted interviews of typical workers from four to six different work sites, there should be enough representative data to complete an affinity diagram. Before the affinity diagramming session, record on average 50-100 observations of each person interviewed. Each observation should be on its own sticky note (be sure that notes reference their original interview transcript, in case a question comes up about it). Once created, notes are posted on a wall that is covered in sheets of large-format paper (which allows the affinity diagram to be moved, if necessary), and the team can begin the rigorous process of interpreting notes and considering the underlying significance of each. Notes that share a similar intent, problem, or issue—or that share an affinity—are clustered together. Out of this work, a story emerges about people, their tasks, and the nature of their problems.

Affinity Diagramming for Usability Tests: Prior to each usability test session, the research team agrees on a different color sticky note for each participant. Once the usability test is in progress, the team (which can include stakeholders, developers, designers, and other researchers) watches the evaluation from an observation room. As the participant talks through the tasks, the team captures specific observations and quotes on the sticky notes, and posts them on a wall or whiteboard. Over the course of a few usability tests, common issues and problems in the interface will emerge. The categories that have usability issues will show many colored sticky notes—indicating several people experienced the same problem. Fixes and priorities to the interface can then be determined: whatever aspect of the design has the most issues is the first to get fixed and retested.

In both variations, affinity diagramming is an *inductive* exercise—which means that instead of grouping notes in predefined categories, the work is done from the bottom up, by first clustering specific, small details into groups, which then give rise to the general and overarching themes. Once complete, the affinity diagram should be referred back to not as a prop, but as the voice of the customer, and a partner in design.[2]

1. Holtzblatt, Karen, and Hugh Beyer. *Contextual Design: A Customer-centered Approach to Systems Design.* San Francisco, CA: Morgan Kaufmann, 1998.

2. See note 1 above.

3. See note 1 above.

Further Reading

The affinity diagram was introduced in the 1960s, alongside the KJ Technique, by Jiro Kawakita, a Japanese anthropologist. See:

Kawakita, Jiro. *The Original KJ Method.* Tokyo: Kawakita Research Institute, 1982.

Kuniavsky, Mike. *Observing the User Experience.* San Francisco, CA: Morgan Kaufmann, 2003.

Behavioral	Quantitative	Innovative	Exploratory	Participatory
Attitudinal	**Qualitative**	**Adapted**	**Generative**	Observational
		Traditional	Evaluative	Self reporting
				Expert review
				Design process

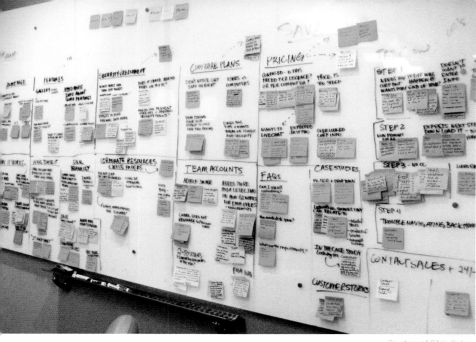

While usability tests are conducted at Citrix, team members in an observation room simultaneously construct an affinity diagram (left) of issues that are detected during the test session. Each color sticky note represents a different participant, and over multiple tests, recurring issues are revealed. The issues with the most sticky notes are the first to get revised and retested.

Courtesy of Citrix Online

In Contextual Design[3], affinity diagramming sessions are scheduled after contextual inquiry interviews. Instead of putting the notes in pre-defined or known categories, the methodology uses a "bottom-up" process for building affinity diagrams. Affinity notes are placed on a wall that is covered in paper large enough to accommodate hundreds (and sometimes thousands) of sticky notes. When planning for a session, InContext uses a metric of 100 notes = 1 person day.

| organizing my information | | | *Green notes describe an overarching area of concern within the work practice.* |

| show me what I have to do | | | *Pink notes describe specific issues within an area of concern.* |

| daily to-do lists help me track progress | I want it printed in front of me | don't interrupt me with non-critical stuff | *Blue notes describe aspects of an issue revealed by clusters of yellow notes.* |

U3 302 likes the prioritization format in her day planner	U2 221 prints calendar several times a day and hangs them next to her computer	U5 523 has his email set so only urgent mail is automatically opened	*Yellow notes represent a single observation, insight, concern, or requirement firmly rooted in research data. These are the building blocks of the affinity diagram.*
U5 518 makes a report for group with day's hot tasks every day	U7 743 transfers meetings from email to wall calendar	U1 12 keeps her inbox behind her so she won't be interrupted	
U1 38 checks things off her to-do list as she finishes them	U3 351 likes getting an email with tasks rather than a phone call so she can print it		

Courtesy of InContext Design

See also 19. Contextual Design • 49. KJ Technique • 94. Content Analysis

04 Artifact Analysis

A systematic examination of the material, aesthetic, and interactive qualities of objects contributes to an understanding of their physical, social, and cultural contexts.

The emphasis of artifact analysis is on the object itself. Artifact analysis asks: what do objects have to say about people and their culture, time, and place? The researcher is attempting to understand the substance of the object and what it says through its material, aesthetic, and interactive qualities.

Material analysis addresses the quantitative inventory of artifacts in the environment under study, and such defining characteristics as the material composition, durability, wear patterns, and disposability.

Aesthetic analysis includes a subjective visual assessment, but also aspects such as historical references, whether the artifact can be identified with a particular era, time, or place. The analysis here can also include the aesthetics of interaction, responding to qualities of experience associated with object use, and an emotional assessment if significant object meaning can be assumed or deciphered.

Interactive aspects of the analysis address the explicit characteristics of operational use and behaviors that the artifact affords, for example, functional or instrumental, mechanical or technological, simple or complex, immersive or multitasked, positive or negative. Interactive aspects should also consider social, shared, or collaborative intent, and whether there is evidence of misuse, adapted use, or adjustments, often suggesting design opportunities.

A final element of analysis should address the location of objects, including public or private, where they are stored, displayed, or carried, if they are part of a larger whole or system, and if they are owned, shared, or communal or corporate property.

All aspects of these interrelated qualities need not be addressed for every analysis, but rather a focused set should be established corresponding to the particular inquiry. A worksheet composed in advance for note taking will guide the researcher in documenting appropriately, and aid in summary and analysis. Visual documentation of artifacts through photographs, video, or sketches is essential.

An artifact analysis can be conducted in participant homes or workplaces, but can also be a useful tool for examining and comparing precedent and competitive products, or for studying specific aspects such as materials and manufacturing processes, colors, brands, or online presence. It can be an informative tool to help understand physical and digital objects.

Further Reading

Artifact analysis owes some of its history to the cultural inventory used in anthropology. See for example:

Collier, Jr., John, and Malcolm Collier. *Visual Anthropology: Photography as a Research Method*. Albuquerque, NM: University of New Mexico Press, 1986.

Objects may also be used as a *means* of analysis. For example, the method of "interaction relabeling" helps participants reinterpret the features of an existing product to suggest possibilities for new aesthetic interactions: mapping the elements of a board game, running shoe, or toy, for instance, with the functions of a digital appointment calendar, various parts representing elements and actions of an imagined system. See:

Djajadiningrat, J. P., W. W. Gaver, and J. W. Frens. "Interaction Relabelling and Extreme Characters: Methods for Exploring Aesthetic Interactions." *Proceedings of Designing Interactive Systems DIS '00*. New York: ACM: 66-71, 2000.

Behavioral	Quantitative	Innovative	**Exploratory**	Participatory
Attitudinal	**Qualitative**	**Adapted**	Generative	**Observational**
		Traditional	Evaluative	Self reporting
				Expert review
				Design process

Artifact analysis is a systematic examination of the material, aesthetic, and interactive qualities of objects in context.

See also **62. Personal Inventories** • **89. Touchstone Tours** • **92. Unobtrusive Measures**

05 Automated Remote Research

Automated remote research is a method that can reveal statistically relevant data about what people are doing on your website, to help identify the usability enhancements with the biggest impact.

Automated remote research enables design teams to leverage web-based research tools and services in order to collect statistically significant information about what people are doing on your website or web application.[1] Once there is enough quantitative data about what users are doing, the research team can triangulate research findings with observed behavioral data to decide which usability enhancements to make to the site.

In automated remote research experiments, the research team's focus shifts from recruiting and observing usability sessions with participants, to planning the appropriate strategy for the study, and then accurately selecting the right automated remote research tools and configuring the logistics of the study. Because there are an ever-growing number of web-based research tools available that are both quantitative and qualitative, it is important to invest some time to understand the automated research landscape.[2]

Many of these automated research tools can be used to further understand specific usability issues the research team is interested in, and to help you to collect quantitative data such as:[3]

- Are participants able to perform a certain task on the website?
- If so, how long does it take them to complete the task?
- If they have trouble completing the task, where are they abandoning the process?
- What is the most common click path that users take through the interface to complete a task?

If your organization puts an emphasis on the value of quantitative information, or if you have enough activity on your site that lends itself to a statistically significant sample, automated remote research may be a good fit for you.[4] However, it should not be used as a replacement or alternative to more qualitative research methods that serve to provide rich insight into *why* site visitors behave the way that they do. It also should not be used interchangeably with *remote moderated research*, which provides qualitative behavior-based data. Even though both are deployed remotely, the resulting data from each method will be very different.[5] It is important to understand these distinctions when selling remote methods internally, to appropriately set stakeholder expectations on research outcomes.

1. Bolt, Nate, and Tony Tulathimutte. *Remote Research: Real Users, Real Time, Real Research*. New York: Rosenfeld Media, 2010.

2. Bolt | Peters maintains an updated list of automated remote research products and services at http://www.remoteresear.ch

3. See note 1 above.

4. See note 1 above.

5. See note 1 above.

Further Reading

Tullis, Tom, and Bill Albert. *Measuring the User Experience*. San Francisco, CA: Morgan Kaufmann, 2008.

Tullis, Tom, Donna Tedesco, and William Albert. *Beyond the Usability Lab: Conducting Large-Scale User Experience Studies*. San Francisco, CA: Morgan Kaufmann, 2010.

Behavioral	Quantitative	Innovative	Exploratory	Participatory
Attitudinal	Qualitative	Adapted	Generative	Observational
		Traditional	Evaluative	Self reporting
				Expert review
				Design process

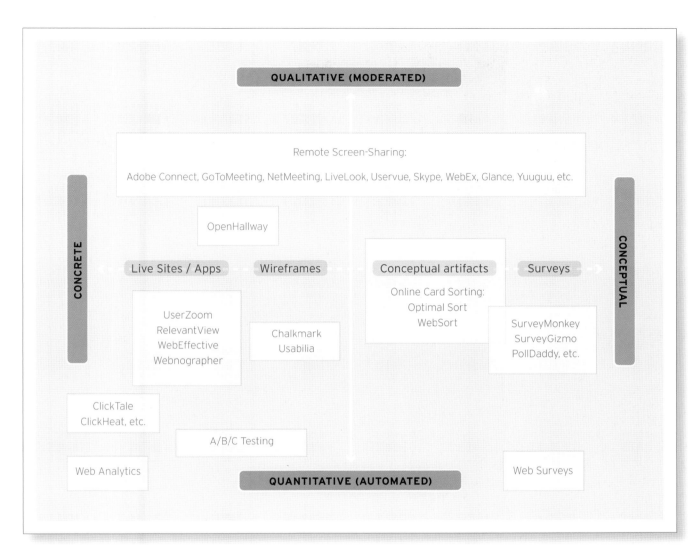

QUALITATIVE (MODERATED)

Remote Screen-Sharing:

Adobe Connect, GoToMeeting, NetMeeting, LiveLook, Uservue, Skype, WebEx, Glance, Yuuguu, etc.

OpenHallway

CONCRETE

CONCEPTUAL

Live Sites / Apps

Wireframes

Conceptual artifacts

Surveys

UserZoom
RelevantView
WebEffective
Webnographer

Chalkmark
Usabilia

Online Card Sorting:
Optimal Sort
WebSort

SurveyMonkey
SurveyGizmo
PollDaddy, etc.

ClickTale
ClickHeat, etc.

A/B/C Testing

Web Analytics

Web Surveys

QUANTITATIVE (AUTOMATED)

In their book *Remote Research*, Nate Bolt and Tony Tulathimutte provide a framework for thinking about the different types of remote research tools and applications available to design teams. Automated remote methods are shown towards the bottom half of the diagram.

Courtesy of Nate Bolt, CEO, Bolt | Peters User Experience

See also **23.** Crowdsourcing • **38.** Experiments • **69.** Remote Moderated Research

06 Behavioral Mapping

Behavioral mapping is used to systematically document location-based observations of human activity, using annotated maps, plans, video, or time-lapse photography.

Behavioral maps are used to document readily observable characteristics, movements, and activities, including approximate ages and genders, whether people are alone or with others, what they are doing, time spent at fixed locations or in transit, and the details of environmental context.

Place-centered mapping is based on observations of people at a site-specific location.[1] Architectural plans may be used as the underlay for documenting observations, but more commonly researchers will construct their own measured diagram, including the basic space layout and architectural features, signage, and any furniture, fixed or portable items that may affect behaviors or interactions. Behaviors may be precoded for ease of recording, for example, with symbols, numbers, or abbreviations assigned to anticipate actions such as standing, sitting, walking, and talking. Alternately, flexible observations may begin with descriptive note taking and annotations of actions as they are witnessed. Maps created from several observations at different times are typically aggregated to indicate summary concentrations of people, place, and feature usage and activities. Common uses of place-centered maps are the analysis of retail stores and service centers, parks, and other public spaces, revealing traffic patterns and key points of interaction to determine or improve space design or service flow.

Individual-centered mapping follows the travel and activities of a specific individual or individuals over time and location.[2] Whereas the emphasis of place-centered mapping is on assessing use of a particular space, the focus of individual-centered mapping is on learning about people, for example, their social behaviors and interactions. This method of behavioral mapping is more intrusive than place-centered mapping, and therefore may require the consent of participants. To minimize reactivity, allow time for the participant to become accustomed to being observed, which may include disregarding initial observations until participants are comfortable.

Place-centered and individual-centered mapping may be used in combination. While behavioral mapping is typically completed in real time, sophisticated research setups can involve time-lapse photography or video. A noted limitation of the method is that often the motivations or reasons for behaviors remain unknown to the observer. In individual-centered mapping, the method can often be supplemented with interviews or debriefing conversations to understand more about behaviors. Alternately, in retrospective mapping, individuals are asked to map their paths and behaviors in a space by simple indications on a floor plan or map, and can simultaneously reveal their motivations for actions.

1. Sommer, Robert, and Barbara Sommer. *A Practical Guide to Behavioral Research: Tools and Techniques.* New York: Oxford University Press, 2002.

2. See note 1 above.

Further Reading

Technology can afford new innovations in methods of behavioral mapping. For example, in an elaborate study of grocery-shopping behavior, Larson, Bradlow, and Fader traced common travel paths using radio-frequency identification (RFID) tags attached to shopping carts. See:

Larson, J. S., E. Bradlow, and P. Fader. "An Exploratory Look at Supermarket Shopping Paths." *International Journal of Research in Marketing* 22, no. 4 (2005): 395–414.

Behavioral	Quantitative	Innovative	**Exploratory**	Participatory
Attitudinal	**Qualitative**	Adapted	Generative	**Observational**
		Traditional	Evaluative	Self reporting
				Expert review
				Design process

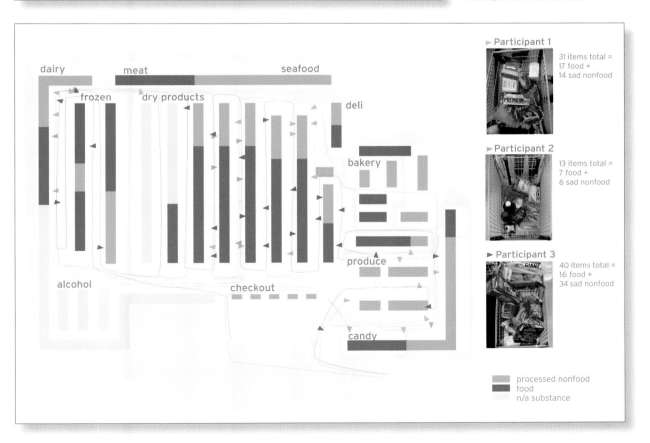

In a study of the relationship between food providers and consumers to create sustainable healthy food communities, behavioral mapping of consumer routes in the grocery store was combined with shadowing observations and conversations to establish a picture of current grocery store design and shopping patterns.

Courtesy of Sarah Calandro © 2011

▶ Participant 1

31 items total =
17 food +
14 sad nonfood

▶ Participant 2

13 items total =
7 food +
6 sad nonfood

▶ Participant 3

40 items total =
16 food +
34 sad nonfood

processed nonfood
food
n/a substance

See also 42. Fly-on-the-Wall Observation • 76. Shadowing • 92. Unobtrusive Measures

07 Bodystorming

Bodystorming situates brainstorming in physical experience, combining role-playing and simulation to inspire new ideas and empathic, spontaneous prototyping.[1]

Bodystorming is physical brainstorming—dynamic, experiential, and generative—situated in methods of *informance*, or informative performance, combining active role-play with simple prototypes.[2] Through bodystorming, designers immerse themselves in user situations through loosely config- ured or simulated contexts, moving through space and situations while paying close attention to decisions, interactive experiences, and emotional responses.[3] The method may be contained within design teams, but can also engage a wider audience of peers or clients, inviting response and dialogue.

Whereas the primary function of traditional role-playing is to gain an empathic sense of users by acting their part, bodystorming encourages active design ideation, concept generation, and even testing of ideas in parallel. During the bodystorm, in addition to props simulating typical products and environmental features that already exist, concept ideas can be integrated and tested in play, and the active situation can inspire the spontaneous creation of additional new product and service concepts. If well executed, bodystorming captures a realistic scenario of use through immersive acting in a simulated context, and the process is seamlessly empathic.

Prototypes or "props" used in bodystorming need not be sophisticated constructions; for example, cardboard or foam core can be used to enclose space; simple boxes or existing furniture can repre- sent fixtures, landmarks, or obstacles; chairs can be airline or car seats; tables become stretchers or beds; and lighting conditions can be manipulated as appropriate. Likewise, while scenarios may be partially scripted from observations using storyboards, the bodystorm is largely spontaneous and encourages improvisation to capture real-world experiences.

1. The Bodystorming method is credited to Interval Research. See:

Burns, Colin, Eric Dishman, William Verplank, and Bud Lassiter. "Actors, Hairdos & Videotape–Informance Design: Using Performance Techniques in Multidisciplinary, Observation-based Design." *CHI 94 Conference Companion*, 1994: 119-120.

The authors define bodystorming as "repping (reenacting everyday peoples' performances)–for living with that data in embodied ways." See: www.baychi.org/calendar/19950808.

2. See note 1 above.

3. http://dschool.stanford.edu/groups/k12/wiki/48c54/Bodystorming.html

Further Reading

Oulasvirta, A., E. Kurvinen, and T. Kanjaunen. "Understanding Contexts by Being There: Case Studies in Bodystorming." *Personal Ubiquitous Computing* 7, no. 2 (2003): 125-134.

For a discussion of variations on the method, see:

Schleicher, Dennis, Peter Jones, and Oksana Kachur. "Bodystorming as Embodied Designing." *Interactions*, November/December 2010: 47-51.

Behavioral	Quantitative	**Innovative**	Exploratory	Participatory
Attitudinal	**Qualitative**	Adapted	**Generative**	Observational
		Traditional	Evaluative	Self reporting
				Expert review
				Design process

Designers bodystorming a contained sound system, with personal bubbles of sound space controlled by mobile devices. Two designers bodystorm the sound bubble; while another "awakens" to music, her "roommate" continues to sleep, undisturbed by the sound.

See also 36. Experience Prototyping • 71. Role-playing • 77. Simulation Exercises

08 Brainstorm Graphic Organizers

Beyond creating lists of new ideas and concepts, brainstorm graphic organizers help in the creation of new knowledge by visually structuring a deep dive into a problem space.

Brainstorming has traditionally been used to spur group creativity with the intention of generating concepts and ideas regarding a specific challenge. "Go for quantity over quality," "withhold judgment and criticism," "build on each other's ideas," and "welcome oddity" are a few of the widely accepted rules of brainstorming.[1] The intention of these guidelines is to create a safe forum for the expression and free association of creative ideas, and quell any inhibitions of the participants by providing a judgment-free zone to explore new concepts.

More recently, brainstorming is also being used to develop one's fluency of thinking.[2] Graphic organizers, or visual representations of knowledge, are frameworks that facilitate teams as they challenge assumptions, experiment with new relationships between accepted components of a problem space, and as they consider unconventional alternatives within a domain.

Design teams can visually communicate the rigor required of most brainstorming sessions using the following visualization frameworks: [3]

Brainstorming Webs Use brainstorming webs when developing a central concept or question and identifying its characteristics, supporting facts, and related ideas. Brainstorming webs can be built by either identifying the center first, then all of the extensions, or by identifying all of the components first, then abstracting them to determine overarching central themes.

Tree Diagrams Use tree diagrams when you need to communicate hierarchy, a classification system, or relationships between main and supporting ideas. Tree diagrams can be constructed from the top down, or from the bottom up. In this way, they require either inductive or deductive thinking while brainstorming a specific topic.

Flow Diagrams Use flow diagrams, or flowcharts, when you need to document a sequence of events, represent the actions or processes of different actors in a system, communicate a process, or show cause and effect of interrelated elements. Flow diagrams usually have a beginning and an end and can support timelines, but they can also be adapted to show cycles for close-looped systems.

The human mind organizes and stores information in a series of networks.[4] Brainstorming webs, tree diagrams, and flow diagrams are three sense-making frameworks that design teams can use to visually brainstorm information in order to disrupt and challenge old patterns of thinking. By using these frameworks, new knowledge and meaning can emerge, with the added benefit that the rigor of the brainstorming session is visually documented within the framework itself.

1. In 1948, *Your Creative Power* by Alex Osborn was published. The book documented the brainstorming technique that had been used at Osborn's famous ad agency, BBDO, since the 1930s. Brainstorming was further popularized in Osborn's book, *Applied Imagination: Principles and Procedures of Creative Problem-Solving*, 3rd ed. Buffalo, N.Y.: Creative Education Foundation, 1993.

2. Hyerle, David. *Visual Tools for Constructing Knowledge*. Alexandria, VA: ASCD, 1996.

3. See note 2 above.

4. Ausubel, David, Joseph D. Novak, and H. Hanesian. *Educational Psychology: A Cognitive View*, 2nd ed. New York: Holt, Rinehart & Winston, 1978.

Further Reading

Clarke, John H. *Patterns of Thinking: Integrating Learning Skills in Content Teaching*. Boston, MA: Allyn & Bacon, 1990.

Sinatra, Richard, et al. "Integrating Computers, Reading, and Writing Across the Curriculum." *Educational Leadership* 48 (1990): 57-62.

Behavioral	Quantitative	Innovative	Exploratory	Participatory
Attitudinal	Qualitative	Adapted	Generative	Observational
		Traditional	Evaluative	Self reporting
				Expert review
				Design process

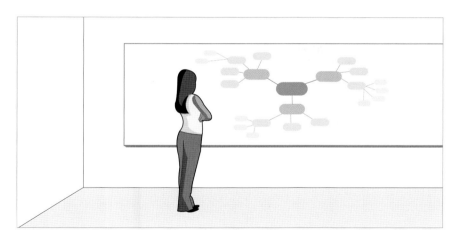

Brainstorming webs are helpful when developing a central concept or question and its identifying characteristics, supporting facts, and related ideas.

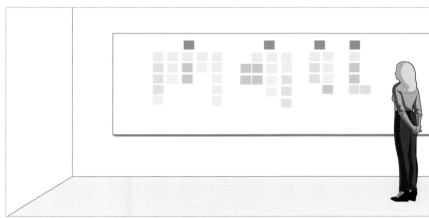

Tree diagrams communicate hierarchy, a classification system, or relationships between main and supporting ideas.

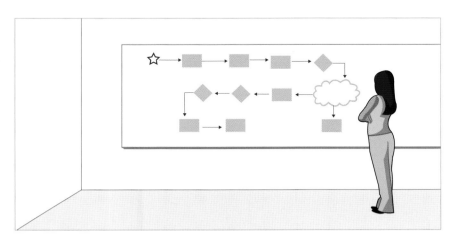

Flow diagrams, or flowcharts, show the actions or processes of different actors in a system, communicate a process, or show cause and effect of interrelated elements within a system.

See also **12. Cognitive Mapping • 16. Concept Mapping • 56. Mind Mapping**

09 Business Origami

Business origami enables teams to paper-prototype the interaction and value exchange among people, artifacts, and environments in a multichannel system.[1]

Business origami is a service design activity that models current and future multichannel systems. It provides a forum in which project stakeholders can come together in a workshop setting to build a physical representation of a system, and then prototype future or alternative states of the same system. The method uses paper-cutout *tokens* to represent the actors, artifacts, environments, and technologies that comprise a system, and a horizontal whiteboard surface is transformed into a *stage* or *set*, where a series of interactions play out to tell a story. By bringing the system elements into the physical dimension, stakeholders can make explicit the value exchange between elements as they occur over time and within the context of a scenario.

The purpose of the method is to articulate a model of the system, particularly the value exchange that happens between tokens on the set. The *tokens* are used to model face-to-face interactions, or interactions that are mediated by technology or artifacts, within a specific environment and context. The interactions between tokens are represented by *arrows* that are drawn on the whiteboard surface with dry-erase markers. The arrows are labeled with the *value exchange* of the interaction, articulating what value people get out of the interaction. If the scenario is to "optimize a shopping experience," an interaction between a customer and a salesperson could show a customer "buying a superior running shoe" and the salesperson "building a relationship" or "making a sale." The method requires a constrained series of *scenarios* that are tied to specific project goals. Scenarios focus participants' thinking and can help identify tangential components of the system that fall outside of the scope of the exercise.

The method works best early in the design process, and should include a multidisciplinary mix of four to six participants. As the team populates the set with tokens that represent people, places, and artifacts, inherent in the method is a structured means to carry on conversation that promotes consensus, understanding of different perspectives, and multidisciplinary collaboration.

Although photos and video "flythroughs" can document the business origami *set*, the experience of modeling the system is the critical deliverable. The final result is a physical representation of the current system design that reveals how the different touch points realistically play out over time. The method gives all participants an equal voice in the prototyping activity, and it can bridge different perspectives by providing a common reference for further discussion.

1. Jess McMullin is the founder of the Centre for Citizen Experience in Canada. He was introduced to the business origami method by Professor Kenta Ono, from Chiba University in Japan. McMullin now teaches the method at design workshops, speaks about it at conferences, and consults with organizations that want to use business origami and value-centered design methods to evaluate and explore system design. See:

www.citizenexperience.com.

Behavioral	Quantitative	Innovative	Exploratory	Participatory
Attitudinal	Qualitative	Adapted	Generative	Observational
		Traditional	Evaluative	Self reporting
				Expert review
				Design process

The name of the business origami method pays homage to the Japanese art of folding paper into symbolic shapes and figures. The paper pop-up tokens that are placed on the set represent people, locations, artifacts, technology (cellphones, computers, laptops, TV, game consoles) things that move people (bicycles, streetcars, cars, buses), channels (Salesforce.com, SAP), third parties (suppliers), social media (Twitter, Facebook), and proprietary tools (databases). These are placed on a horizontal whiteboard, and a dry-erase marker is used to help illustrate relationships between the different tokens.

Courtesy of Jess McMullin, Centre for Citizen Experience

See also 21. Creative Toolkits • 28. Design Workshops • 95. User Journey Maps

10 Card Sorting

When user comprehension and meaningful categorization is critical, card sorting can help clarify.[1]

Card sorting is a participatory design technique that you can use to explore how participants group items into categories and relate concepts to one another, whether for digital interface design or a table of contents. Participants are given cards with printed concepts, terms, or features on them, and are asked to sort them in various ways. One of the most common reasons to do a card sort is to identify terminology that is likely to be misunderstood, either because the terminology is vague or because multiple meanings are associated with it.

The card sorting method can also be used when you want to generate options for structuring your information, as it can identify different schemas for organizing your navigation, menus, and taxonomies. You can use this method to help develop frameworks that maximize the chances of users being able to find the information they need.

Card sorting can also be used to evaluate categories. The method can identify items that may be difficult to categorize or perhaps aren't as important as others. The method validates that the categories in your product or service actually reflect the mental model of your audience, and helps them achieve their goals using words in a context that makes the most sense to them.

When running a card sort, these best practices will help in planning a successful activity:[2]

- Select a moderator who is familiar with the content and participants who are the target audience of the content, and who care about the information.

- Work iteratively with individual participants or small groups of participants (no more than three to five people).

- Limit the total number of participants. After 15 sessions, there are diminishing returns on the insight that can be garnered from card sorts.[3]

- Use 30 to 100 cards, and allow about 30 minutes for each multiple of 50 cards.

- Include blank cards and markers to allow participants to add their own items where needed.

- If there are no consistent patterns emerging after ten card sorts, consider renaming the cards, or reconsider the categories.

Your business goals probably require some sort of action on the part of your customers. However, it can be difficult for customers to act if they cannot find or understand the information you provide. A card sort can uncover how real-world usersmake sense of your "insider" or "expert" understanding. This is especially important if your content is organized with an internal view of your organization.

1. The Wisconsin Card Sorting Task (WCST) was introduced in 1946 as a means to assess patients with frontal lobe injuries, which can affect their ability to organize, plan, search, and shift cognitive sets based on environmental feedback. See:

Berg, Esta A. "A Simple Objective Technique for Measuring Flexibility in Thinking." *The Journal of General Psychology* 39, no. 52, 1948: 15–22.

The Card Sorting technique was later adapted for the purposes of determining web content structure and documented by Jakob Nielsen and Darrel Sano in 1994. See: "Design of SunWeb: Sun Microsystems' Intranet," www.useit.com.

2. Spencer, Donna. *Card Sorting: Designing Usable Categories*. New York: Rosenfeld Media, 2009.

3. Nielsen, Jakob. "Card Sorting: How Many Users to Test?" 2004, www.useit.com.

4. See note 2 above.

Further Reading

Coxon, Anthony Peter MacMillan. *Sorting Data: Collection and Analysis*. Thousand Oaks, CA: Sage Publications, 1999.

Behavioral	Quantitative	Innovative	Exploratory	Participatory
Attitudinal	Qualitative	Adapted	Generative	Observational
		Traditional	Evaluative	Self reporting
				Expert review
				Design process

AN OVERVIEW OF CARD SORTING

Card sorting is a powerful and flexible method that can help you understand how people group information, identify how they perceive and describe different groups of information, and generate a number of possible ideas for primary, secondary, and tertiary navigation categories. Card sorts are also not very complicated to moderate, as illustrated below. The rigor of the method is in its anaylsis.

See also **05.** Automated Remote Research • **18.** Content Inventory & Audit • **29.** Desirability Testing

11 Case Studies

The case study is a research strategy involving in-depth investigation of single events or instances in context, using multiple sources of research evidence.[1]

Case studies have a long history in social science research, and in the teaching practices of law and business.[2] More recently, it has been proposed that this method has value for design practice and education, in both the *use* of case studies for design research and teaching, and in the *writing* of case studies by designers.[3] Case studies are useful in exploratory research for understanding existing phenomena for comparison, information, or inspiration, but can also be used to study the effects of change, new programs, or innovations.

The case study method focuses on gaining detailed, intensive knowledge about a single instance or a set of related instances. These instances, or cases, may be of individuals, organizations, entire communities, events, or processes. The details of cases emerge during data collection and analysis, which typically include the following features:[4]

- Selection of a case or small set of cases for a situation or area of concern
- Study of the case in context, in its social and physical setting
- Collection of information using multiple, triangulated methods such as interviews, observations, unobtrusive trace measures, and document analysis

Case studies are inclusive, assuming that consideration of the whole, covering interrelationships, is more advantageous than a reductionist study of parts, and that this depth compensates for any shortcomings in breadth and the ability to generalize. Furthermore, the case study method does not look for representative instances, but welcomes extraordinary cases and outliers. However, descriptions from a single researcher should be cross verified to enhance the reliability of participant accounts, while still recognizing that each individual point of view may be valid. While single cases are not enough to support or reject hypotheses, they may shed light on theory.[5]

Case studies have been proposed as useful for designers, bearing some resemblance to the design process. Case studies require the researcher to determine a problem, make initial hypotheses, conduct research through interviews, observations, and other forms of information gathering, revise hypotheses and theory, and tell a story.[6] The telling of case studies should in fact be designed, and when well composed, can result in compelling human narratives, meaningful for research yet enjoyable to read, with vivid details that make the case more memorable.[7] Furthermore, the documenting of design process has the potential to contribute to a repository of design case studies.

1. Yin, Robert K. *Case Study Research: Design and Methods*, 3rd ed. Thousand Oaks, CA: Sage Publications, 2002.

2. Harvard Law School introduced the concept of case study beginning in the late 1870s, taking advantage of existing cases natural to the practice of law, and in reaction to traditional teaching methods requiring memorization and recall. By the 1920s, the Harvard Business School followed, with the added challenge of writing its own cases. Harvard Medical School introduced the use of case studies in the 1980s. The adoption of case studies as an educational approach fostered in-depth reading of cases, analysis, and the dialectic of classroom discussion. In professional programs, case studies proved to be a needed bridge between the scholarship of theories, and connections to real-life experience to inform decision making. See:

Breslin, Maggie, and Richard Buchanan. "On the Case Study Method of Research and Teaching in Design." *Design Issues* 24, no. 1 (Winter 2008): 36-40.

3. Breslin, Maggie, and Richard Buchanan. "On the Case Study Method of Research and Teaching in Design." *Design Issues* 24, no. 1 (Winter 2008): 36-40.

4. Robson, Colin. *Real World Research: A Resource for Social Scientists and Practitioner-Researchers*, 2nd ed. Oxford: Blackwell Publishers, 2002.

5. Sommer, Robert, and Barbara Sommer. *A Practical Guide to Behavioral Research: Tools and Techniques*. New York: Oxford University Press, 2002.

6. See note 3 above.

7. See note 5 above.

Behavioral	Quantitative	Innovative	Exploratory	Participatory
Attitudinal	**Qualitative**	Adapted	Generative	Observational
		Traditional	Evaluative	Self reporting
				Expert review
				Design process

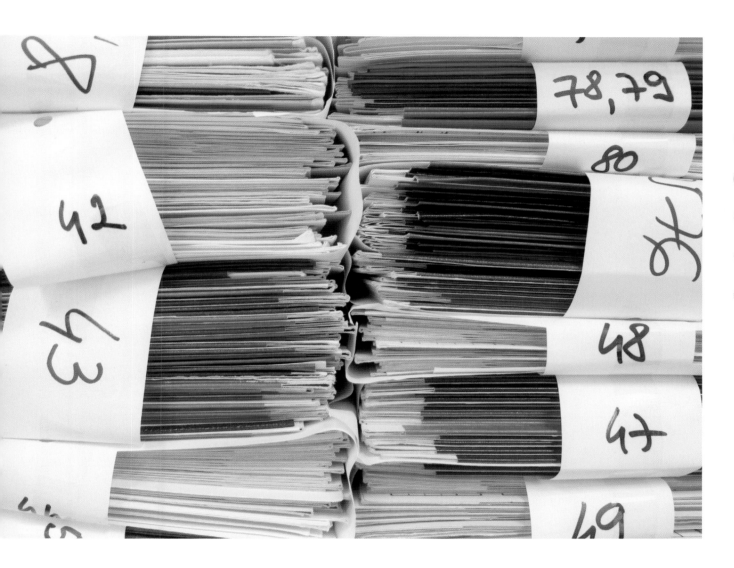

12 Cognitive Mapping

Cognitive mapping is a visualization of how people make sense of a particular problem space. It is most effective when used to structure complex problems and to inform decision making.[1]

Cognitive mapping is an information visualization technique that can be used as a decision- and sense-making tool. Its purpose is to reveal how people think about a problem space, and visualize how they process and make sense of their experience. As the map builds, the participant's subjective patterns of reasoning can be revealed and the underlying nature of the problem exposed.

Like concept maps and mind maps, cognitive maps are visual-thinking tools that represent a network of ideas and associations. All three are used to organize a complicated (and usually messy) information space so that the relationships between concepts can be identified, more fully explored, shared, and reflected upon. However, even though similarities exist across visual-thinking techniques, cognitive maps have a few distinctive qualities. Primarily, cognitive maps were designed specifically as a decision-making tool that can inform strategic direction.[2] The format and structure require no central node (or concept) that works as the focus of the visualization, and they rarely include imagery. Instead, the nodes of a cognitive map are made up of the exact words and phrases spoken by participants.

Each node can have as many incoming and outgoing associations as necessary, and this flexibility is how the most salient concepts are quickly identified.[3] The nature of the links in a cognitive map communicate cause and effect. They are to be read as *node x may lead to node y* or *node x may imply node y*. Another attribute specific to cognitive maps is that concepts can be monopolar or bipolar: which allows for the expression of nuance and "shades of gray."[4] As these poles often represent significant issues or choices, the ability to visually connect them is a powerful means of considering the range of challenges associated with a problem space.[5]

Cognitive mapping can facilitate the note-taking process during interviews, and when transcribing text-based qualitative data. Cognitive mapping gets easier with experience, and novice mappers should try practicing the technique using existing transcripts or taped interviews before applying it in the field.[6] The technique has been used for agenda and strategy development,[7] and when "group" maps are produced that weave together multiple points of view, the maps can serve as a powerful consensus-making tool. The guidelines around building cognitive maps are purposely written to remain flexible. The use of the tool can be considered successful when it provides a scaffolding to think about, explore, and create new constructs of meaning that help people and groups achieve problem resolution.

1. The cognitive mapping technique is grounded in George Kelly's personal construct theory. Personal construct theory holds that in an attempt to anticipate and predict future events, humans make sense of the world by creating subjective classifications—or personal constructs. By differentiating concepts, we create meaning, and can intervene as necessary to get what we want from the world—a "predict and control" view of how the world works. See George Kelly's two-volume opus:

Kelly, George. *The Psychology of Personal Constructs (Volumes 1 and 2)*. New York: Norton, 1955.

2. For an explanation of how to codify text-based documents and create cognitive maps, see:

Ackermann, Fran, Colin Eden, and Steve Cropper. "Getting Started with Cognitive Mapping" in *The Young OR Conference*, *University of Warwick*, 1992: 65-82.

Eden, Colin, and Fran Ackermann. *Making Strategy: The Journey of Strategic Management*. Thousand Oaks, CA: Sage Publications, 1998.

3. "What's In A Name? Cognitive Mapping, Mind Mapping, Concept Mapping," www.banxia.com.

4. See note 3 above.

5. See note 2 (Ackermann, Eden, and Cropper) above.

6. See note 2 (Ackermann, Eden, and Cropper) above.

7. See note 2 (Eden and Ackermann) above.

8. Gomes, Luiz Flávio Autran Monteiro, Luís Alberto Duncan Rangel, and Rogério Lúcio Jeronimo. "A Study of Professional Mobility in a Large Corporation Through Cognitive Mapping." *Pesquisa Operacional* 30, no. 2 (2010): 331-344.

Behavioral	Quantitative	Innovative	**Exploratory**	Participatory
Attitudinal	**Qualitative**	Adapted	Generative	Observational
		Traditional	Evaluative	**Self reporting**
				Expert review
				Design process

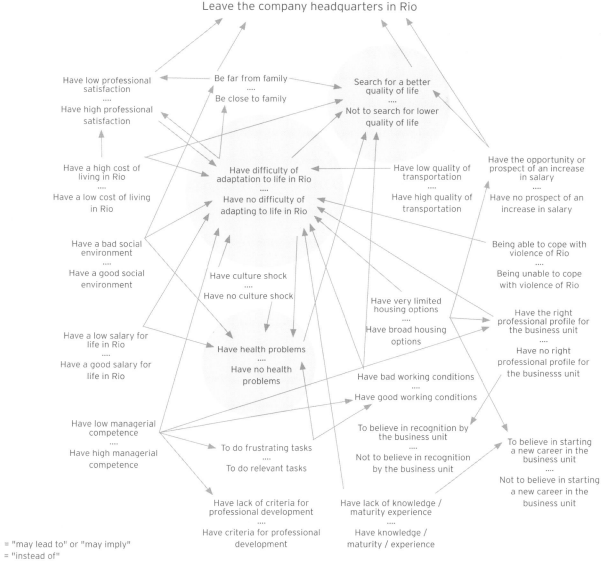

Leave the company headquarters in Rio

Have low professional satisfaction
....
Have high professional satisfaction

Be far from family
....
Be close to family

Search for a better quality of life
....
Not to search for lower quality of life

Have a high cost of living in Rio
....
Have a low cost of living in Rio

Have difficulty of adaptation to life in Rio
....
Have no difficulty of adapting to life in Rio

Have low quality of transportation
....
Have high quality of transportation

Have the opportunity or prospect of an increase in salary
....
Have no prospect of an increase in salary

Have a bad social environment
....
Have a good social environment

Have culture shock
....
Have no culture shock

Being able to cope with violence of Rio
....
Being unable to cope with violence of Rio

Have a low salary for life in Rio
....
Have a good salary for life in Rio

Have health problems
....
Have no health problems

Have very limited housing options
....
Have broad housing options

Have the right professional profile for the business unit
....
Have no right professional profile for the businesss unit

Have bad working conditions
....
Have good working conditions

Have low managerial competence
....
Have high managerial competence

To do frustrating tasks
....
To do relevant tasks

To believe in recognition by the business unit
....
Not to believe in recognition by the business unit

To believe in starting a new career in the business unit
....
Not to believe in starting a new career in the business unit

Have lack of criteria for professional development
....
Have criteria for professional development

Have lack of knowledge / maturity experience
....
Have knowledge / maturity / experience

→ = "may lead to" or "may imply"
···· = "instead of"

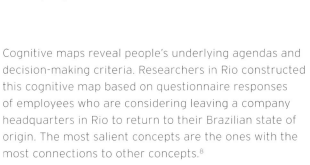

Cognitive maps reveal people's underlying agendas and decision-making criteria. Researchers in Rio constructed this cognitive map based on questionnaire responses of employees who are considering leaving a company headquarters in Rio to return to their Brazilian state of origin. The most salient concepts are the ones with the most connections to other concepts.[8]

Cognitive Map courtesy of Luiz Flávio Autran Monteiro Gomes, Luís Alberto Duncan Rangel, and Rogério Lúcio Jerônimo

See also *17. Content Analysis* • *48. Interviews* • *39. Exploratory Research*

13 Cognitive Walkthrough

Cognitive walkthrough is a method that evaluates whether the order of cues and prompts in a system reflect the way people cognitively process tasks and anticipate "next steps" of a system.[1]

The cognitive walkthrough is a usability inspection method that evaluates a system's relative ease-of-use in situations where preparatory instruction, coaching, or training of the system is unlikely to occur. In these situations—when a person must actively engage with an interface to know what to do next, rather than relying on preexisting knowledge of the system—each step of the interaction with the system can be assessed as a step that either moves the individual closer to or further from his goal. Cognitive walkthroughs provide a systematic way to identify these distinct points during an interaction sequence, and then evaluate whether each step is more likely to fail or succeed in helping people make the next correct decision in the interaction.[2] Systems that meet these expectations are considered to be more usable and more learnable.

Cognitive walkthroughs are particularly well suited for evaluating "walk-up-and-use" systems that are primarily audio- or display-based—such as ATMs, automated parking garage or subway ticketing systems, and automated voice-response phone systems.[3] A series of representative tasks should be selected, all written from the user's vantage point, and outlined in a believable sequence of action steps. The method then sets out to critique each step in the action sequence and evaluate whether it is the right step at the right time. The success of the interface can be judged based on whether the system feedback either helps or hinders users to achieve their goals.[4]

The method's focus on how people solve problems requires that evaluators ask the same four learning theory-based questions for each step in the action sequence.[5]

- Will users want to produce whatever effect the action has?
- Will users see the control (button, menu, label, etc.) for the action?
- Once users find the control, will they recognize that it will produce the effect that they want?
- After the action is taken, will users understand the feedback they get, so they can confidently continue on to the next action?

As the team evaluates each step in a task using the questions above, they will be able to make decisions about which sequence creates the fewest obstacles for the user. Because it cannot be assumed that users will be available for testing every step of the way along the iterative design process, expert reviews like cognitive walkthroughs ensure better use of participants' time. However, because cognitive walkthroughs and usability testing tend to uncover different classes of design issues and usability problems, using them together—rather than in lieu of one another—is always recommended.

1. In the early 1990s, Peter Polson, Clayton Lewis, John Reiman, and Cathleen Wharton from the University of Colorado's Institute of Cognitive Science introduced the cognitive walkthrough method. It was based on a theory of exploratory learning by Polson and Lewis, which is documented in their 1990 *Human-Computer Interaction* article "Theory-based Design for Easily Learned Interfaces." See also:

Polson, Peter G., Clayton Lewis, John Rieman, and Cathleen Wharton. "Cognitive Walkthroughs: A Method for Theory-based Evaluation of User Interfaces." *International Journal of Man-Machine Studies* 36, no. 5 (1992): 741-773.

2. Wharton, Cathleen, John Rieman, Clayton Lewis, and Peter Polson. "The Cognitive Walkthrough: A Practitioner's Guide" in *Usability Inspection Methods*. New York: John Wiley and Sons, 1994.

3. See note 2 above.

4. See note 2 above.

5. See note 2 above.

Lewis, Clayton, and John Reiman. *Task-centered User Interface Design: A Practical Introduction*, 1993, http://www.hcibib.org

Behavioral	Quantitative	Innovative	Exploratory	Participatory
Attitudinal	**Qualitative**	Adapted	Generative	Observational
		Traditional	**Evaluative**	Self reporting
				Expert review
				Design process

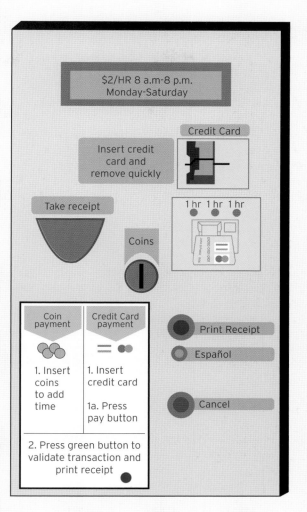

Cognitive walkthroughs are used to evaluate whether an interface is understandable and easy to learn based on the user's problem-solving mental operations, and can be particularly effective in situations where a person is likely to be a first- or one-time user of the system.

The illustrated example shown to the right is based on an actual parking meter machine (see above), that clearly could have benefited from the cognitive walkthrough method.

AN EXAMPLE OF A COGNITIVE WALKTHROUGH TASK:

Task: Pay for 2 hour parking with a credit card

Action 1: Select 2 hour option

1. Will the users be trying to achieve whatever effect Action 1 has?

2. Will the user see the correct action is available?

3. Will the user associate the correct action with the effect (s)he is trying to achieve?

4. If the correct action is taken, will the user understand that progress is being made toward the desired solution?

See also 46. Heuristic Evaluation • 87. Think-aloud Protocol • 99. Wizard of Oz

14 Collage

As inspiration for design teams, collage allows participants to visually express their thoughts, feelings, desires, and other aspects of their life that are difficult to articulate using traditional means.[1]

When prompted by traditional research methods such as questionnaires and interviews, people often find it challenging or uncomfortable to articulate and express their innermost feelings, thoughts, and desires. Collage can help mitigate this challenge, by providing an opportunity for research participants to project personal information onto visual artifacts, then using these results as a tangible reference point for conversation.

A collage kit typically includes card or paper sheets, a preset collection of images, words, and shapes, and glue sticks. Recent studies have also experimented with screen-based collage sessions using custom-made software.[2] Collages are each completed by a single person, but sessions are generally conducted in small groups. A critical component is to have participants present their collages to the group or researcher, to provide clarity and insight about image choices and meaning. Presentations are videotaped for later analysis of footage or transcripts.

Collage is usually instructed openly to allow for participant interpretations. For example, participants may be invited to collage their view on some phenomena (technology, information), or their feelings about particular service experiences (hospital, finances), or their home or work life. A common framework is to include time dimensions to the collage instructions, for instance, experiences past, today, and in an ideal future. Participants may be provided with a blank paper canvas on which to create their collage, or it may have general frames or lines to suggest placing words and images above or below a line, along an axis, or within or outside a shape or outlined object.

The challenge for designers in creating collage kits is to find the right quantity and level of specificity in images and words—ambiguous enough so that they do not bias the participant, yet specific enough to be relevant to the topic being collaged. Blank frames or stickers should be provided, and markers to add participants' own material to the collage.

Qualitative analysis is used to look for patterns and themes within and across several collages. Coding may include the use or nonuse of particular images, words, and shapes, negative and positive use of elements, position of elements on the page, and the relationship between elements. To obtain a level of objectivity and rigor in the analysis, collage interpretations may be compared between the facilitators who attended the session and those who were not there; by individually interpreting collages and then discussing them in design teams; and by analyzing the visual artifact with and without the transcript of the participant.

1. Creative, participatory tools for design, including collage, have been pioneered by Liz Sanders. See, for example:

Sanders, Elizabeth B.-N., and Colin T. William. "Harnessing People's Creativity: Ideation and Expression through Visual Communication" *Focus Groups: Supporting Effective Product Development.* London: Taylor and Francis, 2001.

See additional readings from research and practice at http://www.maketools.com.

2. Stappers, Pieter Jan, and Elizabeth B.-N. Sanders. "Generative Tools for Context Mapping: Tuning the Tools" in *Design and Emotion: The Experience of Everyday Things.* London: Taylor & Francis, 2003: 85-89.

Behavioral	Quantitative	**Innovative**	Exploratory	**Participatory**
Attitudinal	**Qualitative**	Adapted	**Generative**	Observational
		Traditional	Evaluative	Self reporting
				Expert review
				Design process

Collage allows participants to project their thoughts, feelings, and desires onto a visual artifact, providing insight and inspiration for design teams.

Participants working with various collage materials.

Participant engaged in the collage-making process to communicate personal impressions of information technology, today and in the future.

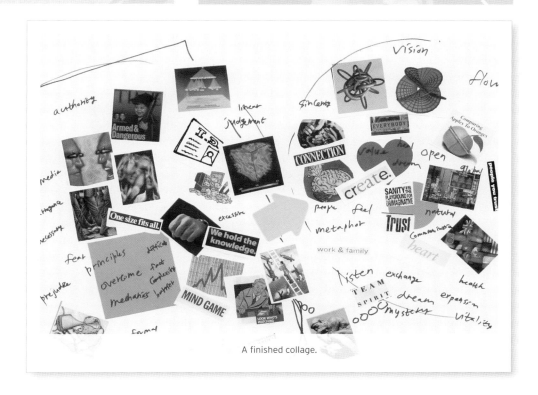

A finished collage.

See also 21. Creative Toolkits • 44. Generative Research • 61. Participatory Design

15 Competitive Testing

Competitive testing is the process of conducting research to evaluate the usability and learnability of your competitors' products.[1]

Keeping a pulse on the competition's business activity is a necessary marketing practice in most organizations. The process includes monitoring a competitor's key business financials such as revenue and operating profit, as well as company size, and product and service mix on an ongoing basis. Although the analysis of competitor information can be helpful when refining a market strategy, these traditional business audits rarely take a user-centered perspective, nor do they consider the social, economic, and technical realities that shape the context in which products and services help people accomplish goals in their day-to-day lives.

Competitive testing provides design teams with an opportunity to assess a competitor's products from the end user's point of view. According to studies, the difference between your site and your competitors' can reveal a 68% gap in usability.[2] Teams inspect how usable and learnable competitors' digital applications are by conducting usability tests on their three to four competitive products, as well as on their own.[3] Unlike other methods that might survey *attitudes* toward competitor products (e.g., surveys or focus groups), competitive testing focuses on end-user *behavior* as they attempt to accomplish tasks that exist across products.

When testing a competitor's digital application, it is likely that you will be able to reuse the same scripts, scenarios, and tasks you use when testing the usability of your product interface.[4] Although identifying the similarities to test between competitor sites is important, it's equally important to isolate and test the features of the competitive product that are different from yours. By understanding the key differences between online, multichannel solutions, gaps can be identified that can provide clues for further market differentiation or specialization.

Researchers must be aware of the potential for introducing bias into competitive testing usability sessions. A best practice should be to not reveal your company name to participants when recruiting for the event. During the event, be mindful that even the subtlest body language—a flinch, a smirk, a nod—can influence a participant's reactions and alter their behavior. To avoid any potential issues, hiring a third-party consultant is worth considering when planning for competitive testing.[5]

Results from competitive tests should be tracked and compared over time. It may be worthwhile scheduling them to recur on an ongoing basis and alongside the marketing department's competitive audits. Together, the results of competitive research that include insights from competitive testing will reveal a fuller, more compelling picture about the competition in your industry, and how they are positioning themselves in the market.

1. Kuniavsky, Mike. *Observing the User Experience*. San Francisco, CA: Morgan Kaufmann, 2003.

2. Nielsen, Jakob. "How Big is the Difference Between Websites?" 2004, www.useit.com.

3. Nielsen, Jakob. "Parallel & Iterative Design + Competitive Testing = High Usability," 2011, www.useit.com.

4. See note 1 above.

5. See note 1 above.

Behavioral	Quantitative	Innovative	Exploratory	Participatory
Attitudinal	**Qualitative**	**Adapted**	Generative	**Observational**
		Traditional	**Evaluative**	**Self reporting**
				Expert review
				Design process

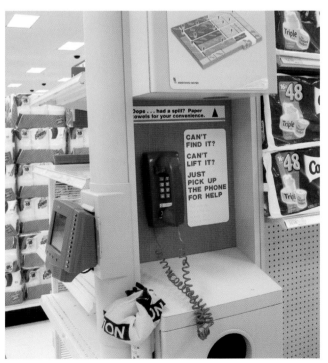

Before designing a shopping assistant for a retail warehouse environment, a design team conducted competitive research of existing, in-store help kiosks.

Courtesy of Ruqian Zhou, Kelly Nash, Theyab Al-Tamimi, Matthew Deutsch, Aesha Shah

See also 50. Kano Analysis • 87. Think-aloud Protocol • 96. Value Opportunity Analysis

16 Concept Mapping

Concept mapping is a visual framework that allows designers to absorb new concepts into an existing understanding of a domain so that new meaning can be made.[1]

A concept map is a sense-making tool that connects a large number of ideas, objects, and events as they relate to a certain domain. It provides a scaffolding that can help designers visualize the complexities of a system, and assists them as they make and break connections, study existing connections, and expand on what is already understood but possibly taken for granted within a particular system.

Concept maps consist of individual *concepts* (a well-understood idea, object, or event; usually a noun or noun cluster) connected by *linking words* (usually a verb). When linking words connect two or more concepts, a *proposition* is formed that creates a meaningful statement. As propositions emerge, some relationships may reflect knowledge that is already understood, but others will represent new knowledge.[2] The power of the concept map is that it brings new connections into focus within the context of already understood information. As new insights are formed, designers can study relationships between old and new concepts, revealing new meaning as it relates to the domain.

To construct a concept map, it is important to have a good understanding of the domain. If one's understanding of the concepts is limited, it will be difficult to make meaningful interconnections with linking words.[3] Also, articulating the correct focus question is a key step that will provide context and structure to the map. "How do people share pictures" and "How do people want to share pictures" should lead to different maps: the former providing a listing of options, the latter, a more exploratory audit suggesting a range of opportunities.

After a focus question is generated, a list of fifteen to twenty-five concepts should be identified and ranked from general to very specific, as they relate to the focus question. Successful concept maps are organized hierarchically based on this ranking, even if it is just a loose organization at first. Once all of the concepts are ranked, the next step is to initiate the construction of a preliminary map using either paper-based or computer-based tools that make it easy to move concepts around. Ideally, the concepts can be moved around by trial and error until the best hierarchy is reached.

Once a strong map is in place, cross-links identify relationships between subdomains in the map, and linking words articulate individual concepts. This can be the most difficult step for the mapmaker.[4] Finally, revise, reposition, and rewrite until a final map emerges that adequately answers the focus questions. Maps that meet the above criteria should help design teams gain new knowledge, and find new meanings in an information space.

1. While researching how children learn new concepts and information, David Ausubel determined that learning is more meaningful when new information is assimilated into existing frameworks that children already grasp. While seeking a better way to represent the learning process, what emerged was the idea of visually representing children's knowledge in the form of a concept map. See:

Ausubel, David P. *The Psychology of Meaningful Verbal Learning*. New York and London: Grune and Stratton, 1963.

2. Ausubel, David, Joseph D. Novak, and H. Hanesian. *Educational Psychology: A Cognitive View*, 2nd ed. New York: Holt, Rinehart & Winston, 1978.

3. See note 2 above.

4. See note 2 above

5. Novak, J. D., and A. J. Cañas. "The Theory Underlying Concept Maps and How to Construct and Use Them" in *Technical Report IHMC CmapTools 2006-01 Rev. 01-2008*, Florida Institute for Human and Machine Cognition, 2008, http://cmap .ihmc.us/Publications/ResearchPapers/ TheoryUnderlyingConceptMaps.pdf

CmapTools, a knowledge modeling kit that is designed to construct concept maps, is available online at cmap.ihmc.us.

Further Reading

Novak, Joseph D,. and D. Bob Gowin. *Learning How to Learn*. Cambridge: Cambridge University Press, 1984.

Preszler, R. W. "Cooperative Concept Mapping Improves Performance in Biology." *Journal of College Science Teaching* 33 (2004): 30-35.

Behavioral	Quantitative	Innovative	Exploratory	Participatory
Attitudinal	**Qualitative**	Adapted	**Generative**	Observational
		Traditional	Evaluative	Self reporting
				Expert review
				Design process

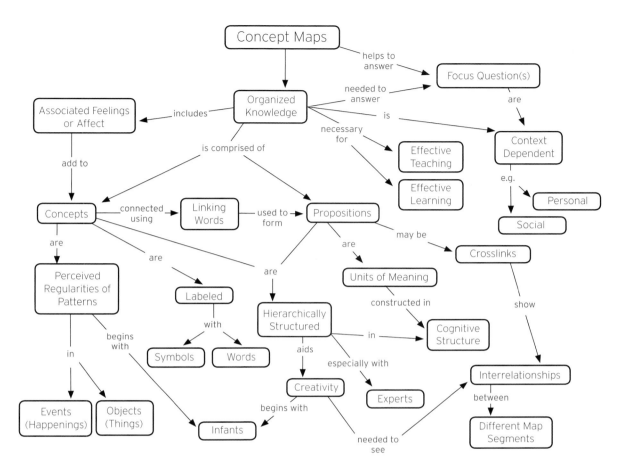

Concept Maps

helps to answer → Focus Question(s)

Organized Knowledge

needed to answer → Focus Question(s)

Focus Question(s) → are → Context Dependent

Associated Feelings or Affect ← includes ← Organized Knowledge

Organized Knowledge → is → Context Dependent

Organized Knowledge → necessary for → Effective Teaching / Effective Learning

Associated Feelings or Affect → add to → Concepts

Organized Knowledge → is comprised of → Concepts / Propositions

Context Dependent → e.g. → Personal / Social

Concepts → connected using → Linking Words → used to form → Propositions

Concepts → are → Perceived Regularities of Patterns

Concepts → are → Labeled

Propositions → are → Units of Meaning

Propositions → may be → Crosslinks

Crosslinks → show → Interrelationships

Units of Meaning → constructed in → Cognitive Structure

Propositions → are → Hierarchically Structured

Perceived Regularities of Patterns → in → Events (Happenings)

Perceived Regularities of Patterns → begins with → Objects (Things)

Labeled → with → Symbols / Words

Hierarchically Structured → in → Cognitive Structure

Hierarchically Structured → aids → Creativity

Hierarchically Structured → especially with → Experts

Creativity → begins with → Infants

Creativity → needed to see → Interrelationships

Interrelationships → between → Different Map Segments

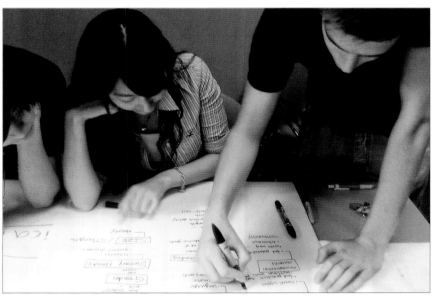

Concept maps are organized in a downward hierarchy, with the focus question at the top of the map and the most general concepts below it.

Concepts are well-understood ideas, objects, or events, connected by *linking words*. When linking words connect two or more concepts, a *proposition* is formed that potentially challenges existing thinking or creates new meaning.[5]

Courtesy of Joseph D. Novak and Alberto J. Cañas, http://cmap.ihmc.us

See also *08. Brainstorm Graphic Organizers* • *12. Cognitive Mapping* • *56. Mind Mapping*

17 Content Analysis

Content analysis is the systematic description of form and content of written, spoken, or visual materials expressed in themes, patterns, and counted occurrences of words, phrases, images, or concepts.

Qualitative research methods that collect rich descriptions such as open-ended responses, narrative descriptions, and visual expressions are often characterized as an "attractive nuisance."[1] On the one hand, the material contains deep accounts of compelling information critical to design inquiry; on the other hand, lengthy text, interview transcripts, and ambiguous images can be challenging and time consuming to analyze. Content analysis provides an established and systematic technique for dealing with qualitative data, whether analyzing existing records and archived documents, or new materials generated by research participants through interviews, questionnaires, or creative methods such as drawing or collage.

Two primary approaches to content analysis are inductive and deductive, the former being preferred and more common. In inductive content analysis, the categories or codes are derived from a systematic reading of a sample set of the materials to be analyzed, gradually establishing the categories that will be used for subsequent analysis of all the materials. For example, in a review of transcripts, as key phrases emerge constituting a common theme, a name is given that characterizes the theme, and then subsequent examples of words or phrases that represent that theme are categorized accordingly.

In deductive content analysis, the codes or categories are derived prior to analysis, often based on a theoretical framework. For example, in a study of product advertising, codes could be established from Maslow's Hierarchy of Needs, looking for textual and visual instances that exemplify physical or social needs, safety, or self-actualization. These codes could have a further indicator of strength, and whether the message was explicit or implicit.

The outcomes of content analysis can be quantitative, most often counting simple occurrences of the units of analysis: words, phrases, images, concepts; but it may also satisfy the needs of the particular analysis to merely identify the common themes and patterns that emerge from the data, supported by a general indication of how dominantly they are represented. Affinity diagrams are useful in clustering units of analysis to derive and subsequently name theme categories.

In addition to content, the analysis method examines form, or structure of communication; for example, the scale and location of images or the font and type size of text on a page or screen or within a document, and the relationships between texts and images. For smaller sample sets, content analysis can be done manually; for larger information sets, software is available for sophisticated analysis and communication of results.[2]

1. Robson, Colin. *Real World Research: A Resource for Social Scientists and Practitioner-Researchers*, 2nd ed. Oxford: Blackwell Publishers, 2002.

2. See QSR International for an overview of qualitative analysis tools such as NVivo at http://www.qsrinternational.com

Further Reading

Sommer, Robert, and Barbara Sommer. *A Practical Guide to Behavioral Research: Tools and Techniques*. New York: Oxford University Press, 2002.

Many academic institutions have writing guides that provide information on content analysis, for example: http://writing.colostate.edu/guides/research/content/index.cfm

Behavioral	Quantitative	Innovative	Exploratory	Participatory
Attitudinal	Qualitative	Adapted	Generative	Observational
		Traditional	Evaluative	Self reporting
				Expert review
				Design process

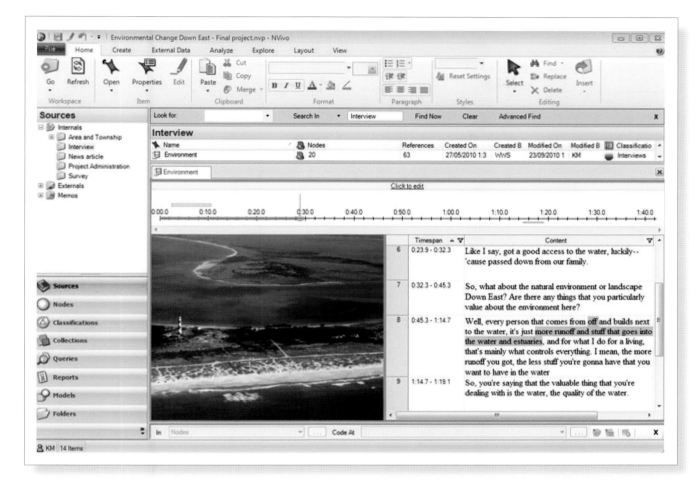

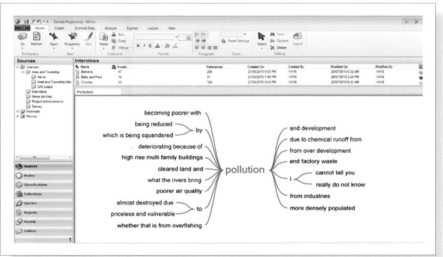

Content analysis helps you extract themes and make meaning out of unstructured information, often with the help of software.

Above: Screenshot of NVivo 9 main window.

Left: Screenshot of a word tree in NVivo 9.

Published with permission from QSR International

See also 03. Affinity Diagramming • 86. Thematic Networks • 100. Word Clouds

18 Content Inventory & Audit

A content inventory tells you what your content is. A content audit makes recommendations as to what your content should be.

Content is more than just text, and it can encompass all the information that you package and publish for your customer's benefit. Everything a customer can read, watch, interact with, or listen to can be considered content, as each of these activities plays an important part in how people will feel about your product or service.

The content inventory and auditing process assumes two things: first, that you have content to index, and second, that you have someone on staff with an affinity for organization and information . If you meet those two requirements, here are a few situations in which to perform an inventory and audit:

- When beginning a website redesign
- When merging multiple sites, or conversely, a site is being split up into smaller, niche sites
- When preparing content for multichannel distribution or a Content Management System (CMS)

A content inventory is a quantitative exercise that aggregates all of your content assets, and is typically organized in a spreadsheet. In content inventory, the spreadsheet's rows usually represent the content items, and columns represent content attributes. During the content inventory stage, the information listed in the table below under "General Information" is recorded.

The content audit is both quantitative and qualitative. The quantitative content audit follows the content inventory, and begins the assessment, or evaluation, of the content using the attributes of "Governance" criteria below. The evaluation of content continues with the qualitative content audit, which rates the criteria in the "Content Quality" column below. The qualitative audit can also identify unifying themes and patterns across content sources.

GENERAL INFORMATION	GOVERNANCE	CONTENT QUALITY (LOW/MED/HIGH SCALE)
Identification/Numbering System	Created by	Credible?
Title/Name	Create Date	Original?
URL or Data Source	Updated Date	Accurate?
Document Type	Owned by	Relevant to Audience?
Comments/Notes	Due Date	Relevant to Business?
	Legal Review Required?	Accessible? (508 Compliance)
	Any TMs or ©	

Although affordable, content inventories and audits can take a lot of time and care to be done well and comprehensively. Once you have established the process, ongoing audits can be used to help you prepare a business case for your next initiative.

Further Reading

Halvorson, Kristina. *Content Strategy for the Web.* Berkeley, CA: Peachpit Press, 2009.

Jones, Colleen. *Clout: The Art and Science of Influential Web Content.* Berkeley, CA: New Riders, 2010.

Rosenfeld, Lou. *The Rolling Content Inventory.* 2006, www.louisrosenfeld.com

Veen, Jeff. *Doing a Content Inventory (Or, A Mind-Numbingly Detailed Odyssey Through Your Web Site).* 2002, www.adaptivepath.com

Behavioral	Quantitative	Innovative	Exploratory	Participatory
Attitudinal	Qualitative	Adapted	Generative	Observational
		Traditional	Evaluative	Self reporting
				Expert review
				Design process

QUALITATIVE CONTENT AUDIT

Content was rated on: Credibility, Originality, Accuracy, Relevance to Business, Relevance to Audience, and Accessibility.

- ■ High quality
- ▪ Medium quality
- ■ Low quality

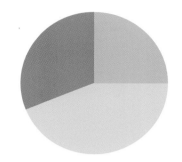

Corporate News	Research & Development	Products & Solutions

QUANTITATIVE CONTENT AUDIT

The following content types were identified per each web site section:

- ■ Text
- ▪ Infographic or Charts
- ▪ Animation
- ■ Video
- ■ Audio

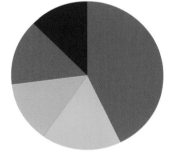

Content inventories and audits can provide both quantitative and qualitative assessments of your current content. Project stakeholders will rarely want to examine spreadsheets to find insights and recommendations, but a few key visualizations can help them understand where their content stands today, and they can begin to get a sense of what has to happen to get it where it needs to be.

Reporting methodology courtesy of Content Science

Corporate News	Research & Development	Products & Solutions

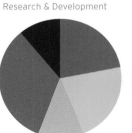

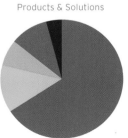

See also 10. Card Sorting • 51. Key Performance Indicators • 78. Site Search Analytics

19 Contextual Design

Contextual design is a customer-centered process that makes the ways in which designers work concrete, explicit, and sharable so that every step is anchored in customer data and feels less like design "magic."[1]

Making the leap from customer-centered data to a sound design direction is a process that involves many methods of data collection, intermediary steps of analysis and synthesis, and a host of research deliverables. Seasoned designers understand this work intuitively—over time, experience and trust in the design process shapes our confidence to execute the work. But to non-designers, this process can seem fuzzy. In an effort to make the work that designers do explicit and sharable, the steps of the contextual design process make our work more predictable and inclusive.

Contextual design prescribes a reliable course of action that guides the team as it transitions through the stages of the design process—starting with user-centered data, through data synthesis and design implications, and ending with an appropriate design direction. Depending on your organization's culture or project directive, contextual design can be adapted to include (or omit) steps that may not translate well to your organization. The recommended steps are:[2]

- *Contextual Inquiry* provides designers with a rich, qualitative understanding of who the customer is, and what it takes to do the customer's work on a day-to-day basis.

- *Interpretation Sessions* are structured debriefing sessions for each customer interview. They enrich the process by creating a framework for everyone to apply their multidisciplinary perspectives when analyzing user data.

- *Work Models and Affinity Diagrams* provide teams with a framework to develop an externalized representation of the complex systems of work. There are five types of work models: flow, sequence, artifact, cultural, and physical.

- *Visioning and Storyboarding* take the implications of the consolidated work models and use them for generating concepts and working out the details, helping the team to invent new or better ways to support the customer's work.

- *User Environment Design* represents a new "floor plan" for a system that augments existing behaviors and supports the natural flow of the customer's work. It documents the structure, function, and flow between "places" in the system.

- *Paper Mock-ups* are used to get feedback from customers on the structure, function, and flow of the proposed design before it is coded and implemented.

The contextual design process can reduce the time it takes to move through the design effort.[3] It is well received in interdisciplinary companies that need a more inclusive and concrete process to follow when responding to customer-centered design challenges.

1. Contextual design is a process created and documented by Karen Holtzblatt, the owner of InContext Enterprises, Inc., and the inventor of the *contextual inquiry* method. See:

Holtzblatt, Karen, and Hugh Beyer. *Contextual Design: A Customer-Centered Approach to Systems Design*. San Francisco, CA: Morgan Kaufmann, 1998.

2. Holtzblatt, Karen, Jessamyn Burns Wendell, and Shelley Wood. *Rapid Contextual Design: A How-To Guide to Key Techniques for User-Centered Design*. San Francisco, CA: Morgan Kaufmann, 2004.

3. See note 2 above.

4. See notes 1 and 2 above.

Behavioral	Quantitative	**Innovative**	**Exploratory**	Participatory
Attitudinal	**Qualitative**	Adapted	**Generative**	Observational
		Traditional	**Evaluative**	Self reporting
				Expert review
				Design process

Contextual design is a customer-centered process that begins with customer data revealed by the contextual inquiry method. The process is intended to help with the transitions between the steps of the design process: moving from (1) discovering what matters to users and characterizing what they do, (2) identifying and articulating new ideas and direction, (3) redesigning activities and technology to provide value, and (4) iterating the system with users to make meaningful improvements.[4]

Courtesy of InContext Design

Contextual Design process steps

Requirements & Solutions	Contextual Inquiry	Talk to specific customers in the field	1
	Interpretation Session	Interpret the data as a team to capture issues	
	Work Models & Affinity Diagramming	Consolidate data across customers for a full market view	
	Visioning	Redesign people's work with new technology ideas	2
Define & Validate Concepts	Storyboarding	Work out the details of particular tasks and roles	
	User Environment Design	Design system to support this work	3
	Paper Mock-Up Interviews	Mock up the interface using interaction patterns for testing	
	Interaction & Visual Design	Design and test the final look and user experience	4

See also 03. Affinity Diagramming • 20. Contextual Inquiry • 82. Storyboards

20 Contextual Inquiry

Contextual inquiry is an immersive, contextual method of observing and interviewing that reveals underlying (and invisible) work structure.[1]

Before design teams can improve the ways in which people work, researchers must observe work where it happens. Spending time where work takes place is a precondition to understanding users' tacit knowledge, and contextual inquiry provides a framework that places the researcher on-site as a participant in the inquiry, and begins the process of exposing underlying work structure.

There are four principles that define the contextual inquiry method:[2]

Context The most basic requirement for contextual inquiry is that researchers must spend time where the work happens. It is critical to understand the "ongoing experience" of the worker rather than just the "summary experience." To discover underlying work structure, the researcher has to observe details about the day-to-day activities of people.

Partnership One of the most powerful characteristics of contextual inquiry is its application of the *master/apprentice* relationship model. Just as an apprentice learns by watching, respectfully asking questions, and seeking to understand *why* things are done a certain way, the master craftsman teaches by doing and talking about tasks as they play out. The transfer of knowledge about work structure happens more reliably when people talk about how they work *while they do the work*. As a result, the research data more reliably reflects reality.

Interpretation What researchers see and hear is just the starting point—all data must be interpreted for meaning before its design implications can be understood. From the data (what was heard or observed), researchers make a hypothesis (or interpretation) about what that data means to the participant. It is critical to double-check your interpretations while on-site with the participant; if this opportunity is missed, the misinterpretation could lead to failed design implications and ideas.

Focus The contextual inquiry researcher must learn to expand the limits of his or her personal focus and see more in the participant's world. Any time a researcher is surprised, finds a participant's behavior idiosyncratic, or picks up on a contradiction, there is an opportunity for the researcher to refocus the interview to see beyond personal experiences.

Use contextual inquiry to understand communication *flows*, *sequence* of tasks, the *artifacts* and tools people use to accomplish work, the impact and influence of the *culture* on the work, and also, the impact and influence of the *physical environment* on the work.[3] A contextual interview is usually completed in a two- to three-hour session. How many people you need to interview depends on the scope of the project and work you want to support, but you need to interview multiple people in different user segments before the synthesis of contextual inquiry findings can begin (see *Affinity Diagramming*).

1. Contextual inquiry is a method adapted from the immersive work of ethnographers. The method was invented by Karen Holtzblatt as part of the contextual design customer-centered process. Karen is a member of the CHI Academy, and in 2010 she received CHI's first Lifetime Achievement Award for Practice for her prolific contributions to the field of human-computer interaction.

2. Contextual inquiry is just one part of the contextual design process, which also includes work modeling, consolidation (which uses affinity diagramming), work redesign, user environment design, and prototyping and testing with customers. Each of these sections is fully defined in Holtzblatt and Beyer's book:

Holtzblatt, Karen, and Hugh Beyer. *Contextual Design: A Customer-Centered Approach to Systems Design*. San Francisco, CA: Morgan Kaufmann, 1998.

3. See note 2 above.

Further Reading

Holtzblatt, Karen, Jessamyn Burns Wendell, and Shelley Wood. *Rapid Contextual Design: A How-To Guide to Key Techniques for User-Centered Design*. San Francisco, CA: Morgan Kaufmann, 2004.

Behavioral	Quantitative	Innovative	Exploratory	Participatory
Attitudinal	Qualitative	Adapted	Generative	Observational
		Traditional	Evaluative	Self reporting
				Expert review
				Design process

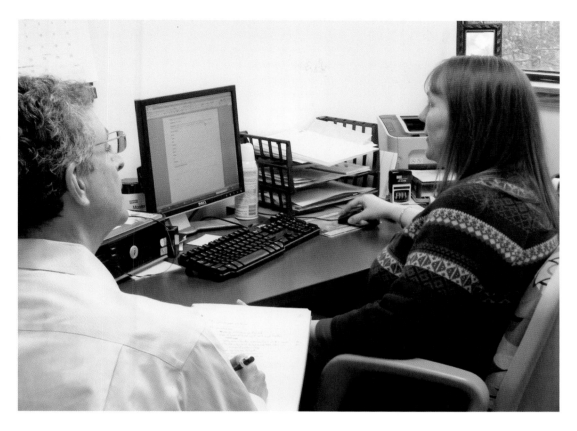

Unless observed, most people will summarize their work activities and speak abstractly about tasks, because typically their processes are invisible to them. Contextual Inquiry provides a way to structure interviews with people that expose specific details about how they work, and helps expose underlying work structure.

Above: an InContext Design researcher is conducting a contextual inquiry interview. Right: after the interview, the InContext Design team works together in an affinity diagramming exercise that helps externalize the complexity of a work system revealed in the interviews.

Courtesy of InContext Design

See also 03. Affinity Diagramming • 19. Contextual Design • 48. Interviews

21 Creative Toolkits

Creative toolkits are collections of physical elements conveniently
organized for participatory modeling, visualization, or creative play
by users, to inform and inspire design and business teams.[1]

Creative toolkits are really a means of conveniently packaging the elements of any of several participatory, generative design methods. Engaging people in creative expression through facilitated
participatory exercises can provide them with a tangible artifact on which to project thoughts,
feelings, desires, and emotions that might be otherwise hard to articulate using traditional
research methods. Creative toolkits can also foster innovation through creativity, and they can
provide a constructive impetus for team building.

The ingredients of creative toolkits are determined by the possibilities of the various activities that they aim to encourage. For example, kits for flexible or Velcro modeling will contain a
significant range of three-dimensional forms, buttons, and ambiguous design elements that can
be easily attached to each other and removed. Interface kits can contain paper or card elements
representing design features for flexible arrangement, for suggesting mock or ideal web or device
interactions. Collage kits can contain an inventory of images and words, or shape and symbol
elements for open interpretation and use relevant to the design inquiry. Drawing kits will contain
various papers, cards, markers, pencils, and pens, accommodating a range of potential exercises
for participants. Large toolkits may combine several or all of these elements to accommodate a
range of participatory design activities.

One goal of toolkit creation is to arrive at a set of elements that can be reused for a variety of
research sessions in participatory design, even if some parts may need re-stocking after each use.
For example, image and word cards in a collage kit could be laminated, and each collage photographed. In this instance, the toolkit could be reused across several participants within the same
design inquiry, but would likely need editing for each new subject matter.

In addition to toolkits that may target specific design activities or subject themes, flexible parts
can also be assembled to encourage play. Depending on the intent of the exercise, play kits can be
built from original materials, or from existing parts, constructive toys, or games.

Another motivating factor in the creation of toolkits is portability, facilitating ease of storage,
transport and use across locations, and the packing and unpacking of parts. This is particularly
useful if participatory design sessions are held in a number of locations, such as private homes, or
for design workshops in several different workplaces.

1. Creative, participatory tools for design have
been pioneered by Liz Sanders. For examples
and readings from research and practice, see:
http://www.maketools.com

2. http://www.seriousplay.com

Further Reading

Sanders, Elizabeth B.-N., and Colin T. William.
"Harnessing People's Creativity: Ideation and
Expression through Visual Communication"
in *Focus Groups: Supporting Effective Product
Development*. London: Taylor and Francis,
2001.

Behavioral	Quantitative	Innovative	Exploratory	Participatory
Attitudinal	Qualitative	Adapted	Generative	Observational
		Traditional	Evaluative	Self reporting
				Expert review
				Design process

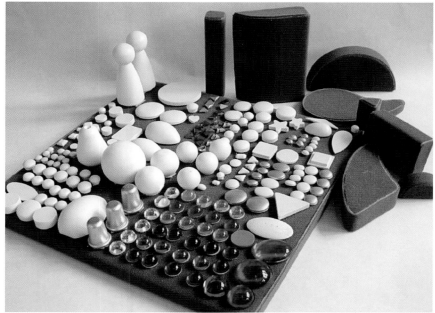

Above: LEGO has predesigned kits for their method of "Serious Play," for building metaphors, creative story making and imagination in business settings, through a series of application workshops. "Based on research that shows that this kind of hands-on, minds-on learning produces a deeper, more meaningful understanding of the world and its possibilities, LEGO Serious Play deepens the reflection process and supports an effective dialogue–for everyone in the organization."[2]

Courtesy of Cecilia Weckstrom, The LEGO Group

Above: A typical Velcro modeling kit with form and element variations designed for physical manipulation and configuration by participants.

Courtesy of Liz Sanders, MakeTools, LLC

See also 28. Design Workshops • 44. Generative Research • 61. Participatory Design

22 Critical Incident Technique

Understanding how users experience your product at critical moments can help you optimize your designs for future users.[1]

Have you ever tried to course-correct a situation to find that the problem was actually made worse by the step that you hoped would fix it? Or what about a time when you made one simple decision, and the outcome delighted you so much that you had to share your positive experience with others?

Both of these situations are "critical incidents," because both are examples of an event taking place, but a gap exists between the anticipated result and what actually happened. Both situations probably made you think, feel, and react in ways that you did not initially anticipate.[2] The Critical Incident Technique (CIT) helps you isolate, study, and make inferences about this class of events.

The method entails asking individuals to retrospectively describe a situation about your product or service that, in their estimation, either ended well or poorly. The research team collects incidents—which are really just positive or negative experiences captured through directed storytelling, interviews, or diary studies. Between 50 and 100 incidents are usually enough to collect for a workable sample size,[3] but depending on the nature of the problem you are studying, you may want to collect more. The CIT will help you to identify:

- *The incident cause:* What were the events leading up to the critical incident?
- *User actions:* What were the behaviors that took place during the incident?
- *User sentiment:* How did the user feel during the incident, and afterward?
- *Incident outcome:* Did the user change how he or she behaved after the incident? What are other possible outcomes if no changes are made?
- *Ideal outcome:* If behaviors change, what are other possible future outcomes?

Each critical incident is considered effective if it helps to solve a problem, or ineffective if it fails to solve a problem, creates new problems, or creates the need for further actions.[4] The purpose of the data analysis stage is to summarize the data in such a way that the findings can be implemented, and inferences can be made to explain both positive and negative incidents. Positive and negative incidents are analyzed and reported separately.

The goal is to generate representative scenarios that cover both the positive and negative critical incidents, generate possible explanations for the different incidents, and include recommendations for improving future outcomes. Teams can then prioritize the recommendations, and triangulate results from other research to gain a better understanding of situations that have a profound impact on future user behavior.

1. Colonel John C. Flanagan developed the technique during World War II as an outgrowth of studies in the Aviation Psychology Program of the United States Army Air Forces. See: Flanagan, John C. "The Critical Incident Technique." *Psychological Bulletin* 5 (1954): 327-358.

2. See note 1 above.

3. Urquhart, Christine, Ann Light, Rhian Thomas, Anne Barker, Alison Yeoman, Jan Cooper, Chris Armstrong, Roger Fenton, Ray Lonsdale, and Siân Spink. "Critical Incident Technique and Explicitation Interviewing in Studies of Information Behavior." *Library & Information Science Research* 25, no. 1 (2003): 63-88.

4. Serenko, Alexander. "The Use of Interface Agents for Email Notification in Critical Incidents." *International Journal of Human-Computer Studies* 64, no. 11 (2006): 1084-1098.

Further Reading

Ryan, Gerry W., and H. Russel Bernard. "Data Management and Analysis Methods" in *Handbook of Qualitative Research*. Thousand Oaks, CA: Sage Publications, 2000: 769-802.

Serenko, Alexander, and Andrea Stach. "The Impact of Expectation Disconfirmation on Customer Loyalty and Recommendation Behavior: Investigating Online Travel and Tourism Services." *Journal of Information Technology Management* (2010): 26-41.

Behavioral	Quantitative	Innovative	**Exploratory**	Participatory
Attitudinal	Qualitative	Adapted	Generative	Observational
		Traditional	Evaluative	**Self reporting**
				Expert review
				Design process

A POSITIVE CRITICAL INCIDENT

A NEGATIVE CRITICAL INCIDENT

The Critical Incident Technique focuses on how people solve problems, with the goal of optimizing and recreating the successful results, and eliminating the negative, counterproductive ones. Here are two examples of Critical Incidents of interactions with a GPS system in a car, one positive, and one negative.

See also 30. Diary Studies • 31. Directed Storytelling • 48. Interviews

23 Crowdsourcing

Crowdsourcing occurs when an undefined, large group of people (a "crowd") voluntarily responds to an open call and completes tasks and microprojects.[1]

Experienced researchers know that planning research takes effort, time, and money to align the necessary tools, participants, and resources. When extra care is taken to properly devise remote user evaluation tasks and experiments, the method of crowdsourcing can be used to elicit a large quantity of data from real people in less time.[2]

Crowdsourcing leverages the "strength of weak ties"[3] in a decentralized model that brings together users and testers—members of the crowd—to evaluate prototypes and submit potential solutions to problems. The "microtasks" that are assigned to volunteers are specifically structured to focus the degree and the nature of effort required from volunteers. A *microtask* is defined as a short task—either qualitative or quantitative—that is accessed via a common platform, and that can be completed by volunteers within just a few seconds or minutes.[4] Once completed, the participants receive some sort of compensation, which can be either monetary (a micropayment) or nonmonetary (e.g., reputation points).

Like most research methods, time and care taken in the design of crowdsourcing evaluations can serve the team well when collecting and analyzing data downstream. When planning crowdsourcing evaluations and microtasks, there are some key design recommendations to consider.[5] First, uncomplicated tasks seem to get the most volunteers to participate, so design tasks to be straightforward. Be sure to include questions that have a bona-fide answer as part of the task. Not only will this prevent volunteers from "gaming" the system by entering nonsense that minimizes their time investment while increasing how much they are rewarded, but also it can help teams to flag suspicious responses as potentially invalid. Devise the tests so that completing them correctly and in good faith requires as much or even less work than entering random, invalid responses.

If your stakeholders value quantitative data and require large, statistically relevant samples to take user-centered research seriously, consider using crowdsourcing as a "gateway" method to open their eyes to the potential of other user-centered research methods. Having access to a global crowdsourcing community has both benefits and drawbacks: on one hand, crowdsourcing provides an opportunity for teams to gather and generalize results to represent a more varied, diverse population. On the other hand, there is a lack of demographic information provided by testers, not to mention other unknowns regarding their expertise or intentions. Ideally, to hedge against these drawbacks, consider triangulation to increase confidence of research outcomes.

1. The term "Crowdsourcing" is a portmanteau of the word "crowd" and the business word "outsourcing." Jeff Howe coined it in "The Rise of Crowdsourcing," a 2006 *Wired* magazine article.

2. Kittur, Aniket, Ed H. Chi, and Bongwon Suh, Palo Alto Research Center. "Crowdsourcing for Usability: Using Micro-Task Markets for Rapid, Remote, and Low-Cost User Measurements," 2007, www.clickadvisor.com

3. See note 1 above.

4. See note 2 above.

5. See note 2 above.

Further Reading

Howe, Jeff. *Crowdsourcing: Why the Power of the Crowd is Driving the Future of Business.* New York: Crown Business, 2009.

Quinn, Alexander J., and Benjamin B. Bederson. "A Taxonomy of Distributed Human Computation." *University of Maryland Technical Report,* 2009.

Behavioral	Quantitative	Innovative	Exploratory	Participatory
Attitudinal	Qualitative	Adapted	Generative	Observational
		Traditional	Evaluative	Self reporting
				Expert review
				Design process

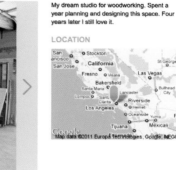

Workbenches

DIY, garage business, artist-in-residence, jobs, school — we all have spaces where we keep and work on our hardware projects. Share your storage triumphs, your multi-use miracles, and stories of how you work where you work. Snap a photo and submit it to the Workbench frogMob — a place we can gather images of where we work, share and find inspirations. We'll look for great ideas, patterns and the unexpected from your images and share them back with you. Open Hardware — Open Workbenches.

TAGS

Audio design Desk Dining Room **Garage** Metal **Multi-use** peg board pegboard printing sewing Shared Use shed Solder **Storage** tools wood Work workbench **Workspace**

More | All

frogMOBSTERS

Celina Pering	15
Michael	8
Jon	5
Alia	3
Vicky	2
Ron	2
Mini	2
Joshua	2
Lori	1
Turi	1
shannon	1

LOCATIONS

San Francisco	18
Austin	16
Brooklyn	9
New York	5
Oakland	3
Berkeley	2
ada, MI	2
Waterfield, CA	2
Palo Alto	1
Milano - Italy	1
Saigon, Vietnam	1
Trecate	1
Bainbridge Island WA	1
Montreal, Canada	1
Santa Monica	1
seattle	1

Santa Monica Woodworking Studio

My dream studio for woodworking. Spent a year planning and designing this space. Four years later I still love it.

LOCATION

Using crowdsourcing, frog's frogmob invites people from all over the world to upload their photographs of interesting trends to inform and inspire designers. The images come together to tell a compelling narrative of how people live in their environments, how they visualize concepts, and the ways in which artifacts create meaning in people's every day lives.

Courtesy of frog, frogmob.frogdesign.com

See also 05. Automated Remote Research • 64. Photo Studies • 91. Triangulation

24 Cultural Probes

Cultural probes are provocative instruments given to participants to inspire new forms of self-understanding and communication about their lives, environments, thoughts, and interactions.[1]

Cultural probes consist of any number of materials designed to inspire people to thoughtfully consider personal context and circumstance, and respond to the design team in unique, creative ways facilitated by the provocations. Cultural probe studies have used postcards, maps, journals, cameras, recording devices, and various pieces of text and imagery to guide personal responses. Cultural probes use several such artifacts, packaged together for participants. The materials, much like the method itself, are intentionally flexible and open-ended. The creators of cultural probes place the method in the artist-designer realm, with an emphasis on being openly subjective, collecting inspirational data to stimulate design imagination.[2]

In a study of interaction techniques to increase the presence of the elderly in three European communities, Bill Gaver et al. created cultural probe kits to gain impressionistic views of participant cultures, preferences, beliefs, and desires.[3] Postcards contained obscure images and were preaddressed for return to the design team, posing open questions about the cultural environment, life, and technology. Several maps printed on various papers asked the elderly to mark zones for meeting others, being alone, dreaming, and going somewhere they could not. Disposable cameras were provided to take images of both assigned and self-selected things, and to use these in telling a story in a small album included in the kit. Finally, a media diary asked about technology interactions and communication.

As an exploratory research method, cultural probes are not intended to be formally analyzed, but rather to serve as inspirational pieces identifying key patterns and themes that might emerge from a participant group or culture. They serve to begin a conversation about possibilities that might exist by design, in tandem with other informative research methods such as observations, site visits, interviews, and secondary sources. In the Gaver et al. study, the results of the returned kits were used as one element to inspire proposals for future possibilities and design conversations, based on the character of each local culture.[4]

Cultural probes are specifically casual and informal, yet thoughtful in their aesthetic craft, message, and delivery, created to inspire delight and respect, response and return. The materials created for probe kits should be varied and imaginative, designed to elicit responses that are relevant to the particular design inquiry. When done well, cultural probes will gain respectable response rates comparable to or exceeding traditional methods, with investment in the exercise by enthusiastic participants, and rich information to inspire great design.

1. The seminal research on cultural probes is by Gaver et al., created for the "Presence Project," examining technology and the increased presence of the elderly in their local communities in Norway, the Netherlands, and Italy. See "Cultural Probes" by Bill Gaver, Tony Dunne and Elena Pacenti, in *Interactions*, January-February 1999, pp. 21-29.

2. See note 1 above.

3. See note 1 above.

4. See note 1 above.

Further Reading

W. Gaver, A. Boucher, S. Pennington, and B. Walker. "Cultural Probes and the Value of Uncertainty" in *Interactions*, Vol. XI.5 (2004): 53-56.

Herd, Kate, A. Bardill, and M. Karamanoglu. "The Co-design Experience: Conceptual Models and Design Tools for Mass Customization" in *Handbook of Research in Mass Customization and Personalization*, vol 1. Singapore: World Scientific Press, 2010.

Herd, Kate, A. Bardill, and M. Karamanoglu. "X-ray Specs, Stickers and Colouring In: Seeing Beyond the Configurator using Design Probes." *Proceedings of 2009 World Conference on Mass Customization & Personalization*, 2009.

Herd, Kate, A. Bardill, and M. Karamanoglu. "Development of a Design Probe to Reveal Customer Touch Points in the Sale of Mass Customised Products." *Design Principles and Practice* 3, no. 3 (2009): 193-208.

Mattelmäki, Tuuli. *Design Probes*. Publication Series of the University of Art and Design Helsinki, 2006, http://www.uiah.fi/publications

Behavioral	Quantitative	**Innovative**	**Exploratory**	Participatory
Attitudinal	**Qualitative**	Adapted	Generative	Observational
		Traditional	Evaluative	**Self reporting**
				Expert review
				Design process

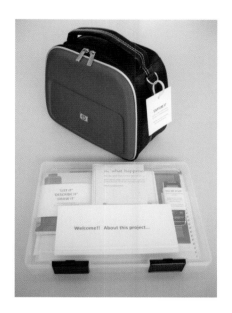

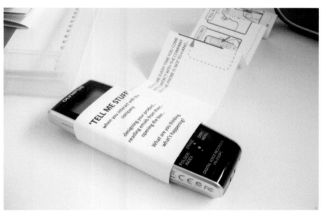

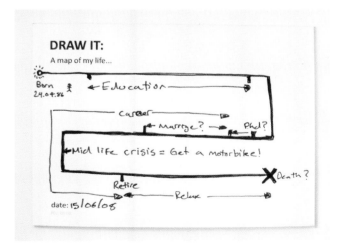

A cultural probe kit for tracking the experience of customers as they move from being consumer to co-designer using mass customizable products. Design probes support empathic understanding through information gathering over a prolonged period, where the researcher cannot be present. The probe kits in this study collected user reflections on experiences through their personal stories, told using digital voice recorders, cameras, postcards, diaries, and stickers.

Courtesy of Kate Herd

See also 30. Diary Studies • 37. Experience Sampling Method • 64. Photo Studies

25 Customer Experience Audit

Customer experience audits capture the day-to-day context in which people engage with your product or service.

Experiences do not exist in a vacuum—rather, they unfold over time, and are shaped by many factors. A customer experience audit captures what customers do, think, and use as they complete a task or set out to achieve a goal that involves your product or service. It provides a framework that design teams can use to isolate specific moments of delight, apathy, or frustration over the course of an entire experience—which includes the *before*, *during*, and *after* phases of an experience. By breaking up an experience into its salient moments, designers and researchers can evaluate how each moment either contributes to or diminishes an experience—regardless of whether it directly or indirectly involves the product or service. Individual moments can then be transformed into the sources of design team inspiration, from which opportunities for innovation can be identified.

When conducting a customer experience audit, it is important for designers to frame their work with rich, qualitative data that reflects people's social, environmental, and financial realities as well as their underlying beliefs, values, and desires. For instance, interviews and directed storytelling can both reveal the journeys people experience and inspire the content of the audit. The fact-based events that comprise an experience audit can only spring to life when the design team understands the context—or frame—of the experience, which may be different for different people. It is only with this understanding that teams can identify which touch points are emotional triggers, which are influenced by contextual factors, where customers need help and where they want to help themselves, and which moments are habitual or "commonplace" (and therefore ripe for innovation). Experience audits can also help researchers isolate the areas where they may need to conduct more research and where gaps in the service or product offering exist.

To keep up with changing social, economic, and technical factors, the customer experience audit should be conducted repeatedly to communicate people's experience with your product over the course of its life cycle. Use it to humanize data, and as a framework to tell a compelling story about people as they interact with your product or service in a larger, real-world context. Ideally, the findings will help design teams to formalize a beginning-to-end commitment to the point of view of the people engaging with a specific product or service as it plays out over time, and ultimately design better products that augment customers' existing contexts and behaviors.

Behavioral	Quantitative	Innovative	Exploratory	Participatory
Attitudinal	Qualitative	Adapted	Generative	Observational
		Traditional	Evaluative	Self reporting
				Expert review
				Design process

CUSTOMER EXPERIENCE WHEEL: LEGO CASE STUDY

Research shows that individuals remember the peaks and troughs of an experience, but are often less capable of detailing the contributing aspects or individual moments of an experience after the event. The LEGO Group designed this three-part tool for recording relevant moments of an experience (Step 1) as they occur, evaluating each moment for consumer relevance and priority (Step 2), and innovating around how to turn the priorities into components of a *Wow experience* (Step 3). Each team member should carry out the assessment in Step 1, in addition to a representative audience of users also charged with the same task. Each assessment contributes to the basis for developing an overview of how the existing experience is perceived, and a shared understanding of the most urgent priorities to improve.

The outcome is a clear, user-centric brief for experience design and the experience wheel can be used continuously throughout the experience design process as components of the new experience are iterated and improved upon. Ultimately it is a litmus test for experience designers to assess whether the intended experience lives up to the user perception and expectations. This tool is part of every experience design project at the LEGO Group, and can be used for assessing and developing product, service, event, online and game experiences, to name but a few.

Courtesy of Cecilia Weckstrom, The LEGO Group

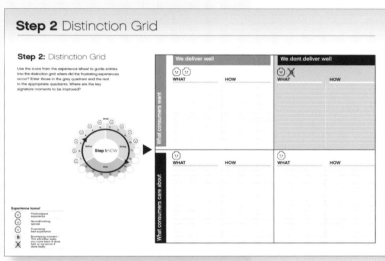

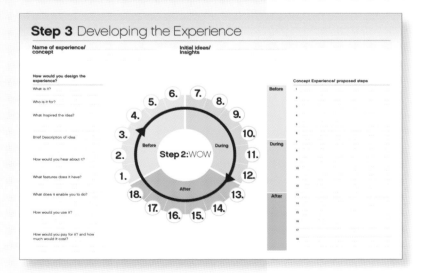

See also 30. Diary Studies • 31. Directed Storytelling • 37. Experience Sampling Method

26 Design Charette

When superior design features and characteristics inspire subsequent rounds of ideas, the end result is more likely to be an optimized design solution.[1]

Design teams flourish when they have a creative environment to explore and share ideas freely, and are expected to leverage and build off each other's best ideas. A design charette is a workshop-style technique that provides a collaborative space that allows for this creation and cross-pollination of design ideas to occur. Designers and non-designers—including project stakeholders, engineers, and users—can participate in a design charette. It can be used to explore ideas about opportunities of a large-scale design challenge, or generate possibilities regarding a very specific interface (where it is more commonly referred to as *parallel prototyping*).[2]

The method is inspired by the process of biological natural selection and genetic algorithms,[3] which seeks to test and select the strongest qualities as the basis for the next generation. This process, when applied over several generations, results in a population (or in the case of a design charette, a design solution) that is optimized for success, given its various requirements.

When planning a design charette, select a physical space that will inspire creativity and the flow of ideas. There should be a public space for participants to come together and discuss the range of ideas, and work spaces for individuals or groups to generate design ideas. At each work space, provide tools to spur creativity: paper templates, pencils, erasers, color markers. The sessions should be decidedly low tech, and a moderator can help to keep things moving, take pictures, and make sure that each group has what they need. Design session outcomes can either be presented, or simply displayed in an area large enough for all participants to congregate and talk about the spectrum of ideas. It should be clearly communicated that each round of designs build off the preferred components identified in the prior cycle.

Oftentimes, more clarity can be achieved not by championing any one particular idea, but through the active comparison and contrast of many ideas.[4] Use design charettes when you want to thoroughly explore a problem space and quickly generate a wide range of ideas. A charette can quickly produce dozens of concepts, but due to the speed of the technique it should be understood that the resulting concepts are rough drafts, or at best, low-fidelity prototypes. The iterative design process can further improve upon the superior design ideas, as can usability testing and other evaluative methods.[5]

1. The National Charrette Institute suggests that the term "charrette" originates from the École des Beaux-Arts in Paris. In the nineteenth century, it was not unusual for student architects to continue working furiously on the illustrations for their design presentations, even while riding in the school cart (*en charrette*) through the streets of Paris en route to submit the projects to their professors. Hence, the term was adapted into the current design-related usage to reflect its rapid pace.

2. McGrew, John F. "Shortening the Human Computer Interface Design Cycle: A Parallel Design Process Based on the Genetic Algorithm." *Proceedings of the Human Factors and Ergonomics Society 45th Annual Meeting*, 2001: 603–606.

Nielsen, Jakob, and Jan Maurits Faber. "Improving System Usability Through Parallel Design." *IEEE Computer* 29, no. 2 (1996): 29–35. Also available online at useit.com.

3. See note 2 (McGrew) above.

4. Tohidi, M., B. Buxton, R. Baecker, A. Sellen. "User Sketches: A Quick, Inexpensive, and Effective Way to Elicit More User Feedback." *Proceedings of NordCHI 2006*, 2006.

5. Nielsen, Jakob, and Heather Dusurvire. "Comparative Design Review: An Exercise in Parallel Design." *ACM INTERCHI'93 Conference Proceedings*, 1993: 414–417.

Behavioral	Quantitative	Innovative	Exploratory	**Participatory**
Attitudinal	**Qualitative**	**Adapted**	**Generative**	Observational
		Traditional	Evaluative	Self reporting
				Expert review
				Design process

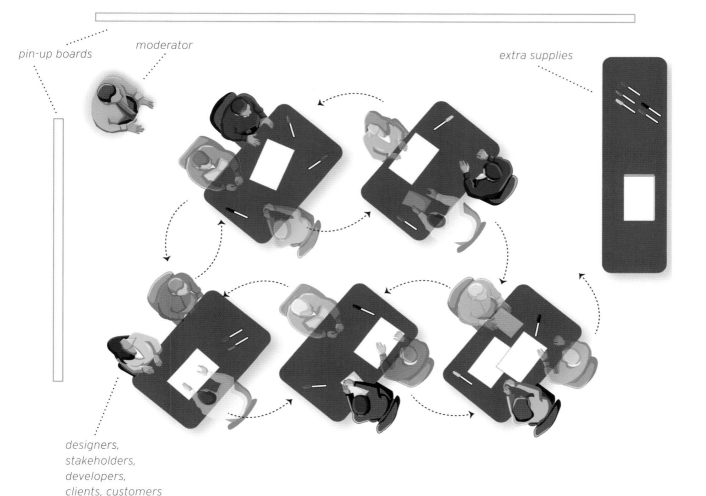

pin-up boards

moderator

extra supplies

designers,
stakeholders,
developers,
clients, customers

HOW A DESIGN CHARETTE WORKS

A creative space is provided for a multidisciplinary group that may consist of designers, stakeholders, and developers to come together and generate potential ideas for a project. Here, small groups of people collaborate at separate tables, and each group is given 10 minutes

to sketch. After 10 minutes, the moderator asks two people from the table to move to different tables, while the third person remains at the table.

Each person brings forward the best ideas from each group, and the cross-pollination of the best

ideas begins to emerge and inform superior design concepts. A benefit of the design charette is that the evaluation and synthesis of ideas happens concurrently over the course of several sessions, and can help everyone involved feel like they are contributing to the final concept.

27 Design Ethnography

Design ethnography approximates the immersion methods of traditional ethnography, to deeply experience and understand the user's world for design empathy and insight.[1]

The intent of exploratory user research in design is clearly exemplified in this definition of ethnography: "The study of people in their natural settings; a descriptive account of social life and culture in a defined social system, based on qualitative methods (e.g., detailed observations, unstructured interviews, analysis of documents)."[2]

While every aspect of the above definition holds true for the motivations of design research, ethnography as practiced by professional ethnographers or anthropologists must be distinguished from design ethnography. While true ethnographers may immerse themselves in a culture or specific population for months or years at a time,[3] designers are more typically seeking sufficient information from time-sampled observations of behaviors. For example, designers conducting immersive ethnographic research may "sample" real experiences of participants through the experience sampling method, diary and photo studies, cultural probes, contextual inquiry, and various forms of observation, including modified versions of participant observation.

Design ethnography is therefore a broad approach encompassing several research methods, focused on a comprehensive and empathic understanding of the users, their lives, their language, and the context of their artifacts and behaviors. The methods of design ethnography are largely qualitative, yet designers can borrow a lesson from the rigor of true ethnographers, as suggested by this description:

"The ethnographer enters the field with an open mind, not an empty head. Before asking the first question in the field, the ethnographer begins with a problem, a theory or model, a research design, specific collection techniques, tools for analysis, and a specific writing style."[4]

Analyses of design ethnography depend on the specific methods used, but are generally focused on a comprehensive view of the users and design territory under investigation, built from deciphering patterns and themes emerging from research materials, and articulated in a set of design implications or guidelines in preparation for generative research and concept development.

1. Seminal work in ethnography derives from social anthropology, and in particular the work of Malinowski. See:

Malinowski, B. *Argonauts of the Western Pacific*. London: Routledge and Kegan Paul, 1922.

Precedent works in design and ethnography include:

"Anthropology: A Research Resource." *Innovation*, special issue. Industrial Designers Society of America, Summer 1996.

Salvador, Tony, Genevieve Bell, and Ken Anderson. "Design Ethnography." *Design Management Journal* (Fall 1999): 35–41.

Sanders, Elizabeth. "Ethnography in NPD Research: How 'Applied Ethnography' can Improve your NPD Research Process." *PDMA Visions Magazine* XXVI, no. 2 (April/May 2002): 8-12.

An extensive ethnography and design bibliography compiled from "Ethnography and Design: Resources for Teaching and Research" by Bruce M. Tharp (ed.), March 2006, is available at designresearch.wikispaces.com/file/view/compiled_ethno_biblio.pdf.

2. Bowling, Ann. *Research Methods in Health: Investigating Health and Health Services*. Buckingham: Open University Press, 1997.

3. LeCompte, Margaret D., and Jean J. Schensul. *Designing and Conducting Ethnographic Research, Ethnographer's Toolkit, Vol. 1*. Walnut Creek, CA: Altamira Press, 1999.

4. Fetterman, David M. *Ethnography Step by Step*, 2nd ed. Thousand Oaks, CA: Sage Publications, 1998.

Behavioral	Quantitative	Innovative	**Exploratory**	Participatory
Attitudinal	**Qualitative**	**Adapted**	Generative	**Observational**
		Traditional	Evaluative	Self reporting
				Expert review
				Design process

DESIGN FOR LEARNING IN EVERYDAY CONTEXTS

Design ethnography of the mechanic's garage, from a study of understanding how technical knowledge and preventative car care might be supported through the design of services and artifacts.

Courtesy of Gretchen Mendoza. Photos by Ivette Spradlin.

See also **24. Cultural Probes** • **39. Exploratory Research** • **59. Participant Observation**

28 Design Workshops

Design workshops are a form of participatory design consolidating creative co-design methods into organized sessions for several participants to work with design team members.

Design workshops are efficient, compelling, fun ways to gain the creative trust and input of stakeholders through activity-based research. Although they can be labor intensive to organize and run, design workshops are worthwhile for their strength in collecting a wealth of insight from participants, and to secure buy-in from team members and clients. Workshops can also be efficient for participants, as they are often brought to the workplace or held in locations convenient to all.

In design exploration, workshops can consist of projective techniques such as collage, mapping, or diagramming exercises, targeted at gaining an understanding of the user's world and establishing design implications. Design workshops are most common in generative research, in participatory sessions focused on co-design exercises such as flexible modeling, contributing to ideation, and verifying design team direction. In evaluative sessions, participants are brought together to collectively review concepts, offer feedback, and contribute insights for design iteration and refinement.

Generally design workshops will entail several activities, planned and orchestrated by design team facilitators. For example, the workshop may begin with an overview of topics and presentation of the agenda, followed by group discussion of concerns, documented or drawn by team members. Individual ideas can be noted by participants on sticky notes, then shared and organized by the group in affinity diagrams. Collages, drawings, or other forms of creative expression can be completed by individuals or smaller teams and presented to everyone. The workshop may include hands-on training of simple design tools, enabling participants to create mock-ups, sketches, or storyboards, or role-play interactions in small teams to exemplify problem solving by design.

The critical features of design workshops are to plan the timing and logistics appropriately for the participants and design team members, gather the necessary materials for the activities planned, stay on track with the plan while remaining adaptable to changing circumstances and team dynamics, and document the session in progress and collect the work outcomes afterward. To successfully meet these goals, design workshops need a balance of design team facilitators relative to the number of participants, with clearly defined roles.

Design workshops are increasingly used to train interested audiences in the methods and processes of design and design thinking. This is currently sought after in corporate training and executive education, where a combination of presentation and hands-on design activities expose participants from business and other roles to the common methods of design research, ideation, thinking, and processes.

Behavioral	Quantitative	Innovative	Exploratory	Participatory
Attitudinal	Qualitative	Adapted	Generative	Observational
		Traditional	Evaluative	Self reporting
				Expert review
				Design process

Design workshops engage participants, often non-designers, in intense creative activity usually centered on assigned problems. Here a three-day workshop on design thinking for business executives is framed by field research and visualization techniques, for the design of new retail and information services.

See also *21. Creative Toolkits* • *44. Generative Research* • *61. Participatory Design*

29 Desirability Testing

When there is disagreement about which design direction to pursue, desirability testing shifts the conversation from which design is "best" to which design elicits the optimal emotional response from users.

First impressions matter, and within seconds of being introduced to a product, people will make judgments about it. Most of the snap judgments are based on how design elements make people *feel*, and designers know that interface elements that trigger an emotional response are difficult for non-designers to identify and articulate. But there is a method designed to explore this emotional space—desirability testing. Desirability testing goes beyond helping teams to simply identify the "best" or "most popular" aesthetic design direction. Instead, it explores the effective response that different designs elicit from people, so that the team can focus design efforts on shaping the exact emotional response they want people to have while using their products.

Desirability testing provides people a way to identify and articulate how a design makes them feel. It accomplishes this by providing participants with a range of positive, neutral, and negative adjectives that help them to tell the story of their experience[1] using simple, handheld tools—index cards with adjectives written on them. To begin, write each adjective/descriptive phrase on its own index card, and place all of the cards randomly on a table. Show participants a prototype mock-up, and ask them to pick the 3, 4, or 5 adjectives that best describes how they feel about the design. Record their selections, and ask the participant to talk about what each card means to them as it relates to the design.

When this process is applied repeatedly with twenty-five or more participants per user segment, the team can begin to compare the words that are most frequently chosen, and explore the groupings of positive, neutral, and negative word clusters. There are multiple ways to visualize the results,[2] and you can continue to refine and retest the design prototypes until there are enough responses that elicit the intended emotional responses.

The method can be conducted using low-fidelity prototypes, or on existing products already in the public domain as a baseline before the team embarks on a redesign. It can also be used to explore the emotional responses people have to competitor websites.[3] If there are too many strong and varied opinions on your multidisciplinary team about the direction a design should go, help everyone refocus their energies on identifying what emotions they want the product to arouse in people. When used this way, the method becomes a helpful consensus-making tool that focuses the team's attention on actual responses from end users, instead of on personal opinions and preferences that often leave teams at an impasse.

1. Desirability testing was first developed at Microsoft and documented by Joey Benedek and Trish Miner in their UPA 2002 paper "Measuring Desirability: New Methods for Measuring Desirability in the Usability Lab Setting." The adjectives and phrases they used to run their studies were chosen from market research, prior user research, and team brainstorming, and were selected to align with specific project goals.

Barnum, Carol M., and Laura A. Palmer. "More Than a Feeling: Understanding the Desirability Factor in User Experience." *Proceedings of CHI 2010* (2010): 4703-4715.

2. See note 1 (Barnum and Palmer) above.

3. Hawley, Michael. "Rapid Desirability Testing: A Case Study," 2010, www.uxmatters.com.

4. Microsoft allows for free use of the cards with the following disclaimer: Developed by and © 2002 Microsoft Corporation. All rights reserved. Permission granted for use.

Further Reading

Williams, Don, Gavin Kelly, Lisa Anderson, Naomi Zavislak, Dennis Wixon, and August de los Reyes. "MSN9: New User-Centered Desirability Methods Produce Compelling Visual Design." *Proceedings of CHI 2004* (2004): 959-974

Behavioral	Quantitative	**Innovative**	Exploratory	Participatory
Attitudinal	**Qualitative**	Adapted	Generative	Observational
		Traditional	**Evaluative**	**Self reporting**
				Expert review
				Design process

MICROSOFT PRODUCT REACTION CARDS: A CASE STUDY

The Microsoft Product Reaction Cards[4] are a powerful tool for gathering qualitative feedback from participants in a single usability study and as a measure of improvement in iterative studies.

In this example, Carol Barnum and Laura Palmer from the Usability Center at Southern Polytechnic conducted three studies of a web-based application for hotel properties worldwide to implement and monitor green initiatives.

User testing of the client's first version demonstrated that the general idea of the application was motivating; however, the product had significant problems that slowed or stopped users from achieving success.

Participants' repeated positive card choices were low with only *comprehensive, professional,* and *usable* selected twice each; but the themes of "Quality," "Appearance," "Ease-of-use," and "Motivation" emerged from participants' card choices. Results from this first study with 14 users led to scrapping this version of the product; yet, the cards proved useful in revealing themes that the developers wanted to retain in the redesigned product.

The second study was of the prototype of the redesigned application. The transformation of the users' experience was from night to day. The positive card choices from 12 users now represented 82% (compared to 42% in the first study) with the most often selected card being *useful*.

With such a positive and significant measurement of change, the development team focused on the remaining issues, and a small test of the pilot version was conducted with four users just before launch. The pilot version results showed that all participants chose only positive words–an astounding 100% positive language choice.

The theme of "Speed" now predominated and confirmed that the earlier negative issue of slow speed was now a positive feeling of fast speed–desirablity testing helped ensure that the application was *fast, time-saving,* and *efficient.*

Courtesy of Carol M. Barnum and Laura A. Palmer

Quality	Appearance	Ease of Use	Motivation	Speed
version 1 (*n=14*)				
Comprehensive (2) Advanced Complex Cutting Edge Integrated	Professional (2) Calm Organized	Usable (2) Accessible Approachable Meaningful Understandable Useful	Compelling Engaging Exciting Fresh Innovative Motivating Novel Stimulating	
version 2 (*n=12*)				
Comprehensive (2) Effective Powerful	Appealing (2) Friendly (2) Professional (2) Business-like Familiar Organized	Useful (5) Usable (4) Clear (2) Collaborative (2) Customizable (2) Flexible (2) Understandable (2) Accessible Controllable Convenient Comfortable Easy to use Meaningful	Relevant (4) Engaging (3) Compelling Creative Fresh Innovative Inspiring Valuable	
version 3 (*n=4*)				
Advanced (2) Comprehensive Creative	Friendly (4) Attractive (2) Organized (2) Clean	Easy to use (6) Useful (5) Clear (3) Accessible (2) Straightforward (2) Collaborative Consistent Helpful Simplistic Usable	Motivating	Fast (3) Time-saving (2) Efficient

See also **91. Triangulation** • **94. Usability Testing** • **96. Value Opportunity Analysis**

30 Diary Studies

Diaries or journals are guiding artifacts that allow people to conveniently and expressively convey personal details about their daily life and events to design teams.

Diary studies are ideal for collecting information from participants across time, sampling their thoughts, feelings, or behaviors at key moments throughout a day, week, or month.

Blank journals are issued to participants in person or by mail. The diary must be designed for portability and ease of use. An overview of the topic of interest is included up front, with instructions on how and when to complete requested entries, and a sample entry. Participants may be requested to document each time they engage in a particular behavior, encounter a product or situation, or have specific types of interactions. Other studies may require regular entries at particular times of day, or a log of items in summary at day's end. When used within experience sampling, diary entries are made at random times when the participant is signaled by a device or alarm.

Each page entry should be guided with a brief question or prompt, with appropriate space for encouraging the desired length of text. Creative page formats can be used to invite other forms of recording as well, such as sketches or drawings, symbols, or photographs, text or visuals that can be circled or checked, or the use of provided stickers. A small set of questions or space for reflections, and a request for demographic information, is sometimes placed at the end of the diary.

Diary studies are useful tools in exploratory research, preparing the designer for further research by contributing to an understanding of participant user groups. While diary studies are typically conducted with a relatively small sample, common themes and patterns can emerge. The synthesized information is intended primarily for inspiration and to indicate design implications for generative design. However, diaries can also be used in generative research. For example, journals are often issued to sensitize participants to research topics leading up to participatory design exercises such as collage, flexible modeling, or co-design workshops. In rare cases, diaries may be used for usability studies or evaluation, as a means of collecting feedback from users testing products in context over time.

While traditionally diary studies have been completed with paper and pen, technology affords novel forms of entries such as digital photos, video, and audio that may be recorded on digital devices, and sent via email or uploaded on provided sites. Digital diaries can also be completed as an integrated component of online or device interactions, with entry forms imbedded directly within software interfaces.

Behavioral	Quantitative	Innovative	Exploratory	Participatory
Attitudinal	Qualitative	Adapted	Generative	Observational
		Traditional	Evaluative	Self reporting
				Expert review
				Design process

Diary studies are used to sample self-reported participant interactions or events over time.

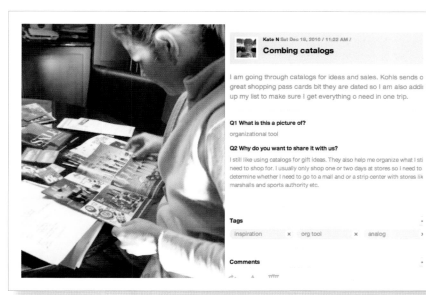

Above: Traditional diary studies are conducted using pen and paper journals, here for a study on skin care regimens..

Diary design by Aya Horiguchi

Left: Digital diary with user photo and text entries describing Christmas shopping experiences.

Courtesy of dscout.com / Gravity Tank

See also 24. Cultural Probes • 37. Experience Sampling Method • 64. Photo Studies

31 Directed Storytelling

Directed storytelling allows designers to easily gather rich stories of lived experiences from participants, using thoughtful prompts and guiding and framing questions in conversation.[1]

Directed storytelling is rooted in the social science method of narrative inquiry, whereby researchers understand people and document their experiences from the personal stories they tell.[2] As a method of design ethnography, directed storytelling is a shorthand means of collecting compelling stories from participants when time or other factors prevent direct observation or longer forms of research inquiry.

Directed storytelling sessions are started with a prompt by the researcher to the storyteller such as "Tell me a story about the last time you..." Guidance from the research leader continues throughout the storytelling session, to keep the storyteller comfortable in flowing narrative. Additional guiding questions are posed in terms of who, what, when, where, and how. For example, if the topic of design inquiry was focused on the last time they were admitted to a hospital, guiding questions for the storyteller might include: With whom did you interact? What means of communication were involved? When did this take place, and how long did the process take? Where did the interaction occur? Were there aspects of the environment that affected your experience? How did you feel about the interactions and experience? While the research leader directs the story, ideally another person on the research team documents the session.

To interpret directed storytelling sessions the documentation is critical. The central ideas of the story need to be identified through the storyteller's own emphasis and interpretation by the documenter. The ideas that emerge from stories can then be clustered using common methods such as affinity diagramming, looking for consistent patterns within and across experiences. Once clusters are formed and named, the themes that characterize experiences can be modeled into a tangible framework, with maps or diagrams serving as a reference artifact for what is most significant about participant experiences. This visible knowledge serves as a critical tool in communication, and in affecting design decisions about the content, hierarchy, and form of information or interactions.

As an exploratory research tool, directed storytelling is most powerful in expressing the essence of experiences for design teams, without a large investment of time or resources. Ideally the results of directed storytelling contribute directly to design decisions. However, the method may provide a more subtle reinforcement and validation of existing design directions, or identify the need for additional research.

1. Evenson, Shelley. "Directed Storytelling: Interpreting Experience for Design" in *Design Studies: Theory and Research in Graphic Design, A Reader*. New York: Princeton Architectural Press, 2006.

2. Clandinin, Jean, and Michael Connelly. *Narrative Inquiry: Experience and Story in Qualitative Research*. San Francisco, CA: Jossey-Bass, 2000.

Behavioral	Quantitative	Innovative	**Exploratory**	Participatory
Attitudinal	**Qualitative**	Adapted	Generative	Observational
		· Traditional	Evaluative	**Self reporting**
				Expert review
				Design process

See also *48. Interviews* • *22. Critical Incident Technique* • *65. Picture Cards*

32 Elito Method

The Elito method is used to develop solid design arguments grounded in research observations and anchored to business directives.[1]

Making the leap from research observations to a clear design direction is challenging for even the most experienced design teams. The Elito method is a rigorous synthesis method designed to help teams bridge the "analysis-synthesis" gap—the "fuzzy" area where designers have to vacillate between analyzing research data and articulating potential design ideas, while anchoring all design decisions to business directives. Ultimately, it helps to shape research findings into a series of fact-based narratives that connect the people for whom we are designing to promising design concepts.

Elito brings the multidisciplinary team together in a working session soon after primary and/or secondary research has been conducted. With the use of a spreadsheet program and a projector, the team captures its work and thinking in a spreadsheet that consists of five columns, each an Elito entity. In many ways, the spreadsheet serves as a catchall and a brainstorming tool that helps to externalize the team's research observations and insights. Together, these five Elito entities create a specific "logic line" or design argument:[2]

- *Observation* asks "What did you see, read, or hear?" The content must be fact-based. Sketches or photos can help make the observation concrete.

- *Judgment* asks "What is your opinion about that observation?" It provides a clear point of view about why the observation matters.

- *Value* asks "What values are ultimately at work?" Values are positive in tone and help to "express a quality of goodness." They communicate what is truly at stake and represent people's deep motivations (e.g., Health, Delight, Privacy).

- *Concept/Sketch* asks "What can the design team do to solve this problem?" It should articulate or visualize a form factor or design direction that solves a problem or creates value.

- *Key Metaphor* asks "What is the hook for this story?" It is a memorable tagline that the team can share to refer to this specific logic line.

Spreadsheet columns do not need to be completed in any methodical way; rather, it is more important to use the Elito spreadsheet to capture the team's random, nonlinear thinking. As the information in the logic line becomes complete, the team can apply lateral thinking to connect arguments, further refine ideas, and organize arguments into observation-based themes.

Elito builds a shared vocabulary and collective memory, and gives team members a sense of ownership in the process. When referred to, the Elito spreadsheet will not be seen as just a document but as a partner in design; a testament of the team's ability to produce sound design arguments.

1. Elito was developed in 2002 as a final project at the Institute of Design, Illinois Institute of Technology (IIT) by Master of Design candidates Trysh Wahlig, Margaret Alrutz, and Ben Singer. The method seeks to provide a structure for designers to cross the "analysis-synthesis gap." The Elito method was named after Eli Blevis, a design researcher and professor, and short for "Eli Toolbox."

2. For a case study of how researchers at Steelcase apply the Elito Method, see:

Ulrich, Emily. "Inclusive Iterations: How a Design Team Builds Shared Insights." *UX Week Podcast*, 2007.

Behavioral	Quantitative	Innovative	Exploratory	Participatory
Attitudinal	Qualitative	Adapted	Generative	Observational
		Traditional	Evaluative	Self reporting
				Expert review
				Design process

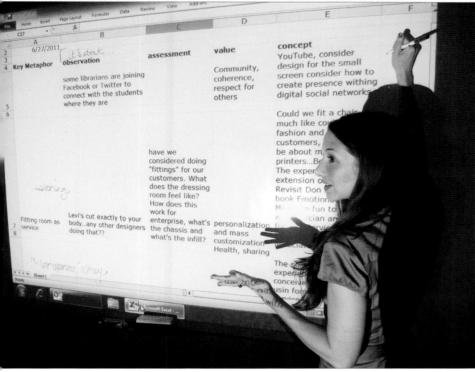

Elito helps teams to articulate an observation-based narrative that explicitly links business logic with design insights. After the design team builds the Elito spreadsheet together, each Elito "logic line" is printed and posted to a board for sorting, clustering, and commenting to further analyze, evaluate, and share the work.

Courtesy of Trysh Wahlig. Recreated with permission.

See also 24. Cultural Probes • 27. Design Ethnography • 89. Touchstone Tours

33 Ergonomic Analysis

Ergonomic analysis provides an assessment of tools, equipment, devices, workstations, workplaces, or environments, to optimize the fit, safety, and comfort of use by people.

Ergonomic analysis is performed as an evaluation of products or environments currently in use to suggest improvements through corrective measures such as adaptations, adjustment, or equipment replacement, or to inspire redesign. It may be conducted as a predesign analysis, through the evaluation of comparable products or systems, or utilizing human studies, literature, and standards, to establish ergonomic criteria for new design.

Five interrelated criteria commonly used in ergonomic analysis are size, strength, reach, clearance, and posture,[1] ranging in scale from micro (finger, hand, tool) to macro (limb, body, environment).

Size Anthropometry is the systematic measurement of people, used in the evaluation of existing tools for size appropriateness, and for designing new tools and systems according to human scale.[2]

Strength The amount of manual force needed for effective use of products and systems encompasses the range of human criteria from finger strength in trigger-based actions, to hand strength for gripping and force requirements, and limb, torso, and body strength for tasks such as lifting.

Reach At a micro level, reach refers to the span of the hand, measured as the distance between touch points in tool and equipment design, establishing grip requirements. At a macro level, reach is used to establish and evaluate effective body positions, for the user to safely, effectively access operator controls, or components of a workstation, appliance, or architectural feature in the environment. Reach thresholds are typically established for the fifth percentile of females, assuming that if the smallest user can grip or access, most users will be accommodated.

Clearance Clearance describes the effective space required within and around tools and machinery for safe, comfortable hand use, and minimum thresholds for avoiding obstacles in the environment. Clearance is commonly based on accommodating the 95th percentile male, on the assumption that this will account for use by all users equal or smaller in size.

Posture In assessing hand postures, tools and systems should avoid excessive deviation (lateral movements left and right) or flexion (movements downward and upward) from a neutral position. For example, ergonomic keyboards attempt to maintain a natural, neutral posture for the wrist. At body scale, a healthy posture and the reduction of bending and stooping are critical to avoid discomfort, fatigue, and long-term injury.

Although ergonomic analyses are usually performed as objective, behavioral evaluations, it is important to also include qualitative assessments. For example, preference measures such as comfort questionnaires can be used to compare and correlate physical measures with subjective perceptions.

1. Tannen, Rob. "Crimping Tools: An Ergonomic Review of the State-of-the-Art." Whitepaper for Thomas & Betts, June 2009. See also:

http: www.designingforhumans.com/idsa/2010/06/ergonomic-analysis-for-tool-redesign.html

2. Extensive data sets of human dimensions are available in print and online. In design, Dreyfuss and Associates is credited as the authoritative resource for human anthropometric data, stemming from the landmark text *The Measure of Man* published in 1959, and updated as *The Measure of Man and Woman*, first published in 1993. See:

Tilley, Alvin R., and Henry Dreyfuss Associates. *The Measure of Man and Woman*. New York: Wiley, 2001.

3. See note 1 above.

Further Reading

Cagan, Jonathan, and Craig Vogel. *Creating Breakthrough Products*. Upper Saddle River, NJ: Prentice-Hall, 2002.

Dul, Jan, and Bernard Weerdmeester. *Ergonomics for Beginners: A Quick Reference Guide*. Boca Raton, FL: CRC Press, 2008.

Pheasant, Stephen, and Christine Haslegrave. *Bodyspace: Anthropometry, Ergonomics and the Design of Work*. Boca Raton, FL: CRC Press, 2005.

Behavioral	**Quantitative**	Innovative	Exploratory	Participatory
Attitudinal	Qualitative	Adapted	Generative	Observational
		Traditional	**Evaluative**	Self reporting
				Expert review
				Design process

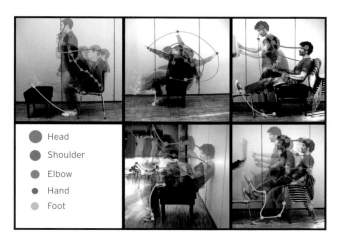

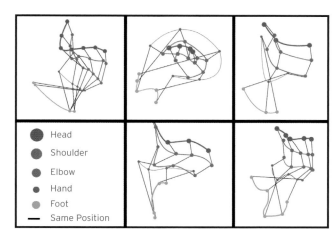

Above: Ergonomic analyses of human postures and movements used to inform the design of library media stations for the Deichmannske main library in Oslo, Norway. www.systemsorienteddesign.net

Courtesy of Birger Sevaldson, AHO

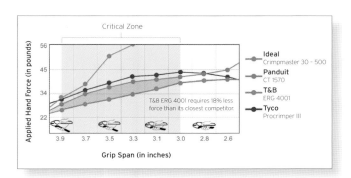

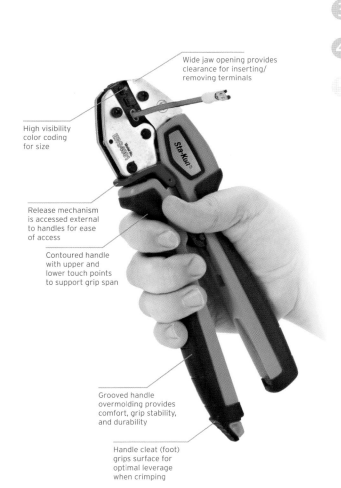

Wide jaw opening provides clearance for inserting/removing terminals

High visibility color coding for size

Release mechanism is accessed external to handles for ease of access

Contoured handle with upper and lower touch points to support grip span

Grooved handle overmolding provides comfort, grip stability, and durability

Handle cleat (foot) grips surface for optimal leverage when crimping

Above and right: Ergonomic analysis of a crimping device hand tool for Thomas & Betts.[3]

Courtesy of Rob Tannen, Bresslergroup

See also *34. Evaluative Research* • *84. Task Analysis* • *94. Usability Testing*

34 Evaluative Research

Evaluative research involves the testing of prototypes, products, or interfaces by real potential users of a system in design development.

Evaluative or evaluation research attempts to gauge human expectations against the designed artifact in question, determining whether something is useful, usable, and desirable. This is the most established form of research in design, stemming from a long history of product and interface testing in human factors, commonly known as "user testing." To avoid connotations that the participants themselves are being tested, the term "product testing" is preferred. Furthermore, whereas testing in the past focused primarily on *performance* measures to gauge variables such as speed and accuracy in task completion, the emphasis in design evaluation is now more comprehensive, collecting feedback on *preference* measures as well, including the aesthetic and emotional response from users. Evaluation research therefore encompasses methods that gauge human factors and ergonomics, usability, aesthetic response, and emotional resonance.

Evaluation research is ideally iterative, based on feedback from potential users in cyclical rounds of concept and prototype development to refine product and interface details. Evaluation should never be reserved only for final product release, when design changes are potentially complicated and expensive. However, evaluation research of existing products may be useful in early stage design research, to inform new product development, for competing products or variations, or for complementary products within a system.

The methodology of evaluation research may be tightly controlled, employing a scientific, experimental model typical in lab testing. The advantage of this model is the control over extraneous variables, but this may come at the expense of realism. Depending on the fidelity of prototypes, testing can also be conducted using flexible evaluations by people using products or prototypes in context or approximate conditions of real-world use. The value of this approach is realism, but it may come at the expense of control over other influencing variables.

New crowdsourcing opportunities afford online testing by volunteers to assess pages, navigation, and how users are engaging with prototype interface designs and wireframes, complete with summarized data analysis and visualizations presented in graphs and heat maps.[1] While evaluation research should always encompass testing with potential users, other methods use expert evaluators to assess products and interfaces, such as cognitive walkthrough and heuristic evaluation.

When evaluation research is conducted following thorough exploratory and generative research, it often needs only to serve a verification purpose, to assess how well designers have responded to input from users as they iterate and refine their designs.

1. See for example:

Kittur, Aniket, Ed H. Chi, and Bongwon Suh. "Crowdsourcing for Usability: Using Micro-Task Markets for Rapid, Remote, and Low-Cost User Measurements." *Proceedings of CHI*, 2008.

See also:

Amazon Mechanical Turk: www.mturk.com
fivesecondtest: www.fivesecondtest.com
navflow: www.navflow.com
clicktest: www.theclicktest.com

Further Reading

Barnum, Carol. *Usability Testing Essentials: Ready, Set . . . Test!* San Francisco, CA: Morgan Kaufmann, 2010.

Hackos, JoAnn, and Janice Redish. *User and Task Analysis for Interface Design.* New York: Wiley, 1998.

Tullis, Thomas, and William Albert. *Measuring the User Experience: Collecting, Analyzing, and Presenting Usability Metrics.* San Francisco, CA: Morgan Kaufmann, 2008.

Behavioral	**Quantitative**	Innovative	Exploratory	Participatory
Attitudinal	Qualitative	Adapted	Generative	Observational
		Traditional	**Evaluative**	Self reporting
				Expert review
				Design process

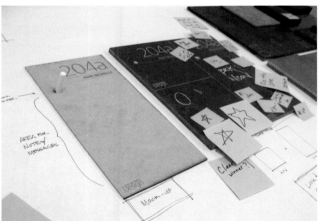

Evaluation research can be conducted through a range of formal and informal means. Here stakeholder evaluations were informally invited through a public display of prototypes for a proposed new signage program in the School of Design at Carnegie Mellon University.

See also *01. A/B Testing* • *46. Heuristic Evaluation* • *87. Think-aloud Protocol*

35 Evidence-based Design

Evidence-based Design is an approach that bases decisions for effective design on the implications of credible research and assessed outcomes, rather than sole reliance on intuition and anecdotal information.[1]

Evidence-based Design (EBD) stems from Evidence-based Research (EBR), which promotes strong connections between evidence and application, or the applied use of known theories validated by research.[2] EBD is most prominent in healthcare, as an initiative to inspire excellence in patient and medical staff experience, including well being, safety, and the reduction of medical errors, through improved environmental and facilities design. The EBD approach to date has primarily involved architects and interior designers, in collaboration with facilities managers, healthcare professionals, patients, and other users, for redesign and new design.

Although currently associated with healthcare, EBD is relevant to many high-performance environments, including schools, prisons, and commercial and industrial buildings and spaces. Furthermore, the approach of EBD is applicable across the spectrum of design disciplines—service design, communication design, industrial design, interaction design—for improving the multitude of service and product touch points within any environment. Gillis, for example, describes how EBD in user experience (UX) design can bridge the gap between two ends of a continuum, avoiding the pitfalls of purely deterministic (predictive) design on the one hand, and open-ended (arbitrary) design on the other.[3]

The primary tenets of EBD are that you enter the problem unbiased, and that you employ traditional research methods and existing factual evidence to influence design decision making. These methods include the use of credible literature reviews and comparative analyses, case studies, and documented post-occupancy evaluations of existing design. As a feature of EBR, systematic reviews carry traditional literature reviews one step further, aimed at being exhaustive, often using statistical techniques or scoring systems to establish the eligibility of study inclusion in the review.[4]

Methods are not limited to secondary research, and as a human-centered approach, EBD should also include documented site visits, interviews, surveys, and other primary means of collecting information. EBD in healthcare involves all stakeholders in the construction process, from the CEO and management team, hospital staff, and patients, to the building contractor and construction crew. Furthermore, as design outcomes emerge, improvements and successes should be tangibly demonstrated through performance measures (building, human, and economic), satisfaction measures, and organizational results. EBD in healthcare, for example, links design decisions to concrete measurable outcomes to justify return on investment, such as reduced infection rates and decreased staff injuries. EBD is therefore not tied to a particular design phase, but is rather an approach to design that overarches the complete design process, from predesign through post-design occupancy or use evaluations.

1. See Hamilton, D. Kirk, and David H. Watkins. *Evidence-Based Design for Multiple Building Types.* Wiley, 2008.

2. www.ehow.com/about_5118300_evidence-based-research-definition.html

3. Gillis, David. "The Art & Science of Evidence-Based Design." *UX Magazine* (online), April 27, 2010, www.uxmag.com/design/the-art-and-science-of-evidence-based-design.

4. For an example of systematic review in healthcare EBD, see:

Ulrich, Roger, Xiaobo Quan, Craig Zimring, Anjali Joseph, and Ruchi Choudhary. "The Role of the Physical Environment in the Hospital of the 21st Century: A Once-in-a-Lifetime Opportunity." Report to The Center for Health Design for the *Designing the 21st Century Hospital Project,* September 2004.

5. Scupelli, Peter, S. R. Fussell, and S. Kiesler. "Architecture and Information Technology as Factors in Surgical Suite Information Sharing and Coordination." *Proceedings of the 1st ACM International Health Informatics Symposium,* 2010: 265-274.

Scupelli, Peter, Y. Xiao, S. R. Fussell, S. Kiesler, and M. D. Gross. "Supporting Coordination in Surgical Suites: Physical Aspects of Common Information Spaces." *Proceedings of the 28th International Conference on Human Factors in Computing Systems.* New York: ACM Press, 2010: 1777-1787.

Behavioral	Quantitative	Innovative	Exploratory	Participatory
Attitudinal	Qualitative	Adapted	Generative	Observational
		Traditional	Evaluative	Self reporting
				Expert review
				Design process

AN EVIDENCE-BASED DESIGN APPROACH TO COORDINATION IN SURGICAL SUITES

Scheduling surgeries is challenging because of frequent urgent schedule changes to accommodate emergencies, transplants, and delays, affecting task coordination, resources, and people within and across staff groups. In surgical suites, the control desk and surgical schedule board become coordination centers, when staff with coordination roles answer questions, resolve conflicts, and keep the surgery schedule up to date there.

Fieldwork in surgical suites and a national survey of surgical suite directors determined that the architecture of the physical space, information availability, and practices influence information sharing and coordination outcomes. Visual access between the shared surgery schedule display and the control desk influenced whether staff groups congregated around schedule boards. Traffic-free areas around the surgery schedule display and up-to-date surgery schedule display information were associated with lower coordination stress.

An evidence-based design approach to the design of a surgical suite coordination location requires that research evidence inform design decisions, design hypotheses be linked to design outcomes, that the design be evaluated once it is built, and that the results of the design evaluation be published.[5]

This material is based upon work supported by the National Science Foundation under Grant No. IIS-0325047. Courtesy of Peter Scupelli.

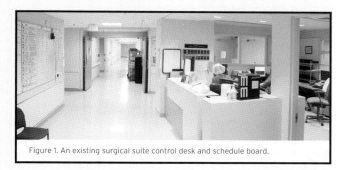

Figure 1. An existing surgical suite control desk and schedule board.

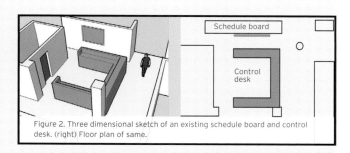

Figure 2. Three dimensional sketch of an existing schedule board and control desk. (right) Floor plan of same.

Figure 3. Three dimensional sketch of new control desk and schedule board. New floor plan of same. Black circles are control desk workers; white circles are information seekers.

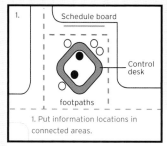

1. Put information locations in connected areas.

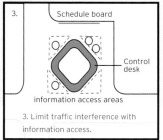

2. Make information locations mutually visible.

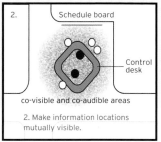

3. Limit traffic interference with information access.

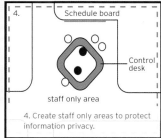

4. Create staff only areas to protect information privacy.

Figure 4. Increased coordination behavior and decreased coordination stress was associated with four design principles.

Design Phase: ① ② ③ ④ ⑤

See also 11. Case Studies • 53. Literature Reviews • 74. Secondary Research

36 Experience Prototyping

Experience prototyping facilitates active participation in design through subjective engagement with a prototype system or service, product, or place.[1]

Prototyping in general is the tangible representation of artifacts at various levels of resolution, for development and testing of ideas within design teams and with clients and users. However, whereas many prototypes only demand passive viewing for concept communication and review, experience prototyping fosters *active* participation to encounter a live experience with products, systems, services, or spaces. Additionally, experience prototyping expands on design development and testing, to embody a means for understanding, exploring, and communicating design ideas and concepts.[2] Experience prototyping can be used as an effective tool for design teams, clients, and end users.

Experience prototyping involves exercises completed by design teams to foster a vivid sense of the user's potential experience. Similar to role-playing, simulation exercises, and bodystorming, low-fidelity prototypes or props are used to help create a realistic scenario of use and activate the felt experiences of designers or users. The method is advantageous for its low cost, and for when situations prevent real-life experiences because of inherent risks and dangers or complicating logistics. For example, design teams could experience a patient intake and surgical preparation process by experience prototyping of a medical environment, including key points of product, system, space, and service interactions.

For exploring and evaluating design ideas, design teams can use experience prototyping internally, and with clients and users. The method here involves typically low-fidelity prototypes in iterative design development, to try things out and gain critical feedback based on realistic scenarios. At the low end, prototypes may include simple props and role-playing sessions; at the higher end, physical or digital prototypes with some level of functionality are tested in realistic field situations.

As a communication tool, experience prototyping is effective for persuading key audiences, whether client or user, of the values inherent in design concepts, through direct and active engagement. This typically implies a level of functionality that allows realistic engagement with a product or system, yet with a caution that the prototype represents a work in progress, and not the final design artifact.

In service design, experience prototyping is an excellent tool for exploring and testing the physical touch points of a system across time and place, for example, with low-fidelity mock-ups representing information kiosks, maps, payment systems, mobile devices and apps, and key personnel roles encountered in the service interaction.[3]

1. The seminal research articulating experience prototyping as a method appears in:

Buchenau, Marion, and Jane Fulton Suri. "Experience Prototyping" in *Proceedings of Designing Interactive Systems (DIS)*. ACM, 2000: 424-433.

2. See note 1 above.

3. See, for example, the service design workshop on creating a citywide bicycle service for the city of Helsinki from October 5, 2009, available at:

www.choosenick.com

4. Davidoff, Scott. "Routine as Resource for the Design of Learning Systems." Ph.D. Thesis: Carnegie Mellon University Technical Report CMU-HCII-11-103, 2011.

Behavioral	Quantitative	**Innovative**	Exploratory	Participatory
Attitudinal	**Qualitative**	Adapted	**Generative**	Observational
		Traditional	Evaluative	Self reporting
				Expert review
				Design process

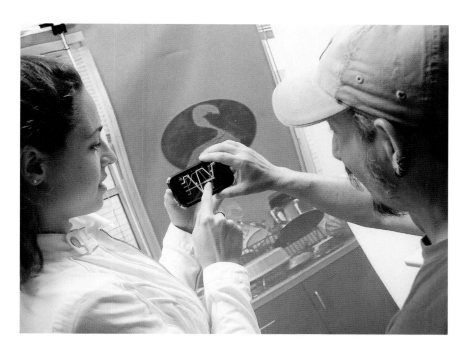

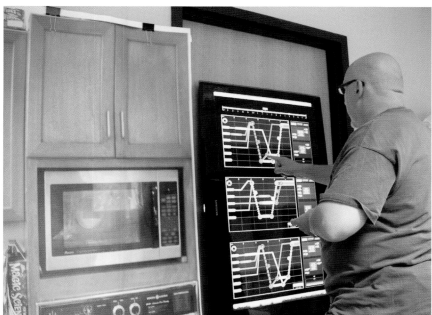

Experience prototypes surround a prototype product or service with a simulated physical and/or social context of use.[4]

Top left: A researcher plays the role of an appointment nurse, simulating the social context of a doctor's office. The user schedules an appointment using a mobile device prototype.

Bottom left: Physical props and large format paper printouts simulate a kitchen. The user receives a call from a researcher playing the role of the spouse, simulating the social context. The user reschedules a doctor's appointment using a large-screen prototype.

Courtesy of Scott Davidoff

See also 07. Bodystorming • 71. Role-playing • 99. Wizard of Oz

37 Experience Sampling Method

Experience sampling allows the designer to collect snapshots of behaviors, interactions, thoughts, or feelings from people who self-report in real time when signaled at random or timed intervals.

Experience sampling is a method well established in the design community, but in fact has a history in the social sciences.[1] The method is extremely useful in exploratory and generative phases of design research, and is often coupled with diary or photo studies. New technologies and software are expanding the possibilities and flexibility of the method.

Experience sampling requires that the participant record or document something specific when signaled, typically by a device alarm. In the past, this signal was sent to a pager carried by the participant, hence the common reference to the method as a "beeper study." Current technology allows other signaling opportunities, including new smartphone applications that can be programmed to alert the participant when it is time to make or send an entry.

The behaviors, interactions, thoughts, or feelings of interest to the design researcher are guided by clear instructions issued in advance, and are entered into a preestablished form, often a diary or journal. The entries may be general, such as "document your feelings right now," or quite specific, such as "list the communication products you are currently using." The journal should be well designed for portability and ease of use in documenting the required items of interest.

Often experience sampling will require the participant to document surroundings or relevant artifacts with quick sketches or photography. In the case of photography, care must be taken to match images to text entries—a simple matter in the past with Polaroid cameras coupled with pen and paper notations—which is more challenging with digital images. However, new technology affords the possibility of documenting (and sending) both photo and text entries through smartphones, or to use audio entries instead of text.

Experience sampling is a form of design ethnography, because it condenses the more traditional time required for extended immersion through the collection of strategic samples of behaviors, interactions, thoughts, or feelings. When done well, these samples can constitute a more comprehensive whole across time or individuals, giving the designer a relatively complete picture of behaviors of interest for any particular design study.

1. Larson, R., and M. Csikszentmihalyi. "The Experience Sampling Method." *New Directions for Methodology of Social and Behavioral Science* 15 (1983): 41-56.

Further Reading

Hektner, J. M., J. A. Schmidt, and M. Csikszentmihalyi (Eds.). *Experience Sampling Method: Measuring the Quality of Everyday Life*. Thousand Oaks, CA: Sage Publications, 2006.

Hsieh, G., I. Li, A. Dey, and J. Forlizzi. "Using Visualizations to Increase Compliance in Experience Sampling" in *UbiComp '08*, ACM, 2008.

Behavioral	Quantitative	Innovative	**Exploratory**	Participatory
Attitudinal	**Qualitative**	**Adapted**	Generative	Observational
		Traditional	Evaluative	**Self reporting**
				Expert review
				Design process

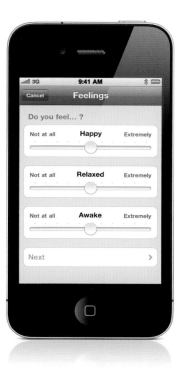

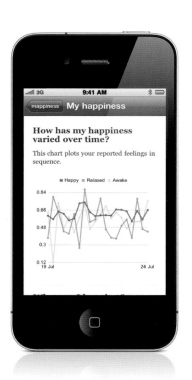

An experience sampling research project in the London School of Economics offers a free app for iPhones that invites participants throughout the United Kingdom to respond when paged to indicate their current feelings, who they're with, where they are, what they are doing, and to take a photo. The information is sent and consolidated as part of a research project mapping how the environment affects people's happiness. See www.mappiness.org.uk.

Courtesy of www.mappiness.org.uk

See also 27. Design Ethnography • 30. Diary Studies • 64. Photo Studies

38 Experiments

Experiments measure the effect that an action has on a situation by demonstrating a causal relationship or determining conclusively that one thing is the result of another.

Experiments can determine cause and effect by meeting three conditions: the presence of two observable and measurable actions or events; the cause event occurring before effect; and elimination of all other possible causes.[1] In a typical experiment, a hypothesis is posed, the exposure to something is manipulated for some participants while held constant for others, and the effect is measured and compared between the two groups, keeping all other conditions of the experiment exactly the same.

The independent or experimental variable is the variable that is manipulated. This can be as simple as something that participants are exposed to (such as a new design), or may be varied in terms of level of exposure (for example, length of time). The dependent variable is then measured to see if there is a significant difference between those exposed to the manipulation, and those not. An operational definition is necessary to define exactly how the dependent variable is being measured. Is a "better" input device, for example, defined by performance speed on a particular task, or a subjective assessment of ergonomic comfort?

Ideally participants are randomly assigned to either an experimental or control group. The experimental group, or treatment group, consists of participants who are exposed to manipulations of the independent variable. The control group is not exposed to manipulations of the independent variable, yet experiences all other conditions exactly the same as the experimental group to rule out the influence of extraneous variables. For example, if testing a new digital interface, the researcher must keep the computer platform and operating system the same in every test for both groups. Likewise, research protocol must be explicitly spelled out so that each test is consistent, whether conducted by the same researcher each time (intra-rater reliability), or by several different researchers (inter-rater reliability). In comparison tests, understanding how exposure can affect outcomes may require that some participants experience design "A" then "B," while others have the reverse presentation (AB | BA) to counteract a potential "order effect."

Quasi-experiments, or natural experiments, occur when the researcher cannot control assignment of participants to conditions (experimental or control groups), for example, when taking measurements before and after an event or change, or when preexisting groups are used for comparison study, such as two classrooms or communities.

1. Sommer, Robert, and Barbara Sommer. *A Practical Guide to Behavioral Research: Tools and Techniques.* New York: Oxford University Press, 2002.

2. Larson, Adam M., and Lester C. Loschky. "The Contributions of Central Versus Peripheral Vision to Scene Gist Recognition." *Journal of Vision* 9, no. 10 (2009): 1-16.

Further Reading

Hanington, Bruce. "Relevant and Rigorous: Human-Centered Research and Design Education." *Design Issues* 26, no. 3 (Summer 2010): 18-26.

Behavioral	Quantitative	Innovative	Exploratory	Participatory
Attitudinal	Qualitative	Adapted	Generative	Observational
		Traditional	Evaluative	Self reporting
				Expert review
				Design process

EXPERIMENTS CASE STUDY: CENTRAL VS. PERIPHERAL VISION

In this experiment, Larson and Loschky investigated whether central or peripheral vision is most useful for categorizing the "gist" of a briefly glimpsed scene (e.g., "Beach," "Street," or "Forest").[2] There were two independent variables: (1) whether central or peripheral information was shown, and (2) how much information was shown or hidden (in terms of the radius of the circular window or scotoma in degrees of visual angle). In Figure 1, the independent variable of central versus peripheral vision was operationalized in terms of the "Window" versus "Scotoma" viewing conditions. The Window condition presented information only centrally (blocking out the periphery), and the scotoma condition was the reverse (blocking out central information, and only presented information peripherally). The control condition presented the entire image. The dependent variable of scene gist categorization was operationalized in terms of participants' accuracy in categorizing briefly glimpsed scenes.

As shown in Figure 2, participants saw images flashed for 1/10th of a second (106 ms). Images were either in the window or the scotoma condition, which randomly varied from trial to trial. Then, after a brief blank, they saw a cue word (e.g., "Beach"), which accurately categorized the image a randomly chosen 50% of the time. If the cue word matched the scene's gist, participants were instructed to respond "Yes," and otherwise "No."

The most interesting result of the study was that scene gist only requires peripheral vision. Specifically, people were just as good at categorizing the gist of briefly glimpsed scenes using only peripheral vision (the 5° scotoma condition) as when seeing the entire image (the control condition).

Courtesy of Lester Loschky and Adam Larson, images reproduced with permission from Journal of Vision, © ARVO

Figure 1: Scene conditions with differing radii in degrees of visual angle.

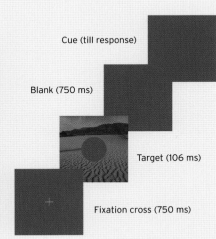

Figure 2: Research trial schematic.

See also 01. A/B Testing • 34. Evaluative Research • 40. Eyetracking

39 Exploratory Research

Exploratory research is defined by user and product studies, intended to forge an empathic knowledge base, particularly when designers may be working in unfamiliar territory.

Exploratory research is typically conducted in the earliest stages of the design process, set by the planning, scoping, and definition phase, and leading to generative concept design. Activities are focused on gaining a solid knowledge base of the design territory and existing artifacts, and forging an empathic sense of the people targeted by the design work.

Exploratory research should be an immersive experience for the designer, inspiring creative momentum and empathy through intense exposure to people and products relevant to the investigation, utilizing a broad variety of diverse yet complementary methods.

Depending on the area of design inquiry, research activities should focus on understanding the nature of the users' world, their daily life routines, challenges, needs, desires, interactions, product preferences, and environmental context and use patterns. Methods should also build a comprehensive knowledge of existing, complementary, and competitive products, systems, and spaces.

Exploratory research encompasses traditional, ethnographic, and other design methods, including:

- Surveys and Questionnaires
- Design Ethnography
- Observation
- Participant Observation
- Experience Sampling
- Touchstone Tours

- Diary Studies
- Cultural Probes
- Contextual Inquiry
- Artifact Analysis
- Personal Inventories
- Unobtrusive Measures

As an exploration, research is purposefully flexible, meaning divergences from planned protocols and the collection of information from spontaneous interactions and observations are encouraged. Synthesis is critical, but targeted toward inspiration rather than the formal analysis of concrete data. Exploratory research culminates in a comprehensive understanding of the people and the area under investigation, and ideally results in a set of tangible design implications or guiding criteria, preparing the groundwork for generative research and concept development.

Behavioral	Quantitative	Innovative	Exploratory	Participatory
Attitudinal	Qualitative	Adapted	Generative	Observational
		Traditional	Evaluative	Self reporting
				Expert review
				Design process

Exploratory research for a service design project on how we decide what meat to buy included an extensive survey, site visits to two farms, interviews with three farmers, and observations and conversations at meat counters with workers, butchers, and consumers.

Courtesy of Kelly Nash.

See also 24. Cultural Probes • 27. Design Ethnography • 57. Observation

40 Eyetracking

Eyetracking gathers detailed technical information on exactly where and for how long participants are looking—and not looking—when using an interface or interacting with products.

Although eyetracking was established for research on the human visual system and in cognitive psychology,[1] the technology has served well to meet the needs of researchers in human computer interaction and product design. Technological advances have further improved opportunities for use of the method, reducing the obtrusiveness of equipment for research participants, and lowering the cost and improving results for researchers.

Eye movements tracked during reading or image-gaze tasks are identified for moments of fixation, and rapid movements from point to point, or saccades, between fixations. Eyetracking technology traces and documents these patterns, generating data for interface and design evaluations, and is widely applied in usability studies. In early eyetracking research participants wore specially designed contact lenses. Current research uses optical methods to capture corneal reflections of infrared light on video using sophisticated cameras. New technology applies small sensing electrodes around the eyes, using electrical signals to precisely detect movements.

As the user reads text and images, fixations and saccades are recorded as an accurate picture of where the eyes travel and rest, creating a scan pattern of where they are looking, and where they are not. While typical tasks involve reading display monitors, eyetracking can also be used to record the eye movements of participants examining printed text and visual materials, engaging with products or product assembly tasks, and navigating environments. For example, eyetracking is used to highlight scanning and reading patterns during website navigation, using a parking kiosk pay system or vending machine, making adjustments or repairs to equipment or machinery, or finding one's way through an unfamiliar building using signage and wayfinding cues. Equipment may vary depending on the task, with a preference for sense electrode technology for mobile recordings of daily life or environmental navigation.

Eyetracking data is used to generate heat maps, aggregating data from several participants for a visual analysis of scan patterns and distributed attention. The color-coded map identifies areas of most intense scanning and fixation patterns in red, with yellows and greens indicating the areas given less attention.

Eyetracking and heat maps are useful in precisely isolating what features of a product or interface may be attended to or not, and for providing a visual reference of summary data. Limitations of the method are that it does not provide the researcher with direct input on user motivations, information processing, or comprehension. As with many methods, it is therefore recommended that eyetracking be triangulated with other confirming or complementary research methods.

1. Rayner, K. "Eye Movements in Reading and Information Processing: 20 Years of Research." *Psychological Bulletin* (1998): 124, 372-422.

Further Reading

Bojko, Aga. *Eye Tracking the User Experience.* New York: Rosenfeld Media, 2012.

Behavioral	Quantitative	Innovative	Exploratory	Participatory
Attitudinal	Qualitative	**Adapted**	Generative	**Observational**
		Traditional	**Evaluative**	Self reporting
				Expert review
				Design process

HEAT MAPS AND SAMPLE SCAN PATTERNS
ON AN EBAY SEARCH RESULTS PAGE

Eyetracking and heat maps are used by eBay to understand where ads could be most effective and useful, and where they had negative impact on the user's ability to utilize the site, helping to shape an advertising strategy.

1. An eyetracking heat map shows how much users looked at different parts of an eBay search results page. Areas where users looked the most are colored red.

2. Scanning pattern on an eBay search results page.

Courtesy of eBay Inc.

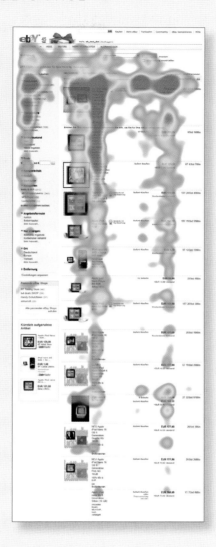

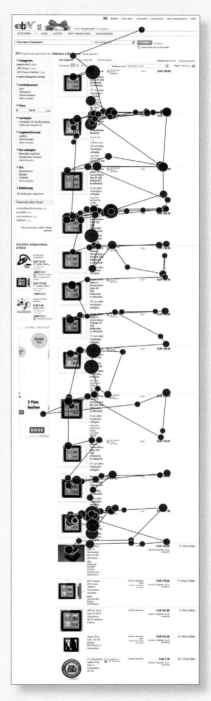

See also 05. Automated Remote Research • 38. Experiments • 34. Evaluative Research

41 Flexible Modeling

Given a component kit of parts, users can provide insight into product or interface configurations as guiding information for designers.

Flexible modeling is a participatory design method that allows users to configure a software interface, product, or environment from a set of predetermined feature elements provided by the designer or researcher. For industrial designers, this method may be most familiar as Velcro modeling, whereby physical product forms and feature sets such as buttons and controls are covered in fabric and Velcro fasteners, for quick and easy attachment in flexible configurations.

For interaction designers, this method may be presented as predetermined interface elements on paper, card, or in digital form for the users to arrange in a way that makes sense to them. This method can give the design team insight into popular interface options and preferred combinations. Flexible modeling can also be used for environmental design and space planning, through flexible configurations facilitated through scale model parts or paper templates of landscape, furniture, or architectural elements.

Components provided for flexible modeling should typically be ambiguous enough that participants can overlay their own meanings onto their use or function. Configurations may represent realistic or ideal (fantasy) artifacts. By communicating directly through the construction and presentation of a tangible form or interface, participants can express their needs and desires not only while they are building the artifact, but also afterward when it is "finished." The discussions provide designers an opportunity to ask questions about specific design decisions and the perceived benefit of those decisions.

For analysis, configured artifacts created through flexible modeling can be collected or photo documented, and then sorted by similar characteristics, common user choices, or themes. Models or layouts resulting from flexible modeling can also be visually translated into refined design artifacts, using the information provided by participants as guiding inspiration for the designer.

Flexible modeling is a good choice and particularly useful when design components are relatively set, but several options exist for their arrangement. It is also a powerful way of finding out which interactive elements or features users prefer for accomplishing tasks. Specifically, pay special attention to elements that elicit joy or delight, as these can be powerful motivators that separate your product from competitive products.

Further Reading

See: http://www.maketools.com.

Sanders, Elizabeth B.-N., and Colin T. William. "Harnessing People's Creativity: Ideation and Expression through Visual Communication." *Focus Groups: Supporting Effective Product Development*. London: Taylor and Francis, 2001.

Curtis, Nathan. *Modular Web Design: Creating Reusable Components for User Experience Design and* Documentation. Berkeley, CA: New Riders, 2009.

Behavioral	Quantitative	Innovative	Exploratory	Participatory
Attitudinal	**Qualitative**	Adapted	**Generative**	Observational
		Traditional	Evaluative	Self reporting
				Expert review
				Design process

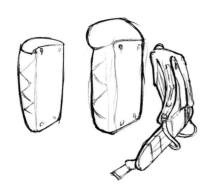

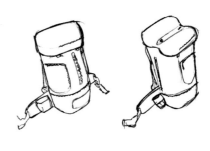

Flexible modeling presents the participant with a kit of ambiguous parts, in this case components of a backpack, to be configured into preferred arrangements. The designer can utilize tangible information provided through mock artifacts and use scenarios within the iterative sketching and modeling process, guiding inspiration for generative concept development.

Courtesy of Luke Hagan

See also 21. Creative Toolkits • 44. Generative Research • 61. Participatory Design

42 Fly-on-the-Wall Observation

Fly-on-the-wall observation allows the researcher to unobtrusively gather information by looking and listening without direct participation or interference with the people or behaviors being observed.

Fly-on-the-wall is differentiated from other types of observation, such as participant observation, because it intentionally removes the researcher from direct involvement with the activities or people under research. Fly-on-the-wall attempts to minimize potential bias or behavioral influences that might result from engagement with users. However, it may also reduce the researcher's ability to connect empathically with people and probe further into motivations behind participant behaviors.

As with other forms of observation, various degrees of structure may be put into place, although generally fly-on-the-wall observation is conducted flexibly, without predetermined criteria to specifically categorize or code observations. However, worksheets or other guiding frameworks may still usefully inform fly-on-the-wall observation (see Observation and AEIOU).

John Zeisel discusses observations from the vantage point of the observer, and suggests two forms that are relevant to fly-on-the-wall.[1] *Secret outsiders* are distant observers, with a vantage point that removes them from participants, minimizing any influence the presence of the researcher or recording equipment may have on behaviors. This form of observation may be limited in capturing individual nuances of interaction and personal depth.

Recognized outsiders have the nature of their research and role as observer made known to the participants being observed, although like a fly-on-the-wall, they position themselves in a natural and unobtrusive way within the environment under study. Despite best efforts to remain distant and unobtrusive when observing, a disadvantage of this method may still be the tendency for people to change their behaviors when they know they are being studied or observed, also known as the "Hawthorne Effect," stemming from a landmark study where this influence was first identified.[2] Another caution is perceived partisanship, if the researcher is associated with particular factions (such as management) within the environment or organization being observed.

When choosing observational methods, let appropriateness for the situation and the research question at hand guide you. For example, fly-on-the-wall might be appropriate when you are observing public places and activities, or when you are studying work processes that may be unduly influenced if interrupted or inconvenienced. Any time you believe that people may edit their speech and actions if observations are intrusive, or the observer's presence will change behaviors, fly-on-the-wall may be a good choice of methods.

1. Zeisel, John. *Inquiry by Design: Environment/Behavior/Neuroscience in Architecture, Interiors, Landscape, and Planning.* New York: Norton, 2006.

2. The Hawthorne Effect is the recognized influence on the behaviors of people because they are under observation or study. The term originates from a study of worker productivity in response to manipulations of lighting levels in the Hawthorne Works of the Western Electric Company in Chicago, in the 1920s and 1930s. Productivity was seen to increase regardless of degree of lighting manipulation and other workplace changes, and drop when studies were concluded, leading to the belief that the intervention itself, or the interest being shown in workers, was responsible for short-term increases in productivity. See, for example:

Landsberger, Henry A. *Hawthorne Revisited.* Ithaca, NY: Cornell University, 1958.

Behavioral	Quantitative	Innovative	**Exploratory**	Participatory
Attitudinal	**Qualitative**	Adapted	Generative	**Observational**
		Traditional	Evaluative	Self reporting
				Expert review
				Design process

See also *57. Observation* • *76. Shadowing* • *92. Unobtrusive Measures*

43 Focus Groups

The dynamic created by a small group of well-chosen people, when guided by a skilled moderator, can provide deep insight into themes, patterns, and trends.[1]

Focus groups are a qualitative method often used by market researchers to gauge the opinions, feelings, and attitudes from a group of carefully recruited participants about a product, service, marketing campaign, or a brand.

The power of focus groups lies in the group dynamic that it creates. When properly recruited, and under the guidance of an experienced moderator, participants can quickly accept one another as peers. In a peer setting (where the fear of being judged is diminished), participants are more likely to share experiences, stories, memories, perceptions, wants/needs, and fantasies. A well-moderated focus group will leverage the nonthreatening group dynamic to get past generalizations and start to peel back what is valuable and important to the group, and what makes the group unique.

A good moderator can get everyone in the group to provide more insight regarding any of the following design-related inquiries:

- reviewing processes that take place over an extended period of time
- explanations of what is not desirable about the current state, or about common misunder-standings with other "personalities" who are tangential to the process
- uncovering the underlying emotions the participants feel while going through a given process (fear, uncertainty, frustration, anxiety)
- work-arounds and hacks participants have invented in order to get a process to work better
- learning how members establish social capital with one another
- understanding constructs and mental models shared by group members

When analyzing focus group data, revisit the logic that participants use to arrive at conclusions. Also, pay particular attention to stories they tell, the metaphors and analogies they use, and how they describe their experiences, preferences, and memories. By looking for recurring topics and themes that produced strong responses, you can analyze for trends.[2]

Based on these trends, a skilled moderator will be able to generate a hypothesis that will usually require more evaluation and inquiry. Focus groups should always be supplemented with well-chosen quantitative and qualitative methods that continue to investigate attitudes and behaviors, and allow you to observe people in the actual context for which your product or service will be used. Results from focus groups should never be extrapolated for how the population in its entirety feels.

1. Originally, "Focused Interviews" were used in the 1930s and 1940s by sociologist Robert Merton and other social scientists to evaluate soldiers' reactions to World War II radio programs and training films. The term "Focus Group" emerged later, in 1956, around the same time when the method was adopted by marketing and advertising agencies.

2. Kuniavsky, Michael. *Observing the User Experience*. San Francisco, CA: Morgan Kaufmann, 2003

Further Reading

Krueger, R. A., and Mary Anne Casey. *Focus Groups: A Practical Guide for Applied Research*, 4th ed. Thousand Oaks, CA: Sage Publications, 2008.

Morgan, David. *Focus Groups as Qualitative Research*, 2nd ed. Thousand Oaks, CA: Sage Publications, 1996.

Behavioral	Quantitative	Innovative	**Exploratory**	Participatory
Attitudinal	**Qualitative**	Adapted	Generative	Observational
		Traditional	Evaluative	**Self reporting**
				Expert review
				Design process

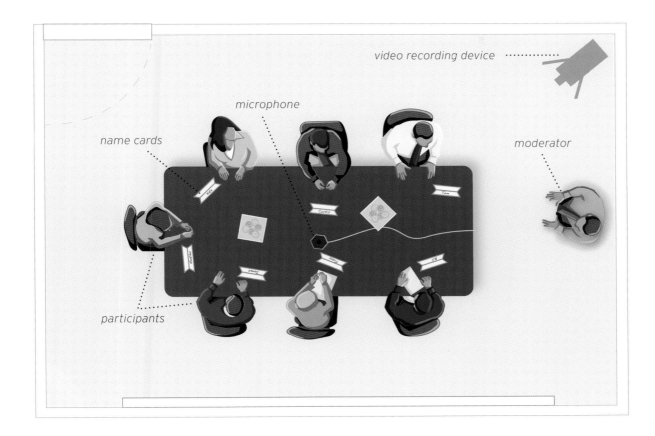

video recording device

microphone

name cards

moderator

participants

BIRD'S-EYE VIEW OF A FOCUS GROUP

A common setup for a focus group involves people sitting around a table, with name cards, and an unobtrusive microphone and camera recording the session. Oftentimes, there is a side room with flatscreens or a one-way mirror where observers and stakeholders can watch the session as it plays out. One of the criticisms of focus groups is the sterile, formal environment in which the sessions often take place. It is important for researchers to be aware of the bias that the setting can introduce, and how it may influence the responses of the participants and, as a result, the analysis of the research data.

See also 31. Directed Storytelling • 52. Laddering • 83. Surveys

44 Generative Research

Generative design exercises engage users in creative opportunities to express their feelings, dreams, needs, and desires, resulting in rich information for concept development.

Generative research opportunities are typically informed by exploratory research, and may even include similar methods, with a consistent emphasis on developing empathy for users. For example, diary studies may be carried over from exploratory research or developed specifically for generative research. These diaries may be issued as an advance probe or instrument to sensitize participants to the area of interest to the design researcher, to help prepare them for participatory exercises. Participatory methods in generative research include co-design activities—a collaborative process between user and designer—such as creative tool kits, card sorting with images or text, collages, cognitive mapping or other diagramming exercises, drawing, and flexible modeling.[1]

Generative research is further distinguished between *projective* and *constructive* methods.[2] Early exercises are typically projective in nature, focusing on expressive exercises enabling participants to articulate thoughts, feelings, and desires that are difficult to communicate through more conventional verbal means. Furthermore, the creation of an artifact around which a participant may talk will act as a trigger for engaged and comfortable conversation. Projective methods are typically ambiguously instructed, and will include the creative range of collage, drawing, diagramming, and image- and text-based exercises.

Constructive methods such as flexible modeling will occur as a later means of concept development, once some concrete parameters are set for product ideation. The key in developing a kit of parts for exercises such as Velcro modeling is to have enough concept variables defined to constrain the field for participants and avoid overwhelming them, without limiting the candid insights that come from flexible, creative play.

A key feature of generative methods is to combine participatory exercises with verbal discussions of work in progress and participant presentations of completed creative artifacts emerging from research sessions. Analysis can then be made of both the visual collateral and transcripts. As the name implies, the focus of generative research outcomes is on the generation of design concepts and early prototype iterations, ultimately preparing for evaluation, refinement, and production.

1. Sanders, Elizabeth B.-N. "Generative Tools for Codesigning." *Collaborative Design*. London: Springer-Verlag, 2000.

2. Hanington, Bruce. "Generative Research in Design Education." *Proceedings of the International Association of Societies of Design Research (IASDR)*. Hong Kong: 2007.

Behavioral	Quantitative	Innovative	Exploratory	Participatory
Attitudinal	Qualitative	Adapted	Generative	Observational
		Traditional	Evaluative	Self reporting
				Expert review
				Design process

PROJECTIVE GENERATIVE RESEARCH

Courtesy of Sonia Wendorf

Left: Participants in a projective generative design session model emotions in clay to inform common design characteristics. Negative states (pain, confusion) are typically modeled as irregular forms; positive states (certainty, happiness) as regular, closed, and symmetrical forms.

CONSTRUCTIVE GENERATIVE RESEARCH

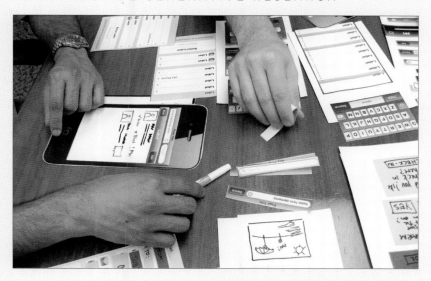

Left: Flexible modeling kits used by participants in constructive generative research, here to propose desired elements for iPhone apps.

See also 21. Creative Toolkits • 41. Flexible Modeling • 61. Participatory Design

45 Graffiti Walls

Graffiti walls provide an open canvas on which participants can freely offer their written or visual comments about an environment or system, directly in the context of use.

The graffiti walls method encourages participation through natural means of facilitating casual, anonymous remarks about an environmental space, system, or facility. Large-format paper is temporarily adhered to a wall or other surface, with markers tied to a string or otherwise made readily available for open-ended comments to be posted. The paper may be left blank, or a guiding question may be posed to direct comments on a particular theme. Depending on the environment, the materials are typically posted in an intentionally casual way.

The method can be used almost anywhere, but it is particularly useful in environments or for situations in which it may be challenging to collect information through traditional methods such as interview or observation; for instance, where respect for privacy or personal behaviors may present an ethical issue. The method has been used effectively for design research projects on public bathrooms, eliciting candid feedback on behaviors and perceptions of current spaces, specific issues such as sanitation, and desires for change. The method is also effective here owing to the natural context of graffiti in public bathrooms.

Photos of each graffiti wall should be taken at regular, daily intervals, as the paper may often deteriorate, or may be mistaken for vandalism and removed by maintenance staff, depending on location. The graffiti wall itself is removed at the end of the study and can be analyzed as a research artifact, for inspiration, comparison, consolidation with "walls" collected from other locations, and content analysis.

Graffiti walls are a low-cost and time-efficient method with which to easily collect information from a range of participants, typically requiring no more materials than large-format paper and pens, and a camera for documenting results. Limitations of the method are that there is little control over who participates in the method, and a lack of clear knowledge about who has contributed to the information collected. However, as an informal method triangulated with other means of exploratory research, graffiti walls are ideal for collecting baseline information and guiding design inspiration.

Further Reading

Hanington, Bruce. "Methods in the Making: A Perspective on the State of Human Research in Design." *Design Issues* 19, no. 4 (Autumn 2003).

Behavioral	Quantitative	**Innovative**	**Exploratory**	Participatory
Attitudinal	**Qualitative**	Adapted	Generative	Observational
		Traditional	Evaluative	**Self reporting**
				Expert review
				Design process

Graffiti walls are an ideal method for capturing informal opinions about an environment directly in the context of use. Here the method has been used effectively for research on perceptions and attitudes about public bathrooms, by facilitating an opportunity for participants to express themselves. Walls collected from various locations can be compared and consolidated to look for common themes and patterns.

Images based on work from Purin Phanichphant.

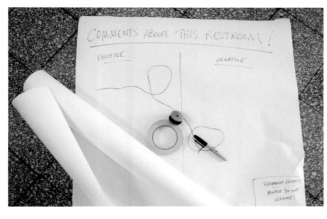

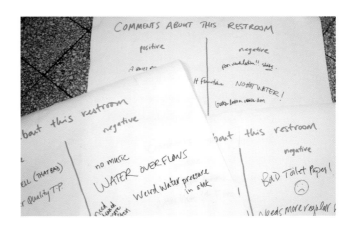

See also 39. Exploratory Research • 57. Observation • 92. Unobtrusive Measures

46 Heuristic Evaluation

An agreed-upon set of usability best practices can help detect usability problems before actual users are brought in to further evaluate an interface.

A heuristic evaluation is an informal usability inspection method[1] that asks evaluators to assess an interface against a set of agreed-upon best practices, or usability "rules of thumb." Unlike usability tests that require participation of actual users, heuristic evaluations enlist members of the team— from the novice computer programmer to the expert usability professional—to inspect an interface and detect the baseline usability problems that should be fixed before user testing begins.

When heuristics are thoughtfully written, and applied repeatedly during an iterative design process, the team's knowledge of usability heuristics can create a disciplined yet practical culture to finding and fixing certain classes of usability problems. Rather than making design decisions based on intuition and personal preferences, a set of manageable and meaningful principles can focus the team's efforts regarding the types of changes to fix. Over time, the principles will become more intuitive to everyone on the interdisciplinary team.

Even though double experts—evaluators who are familiar with the subject matter domain as well as in usability practices—may be the most likely to identify usability issues,[2] the method was designed to be used by experts and novices (who are trained on heuristics) alike. In an attempt to hedge against the bias any one evaluator can bring (based on their mindset or experiences), it is recommended that three to five evaluators independently perform assessments of the interface first, then aggregate their findings into a single report.[3]

Although the heuristic evaluation method will rarely provide opportunities to identify breakthrough opportunities in the design, it can help to detect critical but missing dialogue elements early in the design process.[4] Heuristic evaluation reports list which problems are inconsistent with the heuristics, and include plenty of screenshots and call outs. It is also common to include examples and screenshots of heuristics that are working well in the report. Visually reporting both the positive and negative findings brings balance to the report, recognizes the good work that is already represented in the design, and serves as motivation to keep doing more heuristic evaluations.

When used in the middle phases of the design process (or even as soon as low-fidelity prototypes are available) heuristic evaluations can identify baseline usability problems that can be fixed before actual participants are brought in, which will make the usability tests more effective. Not only that, but as team members *observe* more usability tests, it is likely they will become better at detecting usability problems for heuristic evaluations—a likely indication that attitudes toward user-centered design improve with the experience of observing people using the products that we design.

1. Heuristic evaluation is widely acknowledged as one of Jakob Nielsen's *Discount Usability Engineering* methods. The benefit of discount usability methods is twofold—not only do the users benefit from a more usable product, but it may also cost less and is less resource intensive for organizations to perform.

2. Nielsen, Jakob. "Finding Usability Problems Through Heuristic Evaluation." *Proceedings of the SIGCHI Conference on Human Factors in Computing Systems*, 1992.

Desurvire, Heather, Jim Kondziela, Michael E. Atwood. "What is Gained and Lost When Using Methods Other Than Empirical Testing." *SIGCHI Conference on Human Factors in Computing Systems*, 1992.

3. Nielsen, Jakob, and Rolf Molich. "Heuristic Evaluation of User Interfaces." *ACM CHI '90 Conference Proceedings*, 1990.

4. See note 3 above.

5. Nielsen, Jakob. *Usability Engineering.* Boston, MA: Academic Press, 1993.

6. Ginsburg, Suzanne. *Designing the iPhone User Experience.* Boston, MA: Addison Wesley, 2010.

Further Reading

Nielsen, Jakob. *Usability Inspection Methods.* New York: John Wiley & Sons, 1994.

Behavioral	Quantitative	Innovative	Exploratory	Participatory
Attitudinal	Qualitative	Adapted	Generative	Observational
		Traditional	Evaluative	Self reporting
				Expert review
				Design process

Heuristics should be thoughtfully written and carefully considered to reflect the context of the product. A good place to start is Nielsen's 1994 heuristics,[5] which are adapted here and applied to iPhone apps.[6]

1. Visibility of app status
The Redfin app keeps people informed about how quickly their images are downloading.

2. Match between app and the real world
The iHandy app acts the way a traditional level does, providing measurements about the user's environment.

3. User control and freedom
The iPod provides users volume, fast forward, reverse, next, and previous song at all times.

4. Error prevention
The Amazon app requires two confirmations before removing a book from your wishlist.

5. Consistency and standards
Whether you are using Netflix on a computer, TV, or as an app, the language and behaviors are consistent.

6. Recognition rather than recall
iPod provides visuals of all songs and albums to facilitate selection.

7. Flexibility and efficiency of use
Maps provide car, public transportation, and walking routes depending on the user's method of transit.

8. Aesthetic and minimalist design
Facebook's "Upload Images" functionality contains no superfluous buttons or information.

9. Help users recognize, diagnose, and recover from errors
If you aren't using Location services, Bump tells you both the issue and solution in plain language.

10. Help and documentation
If you need help using the iHandy Level app, instructions are contextual, concise, specific, and visual.

See also **13. Cognitive Walkthrough** • **34. Evaluative Research** • **66. Prototyping**

47 Image Boards

A collage of collected pictures, illustrations, or brand imagery can be used to visually communicate an essential description of targeted aesthetics, style, audience, context, or other aspects of design intent.

Image boards, or mood boards, are a long-standing tradition used by a variety of design professions for a range of reasons, built from inspiration and serving to inspire and sell. The image board is typically created once the designer or team has decided on a general focus for design aesthetics, style, context, or audience. Images are then collected that are representative of that defined aesthetic, context, or user group, and these images are edited and collaged. The image board bears some resemblance to sample boards used by interior designers, whereby color, material, and sometimes hardware and product swatches are presented together to communicate a proposed design system.

For example, to create an image board to visually define the meaning of a chosen design aesthetic verbally described as "urban chic," images that convey the particular styles, colors, products, brands, and environments associated with the designer's interpretation of that aesthetic would be collected, edited, and collaged. For more specific design purposes, image boards can be created to describe targeted users or environmental context. For a user-based image board, the visuals might portray types of people that define an audience target, profiling their age demographics and tastes and preferences as conveyed through clothing, products, preferred brands, environments, activities, transportation, and social interests. An environment-based image board might visually define the typical surroundings for which a product design is appropriately intended, showing sample interiors, furniture, lighting, fixtures, and conveying color palettes and atmospheric tone.

As an internal tool, image boards can serve as a tangible focus for the designer, a visual reminder of the aesthetic context or audience for inspiring their design efforts. Image boards can also serve well as a consensus artifact for design teams, visually representing an agreed-upon version of a design aesthetic or context. To this end, the act of creating the image board can itself be an important tool, managed through team contributions so that all members take ownership of the decided-upon visual definition for design focus. Externally, image boards are powerful tools for effectively communicating design intent to clients, visually clarifying an aesthetic direction or targeted audience.[1]

1. Most image boards are created by hand as physical artifacts, but software tools can also be used, and online services for the digital creation of mood boards are available. See, for example, http://www.sampleboard.com and http://www.moodshare.co

2. Hughes, Kristin. "Design to Promote Agency and Self-efficacy through Educational Games" in *Beyond Barbie and Mortal Kombat: New Perspectives on Girls and Games.* Cambridge, MA: MIT Press, 2008: 231-246.

Behavioral	Quantitative	Innovative	**Exploratory**	Participatory
Attitudinal	**Qualitative**	**Adapted**	Generative	Observational
		Traditional	Evaluative	Self reporting
				Expert review
				Design process

Left: These image boards were produced to help the design team better understand the pop culture, likes, and dislikes of teenage girls. Collage was a great method to use, helping capture the DIY spirit of teenage girls. The boards helped to inform the visual brand/identity and verbal language for a large scale, city-wide, role playing game.[2]

Image boards created by Rebecca Bortman and Michael Sui, courtesy of Kristin Hughes

Below: This image board was created to capture the styling and design intent for a series of wooden vessels. It is used as a reflection piece to show previous typologies of vessel forms in this series and to help inform future design iterations.

Courtesy of Mark Baskinger © 2011

okapi vessels

See also 56. Mind Mapping • 80. Stakeholder Maps • 85. Territory Maps

48 Interviews

Interviews are a fundamental research method for direct contact with participants, to collect firsthand personal accounts of experience, opinions, attitudes, and perceptions.

Interviews are one of two methods of survey research, the other being questionnaires. Interviews are best conducted in person so that nuances of personal expression and body language are recognized in conversation, but they may be conducted remotely by phone or using social media.

Interviews may be structured and follow a script of questions, or relatively unstructured, allowing for flexible detours in a conversational format. However, even in unstructured interviews, the researcher typically has a guiding set of topics that he or she hopes to address in the session. Unstructured interviews have the advantage of being conversational and more comfortable for participants, but rely on the researcher to guide the session and collect the necessary information within an allotted time. Structured interviews may be perceived as formal and impersonal, but are easier to control in terms of questions and timekeeping, and are easier to analyze.

Questions asked during interviews will vary depending on the nature of the design inquiry. If the research is designed for exploratory purposes, then the unstructured format and flexible diversions are fine. However, if designed for more rigorous purposes where consistency across sessions is required, questions should be read exactly as scripted by each interviewer, to avoid the introduction of subtle bias or altered interpretations by the researcher or respondent. In all forms of interviews, the researcher needs to be personally sensitive and adaptable, yet organized and responsible in adhering to the protocol of the session.

Targeted audience is another way to distinguish types of interviews. For example, stakeholder interviews focus on information from specific roles or people who may have a vested interest in the particular inquiry. Key informant interviews concentrate on people who have specialized or expert knowledge to contribute. Interviews may also be conducted individually, with couples, or with strategic groups. Paired or group interviews are efficient and often provide more natural conversation, with participants reminding or challenging each other about details and history. However, the researcher must also be aware of the undue influence that one person can have over another, and find ways to moderate the risk of dominated interviews or conversations.

Interviews are often one component of a research strategy utilizing complementary methods such as questionnaires or observations, to verify and humanize data collected using other means. Interviews can be made more productive when based around artifacts, the inspiration behind integrated methods such as touchstone tours, personal inventories, and picture cards.

Further Reading

Kuniavsky, Mike. *Observing the User Experience: A Practitioner's Guide to User Research*. San Francisco, CA: Morgan Kaufmann, 2003.

Behavioral	Quantitative	Innovative	**Exploratory**	Participatory
Attitudinal	**Qualitative**	Adapted	**Generative**	Observational
		Traditional	**Evaluative**	**Self reporting**
				Expert review
				Design process

See also *20. Contextual Inquiry • 67. Questionnaires • 83. Surveys*

49 KJ Technique

When the traditional meeting format fails to achieve group consensus, the KJ Technique can be used to help teams work through a problem space and prioritize what should be focused on first.[1]

The KJ Technique is a consensus-building exercise that helps teams organize a complicated range of ideas and information. When used as a format for a team meeting, the KJ Technique is an effective way to externalize all of the information that is in everyone's heads, and then organize and prioritize the data in a way that builds group consensus.

In traditional meetings, there is rarely enough time for a problem space to be described, let alone be better understood. This is not a symptom of team dysfunction; rather, it is a limitation of the traditional meeting format. The KJ Technique is designed to succeed in ways that typical meetings fail because it focuses the team on one focus question, and then sets everyone to work on the same task at the same time. Other key strengths of the KJ Technique include:

The KJ Technique is silent. Everyone in the group is provided with blank sticky notes and markers, and then asked to write as many problems, insights, data, or opinions as they can think of—in silence. This way, everyone is provided with an equal opportunity to express his or her points of view, and has the assurance that their issues are being represented and shared.

The KJ Technique makes effective use of time. In traditional meetings, only one person can speak or draw on the white board at a time. With the KJ Technique, all of the sticky notes are posted simultaneously, opening up the opportunity for a holistic assessment of the problem space. This process helps everyone to understand that it is not about "my opinions" versus "your opinions," but rather "how do my opinions relate to yours, and how do our concerns paint a broader picture of our challenge?"

Group pressure won't affect outcomes. The KJ Technique promises equal representation, regardless of the politics and personalities involved. It doesn't matter who has the most power or who can most eloquently argue their point of view. By providing a framework where everyone silently works together as a team, decisions are made democratically, with little or no opportunities for coercion.[2]

Within one to two hours, a team can organize their notes into an *affinity diagram*, which is a relational visual representation of a team's observations, knowledge, concerns, and ideas. Although results of the KJ Technique are subjective and qualitative, it is a powerful way for teams to come together, solve problems, and prioritize next steps.

1. Jiro Kawakita, a Japanese anthropologist, created the KJ Technique in the 1960s. It is one of the seven management and planning tools used in Total Quality Control. See: Kawakita, Jiro. *The Original KJ Method*. Tokyo: Kawakita Research Institute, 1982.

2. Spool, Jared. "The KJ-Technique: A Group Process for Establishing Priorities," 2004, http://www.uie.com

Further Reading

Kuniavsky, Michael. *Observing the User Experience*. San Francisco, CA: Morgan Kaufmann, 2003.

Behavioral	Quantitative	Innovative	Exploratory	Participatory
Attitudinal	**Qualitative**	Adapted	**Generative**	Observational
		Traditional	Evaluative	Self reporting
				Expert review
				Design process

EVERYONE WRITES ALL OF THEIR CONCERNS...

...THEN, NOTES ARE SORTED IN SILENCE...

GOOD PLAN

Meetings that use the KJ Technique are completed in silence. Team members independently identify their respective concerns and project requirements on sticky notes, and then silently cluster similar concerns and challenges. It is effective in helping teams reach consensus and externalizes the range of issues that teams need to work together to solve.

See also *03. Affinity Diagramming • 96. Value Opportunity Analysis • 98. Weighted Matrix*

50 Kano Analysis

Not all product attributes are equally important to the customer. Use Kano Analysis to determine which product attributes have the greatest impact on customer satisfaction.[1]

Kano Analysis is based on the philosophy that the constant addition of new features—the "more is better" approach—is an ineffective strategy when trying to improve customer satisfaction.[2] Instead, when the Kano model is used in surveys and interviews, design teams have a framework to determine and prioritize which product attributes are more important to the customer. By assigning each product attribute (e.g., features, offerings, and benefits) to one of five categories, customer values regarding satisfaction can be revealed. The five product attribute categories are:[3]

Required (atari mae or "quality element")	Required attributes are the baseline features for the product and, once identified, must be included in the product. Threshold assurances like privacy, safety, security, and legislative requirements are required attributes. Features in this Kano category may not increase customer satisfaction, but their absence can definitely have a negative impact.

Desired (ichi gen teki or "one-dimensional quality element")	There is a linear relationship between desired attributes and customer satisfaction: When desired attributes are included, the perceived value of the product will go up. When excluded, the perceived value of the product will decline. Once identified, desired attributes are best to include in the product.

Exciter/Delighter (mi ryoku teki or "attractive quality element")	Exciter/delighter attributes are a source of delight and surprise to customers, and will improve measures of customer satisfaction. However, unlike *required* or *desired* attributes, if exciter/delighters are not represented, they generally won't be a source of disappointment or frustration for customers. Exciter/delighter represent latent customer needs—most people will not think to ask for them.

Neutral (mu kan shin or "indifferent quality element")	Neutral attributes represent features that customers don't have strong feelings for either way. Their presence or absence will not impact customer satisfaction ratings positively or negatively.

Anti-feature (gyaku or "reverse quality element")	Anti-feature product attributes provide insight into what you should leave out of a product. Including them can negatively impact customer satisfaction, and sometimes customers will pay more to not have to deal with them (e.g. a free app that includes ads, but the paid version does not), or pick a competitor product that does not use the anti-feature.

The Kano Analysis will not only help you assign your features to a product attribute category, but it can also help you reassess your product offerings over time. Use it repeatedly, particularly when there are cultural, economic, or technological shifts, as these can change customers' attitudes.

1. Dr. Noriaki Kano, an expert and lecturer in the field of Quality Management, laid the foundation for the Kano Method in the 1970s and 1980s. His efforts worked to show how improving or adding certain types of product attributes and excluding others can reliably produce higher levels of customer satisfaction. See:

Kano, Noriaki, Nobuhiku Seraku, and F. Takahashi. "Attractive Quality and Must-be Quality." *Journal of the Japanese Society for Quality Control* 14, no. 2 (1984): 39–48.

2. See note 1 above.

3. See note 1 above.

Zultner, Richard E., and Glenn H. Mazur. "The Kano Model: Recent Developments." *The Eighteenth Symposium on Quality Function Deployment*, 2006.

Further Reading

Spool, Jared. "Understanding the Kano Model: A Tool for Sophisticated Designers," 2011, www.uie.com.

Behavioral	Quantitative	Innovative	Exploratory	Participatory
Attitudinal	**Qualitative**	Adapted	Generative	Observational
		Traditional	**Evaluative**	**Self reporting**
				Expert review
				Design process

HOW TO PERFORM THE KANO ANALYSIS

The Kano Analysis can help you make informed decisions about which features to improve first, or in what order to add features.

For each product attribute or feature you want to evaluate, write two questions (a question pair) about it—the first asking a customer how she would feel if the product attribute was *present*, and the second, asking how she would feel if the attribute was *absent*. For instance:

Question 1:
If the hotel's Wi-Fi offering is free, how would you feel?

Question 2:
If the hotel's Wi-Fi offering isn't free, how would you feel?

For each question, customers have to select one of the following three responses: "satisfied," "neutral," or "dissatisfied."

Once you have customer responses for each question, cross-reference the question-pair using Figure 2 to determine which Kano product attribute category each feature maps to. Repeat this process for each question pair.

Each product attribute can then be plotted into a Kano category in Figure 1. Where it falls on the matrix can help you decide whether the product attribute will ultimately delight or disappoint the customer.

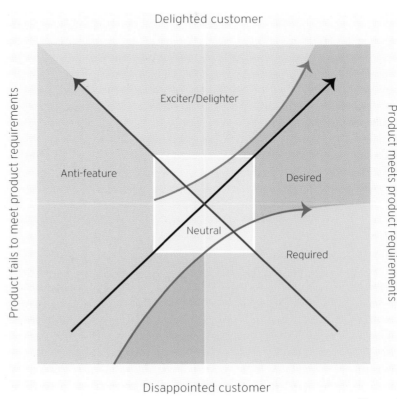

Figure 1

Question 1:
If product attribute is present, the customer feels...

		Satisfied	Neutral	Dissatisfied
Question 2:	**Satisfied**	Questionable	Anti-feature	Anti-feature
If product attribute is absent, the	**Neutral**	Exciter/Delighter	Neutral	Anti-feature
customer feels....	**Dissatisfied**	Desired	Required	Questionable

Figure 2

See also **29. Desirability Testing** • **83. Surveys** • **96. Value Opportunity Analysis**

51 Key Performance Indicators

When you need to keep a pulse on critical success factors for your product or service, a few well-selected KPIs can keep you informed and guide you when you need to course-correct.[1]

Key Performance Indicators (KPIs) are measurements of how well you are doing against quantifiable, widely accepted business goals. KPIs measure where you were yesterday and where you are today, showing both in relationship to where you are trying to go in terms of some predefined business objective. In this way, KPIs provide relative measurements that provide stakeholders with data regarding how people are using—or not using—their products and services.

Although KPIs are quantitative measures, they should be selected for one reason alone: they are fundamentally action-oriented. KPIs can help you to:[2]

- recognize, prioritize, and react to issues as they occur (revenue-based fluctuations are always addressed first, usability metrics second)
- meaningfully summarize and compare data and use it to your advantage
- document a business case for change to senior management
- foster an ongoing organizational understanding of how people are responding to your product or service

It's important to remember that KPIs reflect the activities of real people. Each KPI is ultimately some measurement derived from an individual's interaction with your product or service. Although it can be hard to quantify attitudes with KPIs (for instance, assessing customer sentiment about a new campaign), KPIs are perfect for quantifying behaviors, or behavior metrics (e.g., the ratio of people who abandoned their shopping cart last week versus those who completed the process).[3] KPIs can also report on value metrics (e.g., average cost per visitor or conversion).

Implementing and championing KPIs is an ongoing process. Always respond positively to requests for more data, as being open to suggestions will improve your organization's relationship with data in a way that guides and informs action. Remember that providing a simple KPI spreadsheet to stakeholders is more likely to get them to pay attention to KPIs than forcing them to adopt yet another technology dashboard. The goal is to keep the data concise and immediately actionable, not to bombard people with data or software they don't know how to use. Providing KPI data once a quarter, or just before staff meetings, is not enough. The KPI reporting process needs to be frequent enough so that fluctuations can be immediately course-corrected—daily or weekly reports are best.[4]

1. D. Ronald Daniel of McKinsey and Company introduced the concept of "Key Performance Indicators" and "Critical Success Factors" in the 1960s. See:

Daniel, D. Ronald. "Management Information Crisis." *Harvard Business Review* 39, no. 5 1961.

2. Peterson, Eric. *The Big Book of Key Performance Indicators*, 2006, http://www.webanalyticsdemystified.com

3. See note 1 above.

4. See note 2 above.

Further Reading

Peterson, Eric. *Web Site Measurement Hacks: Tips & Tools to Help Optimize Your Online Business.* Sebastopol, CA: O'Reilly, 2005.

Behavioral	Quantitative	Innovative	Exploratory	Participatory
Attitudinal	Qualitative	Adapted	Generative	Observational
		Traditional	Evaluative	Self reporting
				Expert review
				Design process

ASSIGNING KPIs

In *The Big Book of Key Performance Indicators*, Eric Peterson asserts that KPIs are a reflection of what your business does online. He also suggests that you should assign only a few well-chosen KPIs to internal team members who can directly act on or react to the data. If they can't immediately do something about either a spike or a drop in the data, don't add it to their list of responsibilities. Here are the recommended KPIs for four popular business models and his recommendations for which internal team should monitor them.

Senior Strategists

Mid-tier Strategists

Tactical Team Members

Content Sites

Senior Strategists	Mid-tier Strategists	Tactical Team Members
Average page views per visit	Average visits per visitor	% of visitors using search
Average cost per visit	Ratio of new to returning visitors	% high, med, low click depth visits
Average revenue per visit	% high, med, low time spent visits	Landing page bounce rate
% high, med, low frequency visitors		RSS/email subscription conversion rate

Marketing Sites

Senior Strategists	Mid-tier Strategists	Tactical Team Members
Lead generation conversion rate	Average number of visits per visitor	Landing page bounce rate
Average cost per lead generated	% of high, medium, low time spent	Average searches per visit
Average (estimated) revenue per visit	% high, medium, low recency visits	% zero yield searches
Average cost per lead generated	Ratio of new to returning visitors	Lead generation rate for campaigns

Customer Service Sites

Senior Strategists	Mid-tier Strategists	Tactical Team Members
Average time to respond to email inquiries	Information find conversion rate	% high, medium, low click depth visits
% high, low customer satisfaction	% visitors using search	% zero yield searches
% new and returning customers	% high to low of visitors across products	Form completion rates
	% high to low of visitors across product categories	Download completion rates

Online Retailers

Senior Strategists	Mid-tier Strategists	Tactical Team Members
Order conversion rate	Ratio of new to returning visitors	Search to purchase conversion rate
Buyer conversion rate	New, returning visitor conversion rates	% of low recency visitors
Average revenue per visit	% revenue from new customers	Cart and checkout completion rate
Average cost per conversion	% revenue from returning customers	Order conversion rate by campaign type
% high, low satisfaction customers	Key campaign landing pages bounce rate	Zero yield searches

See also **78. Site Search Analytics** • **97. Web Analytics**

52 Laddering

Use laddering to reveal the connection between a product's obvious physical characteristics and the deeper, more profound personal values that it reinforces in a customer's life.[1]

Laddering is a one-on-one interviewing technique that helps researchers make explicit connections between product attributes, the benefits and consequences of using a product, and the personal values the product reinforces.[2] Laddering builds on Means-End Theory, which posits that people make purchasing decisions based on consequences afforded by using the product, and that each consequence reinforces an underlying value that is meaningful to the individual. It is possible, then, that laddering can reveal the underlying motivations driving loyalty within a product category.

Research has found that the following seven values are often the unspoken motivation behind purchasing behavior: *self-esteem*, *accomplishment*, *belonging*, *self-fulfillment*, *family*, *satisfaction*, and *security*.[3] Laddering connects a product's obvious physical characteristics to these values by asking the question *"Why is that important to you?"* By repeatedly asking a series of directed probes, researchers can explore the links among product attributes, consequences, and values.

- *Attributes* are the physical and obvious product characteristics (for example, antiaging ingredients in beauty creams).

- The *consequences* are the benefit, or the impact that the product has on a person, and reveal another layer about what is important to the person (antiaging creams are used to feel youthful).

- *Values* expose the root cause behind why a product resonates profoundly with a person (antiaging creams promote a sense of health, well-being, and longevity).

Each time "Why?" questions are asked in succession, the conversation slowly shifts focus away from physical product characteristics, and digs into the personal relevance it has in an individual's life. As the conversation builds on itself to reveal what a person values, the "ladder" is constructed that connects attributes to consequences, to values.

Laddering works best when conducted early in the design process, or any time an organization's internal discussions become fixated on a product's features and characteristics. It can also be used once a product is available in the marketplace, to reveal the reasons behind why people are buying it. The results from laddering research help to shape winning marketing campaigns (usually, the *consequences* that are revealed are the key to a brand-marketing platform), to differentiate a product from the competition, and to train adaptive selling techniques to sales teams.[4] The goal of the method is not to focus on the attributes of a product or service (even though laddering interviews usually begin that way). Instead, it should be used to make explicit the connection between product attributes and the personal (and usually unspoken) motivations that shape and inform why people buy.

1. Laddering was popularized in the 1980s by marketers and consumer researchers, and its foundations are the Means-End Theory (1982) and Expectancy-Value Theory (1956). See:

Reynolds, Thomas J., and Jonathan Gutman. "A Means-End Chain Model Based on Consumer Categorization Processes." *Journal of Marketing* 46, no. 2 (1982): 60-72.

For Expectancy-Value Theory, see:

Rosenberg, Milton. "Cognitive Structure and Attitudinal Affect." *Journal of Abnormal and Social Psychology* 53 (1956): 367-372.

2. Reynolds, Thomas J., and Jonathan Gutman. "Laddering Theory, Method, Analysis, and Interpretation." *Journal of Advertising Research* 28 (1988): 11-31.

3. Wansink, Brian, and Nina Chan. "Using Laddering to Understand and Leverage a Brand's Equity." *Qualitative Market Research– An International Journal* 5, no.2 (2002).

4. See note 3 above.

Further Reading

Hawley, Michael. "Laddering: A Research Interview Technique for Uncovering Core Values," 2009, http://www.uxmatters.com

Reynolds, Thomas J., and Jonathan Gutman. "Laddering: Extending the Repertory Grid Methodology to Construct Attribute-Consequence-Value Hierarchies" in *Personal Values and Consumer Psychology*, Vol. II. Lexington, MD: Lexington Books, 1984.

Behavioral	Quantitative	Innovative	**Exploratory**	Participatory
Attitudinal	**Qualitative**	**Adapted**	Generative	Observational
		Traditional	Evaluative	**Self reporting**
				Expert review
				Design process

53 Literature Reviews

Literature reviews are an integral part of academic papers, but are also a useful component of any design project, to collect and synthesize research on a given topic.

Literature reviews are a familiar method of secondary research to any student who has written a term paper or report, yet they can also be critical to design projects in both research and practice. The literature review is intended to distill information from published sources, capturing the essence of previous research or projects as they might inform the current project. The review need not summarize everything from each source, but should begin to converge the information in a synthetic way, such that connections are drawn between references, while maintaining relevant focus on the design project. Literature reviews may be freestanding, but are more typically one component of a larger research paper or project.

Internet resources have expedited literature searches significantly, allowing the researcher to access libraries from around the world using online tools, digital journals, email, and interlibrary loans. However, the good researcher is still discerning in the choice of references for the review, ensuring that the research and literature selected for inclusion are not only relevant, but from credible sources. Particular caution should be exercised if including website or blog resources, often not vetted or peer-reviewed for credibility. Nonetheless, literature reviews for design may include a diverse range of references, including, but not limited to, books, chapters, journal and magazine articles, theses and dissertations, corporate and academic websites and blogs, and documented design projects.

It is often useful in literature reviews to organize the material by research categories. For example, if the focus of the design project is a new digital application for teenagers, the literature could be sectioned into topics related to technology, generational trends, and game design. Other organizational strategies include chronological, thematic, or methodological.

The guiding factor in selecting literature for the review should be relevance to the project, clearly suggesting *how* it informed or informs the design investigation. In rare cases in design, literature reviews attempt to be completely exhaustive, or "systematic reviews," even using statistical techniques or scoring systems to establish the eligibility of study inclusion in the review (see evidence-based design). In all cases, literature reviews should be accurately referenced using consistent footnoting or endnoting, and bibliographic style, although there is no single agreed-upon system for design.

Further Reading

Booth, Wayne C., Gregory G. Colomb, and Joseph M. Williams. *The Craft of Research*, 3rd ed. Chicago, IL: The University of Chicago Press, 2008.

A number of good resources in standard research and writing textbooks can help guide the literature review process. Additionally, many colleges and universities publish online guides, for example, the Writing Center at the University of North Carolina at Chapel Hill: http://www.unc.edu/depts/wcweb/handouts/literature_review.html

Behavioral	Quantitative	Innovative	Exploratory	Participatory
Attitudinal	Qualitative	Adapted	Generative	Observational
		Traditional	Evaluative	Self reporting
				Expert review
				Design process

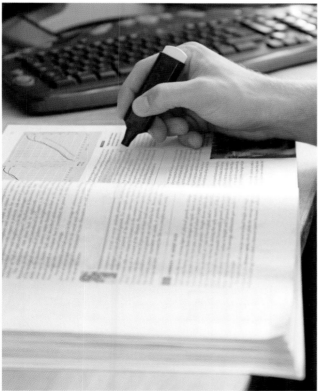

Extracting salient information from precedent research and projects through comprehensive literature reviews is a critical step in laying the foundation and contextualizing the design inquiry.

See also **35.** *Evidence-based Design* • **74.** *Secondary Research* • **92.** *Unobtrusive Measures*

54 The Love Letter & the Breakup Letter

A personal letter written to a product often reveals profound insights about what people value and expect from the objects in their everyday lives.[1]

The love letter, and its counterpart, the breakup letter, are two methods that allow people to express their sentiments about a product or a service using a medium and a format that are immediately understood. Instead of writing to a person, however, participants are asked to personify a product and write a personal message to it. The results are often unexpectedly deep and revealing about the relationships people have with the products and services in their lives.

The Love Letter gets at the heart of what people feel during those magical moments of connection with a product. Descriptions of what elicits delight, infatuation, and loyalty are common themes. As researchers, you will hear about what those first moments of connection are like, and insights into why people stay with a product, even as other products compete for their attention.

The Breakup Letter alternatively provides insight about how, when, and where a relationship with a product turned sour, and can be used to gain insight into why people abandon a brand or a product. People will share information about what new product they are now happy with, and what the new product has that the abandoned product does not.

Both exercises in letter writing are great techniques to use in a group dynamic, such as in design workshops, group interviews, and even icebreaker sessions. Ask participants to spend no more than ten minutes writing a letter (usually, longer timeframes will make participants over-think its contents) and then ask for volunteers to read their letters out loud in front of the other participants.

It is important to capture recordings of participants reading their letters on video: both the participants' expressions and voices provide nonverbal cues that the letters alone do not, and video editing sessions with project stakeholders can also create thoughtful conversation on multidisciplinary teams. The physical, handwritten letters are also important to preserve as research artifacts. Surprising care often goes into their construction, which conveys people's sentimentality and depth of emotion toward a product that they either love or that has disappointed them.

Traditional marketing campaigns used to build brand loyalty are slowly becoming less effective, as they are no longer the only "voice" people will hear when considering whether to buy or stay loyal to a specific product or service. Methods like the love letter and the breakup letter build our empathic knowledge base of how people experience and personify designs. By using them, we can understand what creates moments of connection and delight.

1. In 2009, Smart Design created this method based on a familiar format in which to express thoughts and feelings about a product or a service in an informal, accessible way. The collective insights in the letters continue to influence and inspire the designers at Smart Design on both new and ongoing design projects. www.smartdesignworldwide.com

See Smart Design's video at http://www.vimeo.com/smartdesign/breakupletter for an example of Love and Breakup Letters.

Behavioral	Quantitative	**Innovative**	**Exploratory**	Participatory
Attitudinal	**Qualitative**	Adapted	Generative	Observational
		Traditional	Evaluative	**Self reporting**
				Expert review
				Design process

The Love Letter and Breakup Letter method allows design workshop participants to express their thoughts and emotions in a familiar format—a handwritten letter—addressed to a product or a service that they either love, or has recently disappointed them. More often than not, participants will share stories that are situated in real life experiences about the meaning and place that a particular product plays (or once played) in their lives.

See also 28. Design Workshops • 29. Desirability Testing • 96. Value Opportunity Analysis

55 Mental Model Diagrams

People tend to behave in ways consistent with dearly held beliefs.[1]
The mental model diagram can help you articulate root causes behind
behaviors and develop solutions that deeply resonate with people.

A mental model diagram is a rigorous framework for analysis that aligns the behaviors, beliefs, and emotions people have as they set out to accomplish a task (the top half of the diagram) against your features, product, and service offering (the bottom half of the diagram). The goal is to help teams make appropriate product development strategies that align with how people already approach problem solving in their daily lives, as opposed to building a product that neither resonates with them nor augments their existing patterns of behavior.

When creating a mental model diagram, you must identify the group to study, called the *task-based audience segments*. Constructing the diagram then becomes an instrument used to assess whether an existing product or service offering actually benefits and empowers people in this segment.[2] Later on, these task-based audience segments can be used when recruiting for future research studies such as interviews, card sorts, and usability tests. For each task-based audience segment, try to study *at least* four people.[3]

Mental model diagrams are built from the bottom up, using singularly focused behaviors, beliefs, and emotions as its building blocks. Each of these are derived directly from interview transcripts (or very thorough interview notes), and diary studies of your task-based audience segment. A *task* can be thought of as the "actions, thoughts, feelings, and motivations—everything that comes up when a person accomplishes something, sets something in motion, or achieves a different state."[4] When combing the transcripts, look for ways in which audience segments behave differently when trying to accomplish the same thing, and then organize their tasks into groups that represent those differences. Between 60 and 120 behaviors will be derived per person interviewed.[5]

The purpose of identifying behaviors, beliefs, and emotions, and then teasing them apart to represent differences, can illuminate what people are trying to accomplish regardless of the tools, products, and services they use. The process of building a mental model diagram is focused on uncovering the root causes behind why people complete a task the way they do, by inspecting their behaviors and the philosophical underpinnings they rely on as they go about their daily lives.

Use this research method when you have multiple audience segments that do similar things but accomplish them in different ways. Instead of attempting to build one product that meets everyone's needs, mental models can help you build streamlined, appropriate offerings that align with the behaviors of the different types of people who use your products and services.

1. One of the seminal works on mental models comes from the cognitive sciences. See:

Johnson-Laird, Philip. *Mental Models: Towards a Cognitive Science of Language, Inference, and Consciousness*. Cambridge, MA: Harvard University Press, 1983.

2. Young, Indi. *Mental Models: Aligning Design Strategy with Human Behavior*. Brooklyn, N.Y.: Rosenfeld Media, 2008.

3. See note 2 above.

4. See note 2 above.

5. See note 2 above.

Further Reading

For insight into how Indi Young's Mental Model technique came into existence, read "Appendix B: The Evolution of the Mental Model Technique," available at http://www.rosenfeldmedia.com

Behavioral	Quantitative	Innovative	Exploratory	Participatory
Attitudinal	Qualitative	Adapted	Generative	Observational
		Traditional	Evaluative	Self reporting
				Expert review
				Design process

READING A MENTAL MODEL DIAGRAM

The white building blocks in the top half of the diagram each represents a behavior, belief, or emotion. Each is a verb-driven representation of what people are doing, thinking, and feeling, and is tied closely to the content in the transcripts.

Groups of similar behaviors form the towers in the top half of the diagram (highlighted in yellow). Towers represent general patterns that evolve naturally as related behaviors, beliefs, and emotions are grouped together, from the bottom up. In this example, they form the different

mental spaces common to movie-goers, that include "Choose a Film," "Choose a Theater," and "Choose a Time."

The bottom half of the diagram represents the features, services, or products available in your current offering. They are aligned to the towers that are best matched to the behaviors within the tower.

Choose a Film

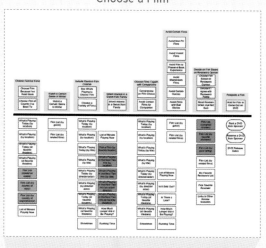

Choose a Theater

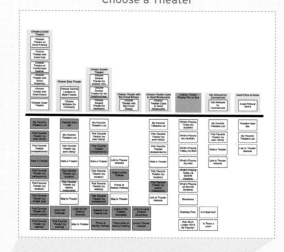

Choose a Time

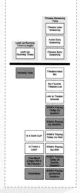

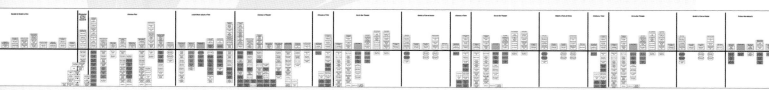

Courtesy of Indi Young. Actual size 85 x 8.5"

See also 30. Diary Studies • 48. Interviews • 84. Task Analysis

56 Mind Mapping

When a topic or a problem has many moving parts, mind mapping provides a method of visually organizing a problem space in order to better understand it.

Mind mapping is a visual thinking tool that can help generate ideas and develop concepts when the relationships among many pieces of related information are unclear. It provides a nonlinear means of externalizing the information in our heads so that we can consolidate, interpret, communicate, store, and retrieve information. Because of its visual, diagrammatic nature, it is a powerful mnemonic device, and can be used to promote understanding and enhance recall of a problem space.

Because the way people think is rarely linear, and complicated problems do not follow a neat pattern of steps that can be isolated from one another, mind maps reflect how we think through complexities of a given problem. As the map takes shape, it allows us to summarize and test assumptions, make and break connections, and consider alternatives while we shape the data into meaningful themes and patterns.

By limiting mind maps to one side of one sheet of paper, the process of freely mapping associations should not feel overwhelming. To draw a mind map, follow the steps below:[1]

1. Identify a focus question to serve as the central theme and keep the mapping process from straying off topic. Draw the subject in the center of a sheet of paper, and circle it.

2. Start drawing extensions outward from the center of the map, and label them with simple verb-noun pairs or noun clusters. The closer a word or image is to the center, the more importance it takes on in your map. These are your primary connections.

3. As the spokes of primary connections are identified, each will reveal deeper, more granular levels of secondary information. Connect primary and secondary connections with lines. It is the connections of concepts that create meaning.

4. Continue this process of making free associations until all relevant pieces of information are represented. As new information comes up, add it to the map.

5. Before declaring the map complete, stay with it for a while. The idea is to strengthen concepts and their interconnections with hopes of creating new knowledge and understanding.

By providing people a means to visually represent their unique thinking patterns in a nonlinear, visual way, researchers can better understand different ways that people prioritize and organize information. After the map is complete, have the user explain the pieces of the map, and its meanings. When mind mapping is used in this manner, it would fall under a "self-reporting" method, and should be further vetted with additional observation-based research. Nonetheless, it can be used to reveal basic, idiosyncratic patterns of thinking.[2]

1. Hyerle, David. *Visual Tools for Constructing Knowledge*. Alexandria, VA: ASCD, 1996.

2. See note 1 above.

3. See note 1 above.

Further Reading

Buzan, Tony. *The Mind Map Book*. New York: Plume, 1996.

Buzan, Tony. *Use Both Sides of Your Brain*, 3rd ed. New York: Plume, 1991.

Wycoff, Joyce. *Mindmapping: Your Personal Guide to Exploring Creativity and Problem-Solving*. New York: Berkley Books, 1991.

See www.mindmapinspiration.com.

Behavioral	Quantitative	**Innovative**	**Exploratory**	Participatory
Attitudinal	**Qualitative**	Adapted	Generative	Observational
		Traditional	Evaluative	**Self reporting**
				Expert review
				Design process

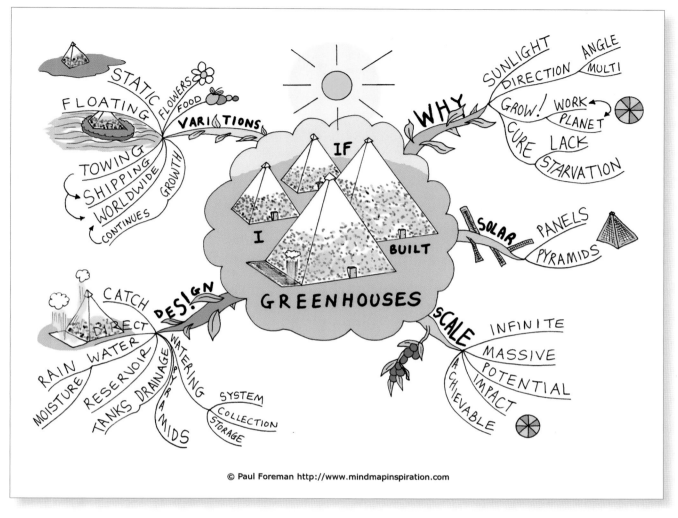

© Paul Foreman http://www.mindmapinspiration.com

When used as a method of analysis and sense-making, mind mapping allows us to simultaneously identify the subject of the map, relationships between the components, and understand the relative importance of the information that is represented. The ability to understand the boundaries, and at the same time understand the interconnecting parts within the system, reflects our human capacity for systems thinking at work.[3]

Use single words or simple noun clusters, common symbols, hand-drawn images, and group-related information with starbursts or clouds. These visual cues serve to transform the map to a mnemonic device that can more readily trigger recall of the information space.

See also 08. Brainstorm Graphic Organizers • 14. Collage • 16. Concept Mapping

57 Observation

A fundamental research skill, observation requires attentive looking and systematic recording of phenomena—including people, artifacts, environments, events, behaviors and interactions.

For design purposes, observational methods may be characterized by their degree of formality, based on the level of prestructuring of the observations and recording methods, and their intended use.

Semistructured, or casual observation, typically describes ethnographic methods in the exploratory phase of the design process, where the intent is to collect baseline information through immersion, particularly in territory that is new to the designer. The researcher may have a guiding set of questions, but is primarily observing with an open mind, and departures from the plan are allowed in response to unexpected events during observation. Despite the informal structure, ethnographic observations should still be systematic, careful, and well documented with notes, sketches, photographs, or raw video footage. Information from semistructured observations is typically synthesized for guiding design inspiration; however, more rigorous forms of qualitative analysis such as content analysis may be performed to uncover common themes or patterns.

Structured, or systematic observation, is formalized by the degree of prestructure imposed upon research sessions, utilizing worksheets, checklists, or other forms for codifying behaviors or observed artifacts and events. Structured coding is ideal where environmental or behavioral elements are targeted and well defined, often through previous semistructured pilot observations. Existing frameworks can be used to guide structured observations (see, for example, AEIOU).

Examples of prestructure include regular time intervals for observations, predetermined types of interactions or behavioral categories for coding observations, or counted successes and errors when observing use of an interface, prototype, or product. Caution should be exercised to avoid the natural tendency to "find what you are looking for," or for artificially assigning observations to preset categories. The inclusion of an "other" category is therefore recommended. If sample sizes are large enough, results can be quantified for analysis, otherwise it is common to look for patterns or trends across observations.

Observations should differentiate between factual behaviors witnessed, and inferences, speculating the meaning and motivations behind actions. Inferences can be verified through interview questions with participants during or following observations.

1. Zeisel, John. *Inquiry by Design: Tools for Environment-Behavior Research.* Cambridge University Press, 1981.

Zeisel, John. *Inquiry by Design: Environment/ Behavior/Neuroscience in Architecture, Interiors, Landscape, and Planning.* New York: Norton, 2006.

Further Reading

Hackos, JoAnn, and Janice Redish. *User and Task Analysis for Interface Design.* New York: Wiley, 1998.

Kuniavsky, Mike. *Observing the User Experience: A Practitioner's Guide to User Research.* San Francisco, CA: Morgan Kaufmann, 2003.

Sommer, Robert, and Barbara Sommer. *A Practical Guide to Behavioral Research: Tools and Techniques.* New York: Oxford University Press, 2002.

Behavioral	Quantitative	Innovative	**Exploratory**	Participatory
Attitudinal	**Qualitative**	Adapted	Generative	**Observational**
		Traditional	Evaluative	Self reporting
				Expert review
				Design process

Right: Classic image showing essential elements of environmental behavior observation. "Each observation comprises a relationship between an actor and a significant other to which the physical setting contributes in some way."[1]

Courtesy of John Zeisel, 1981, 2006

Below: Contextual observations documented from a customer-centered study of the library experience to inform redesign.

Courtesy of MAYA Design

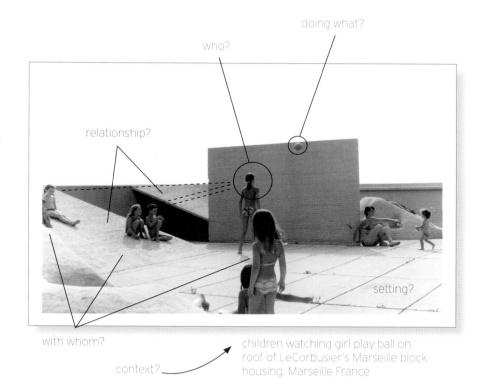

relationship?

who?

doing what?

setting?

with whom?

context?

children watching girl play ball on roof of LeCorbusier's Marseille block housing, Marseille France

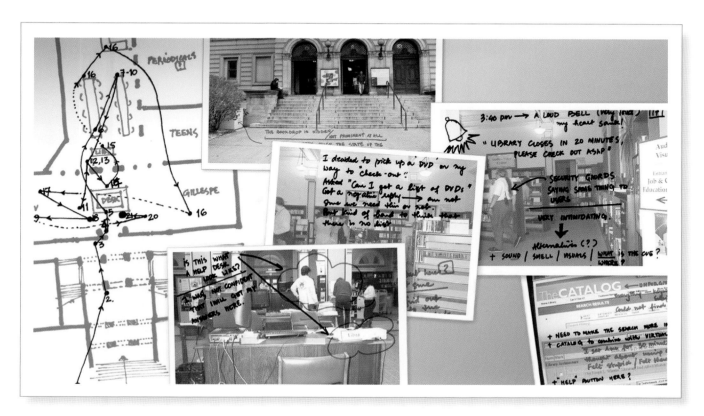

See also 02. AEIOU • 42. Fly-on-the-Wall Observation • 59. Participant Observation

58 Parallel Prototyping

Simultaneously exploring multiple design opportunities can help teams keep from fixating on a design direction too early, improve the nature of design critiques, and lead to more effective design results.[1]

Parallel prototyping is the process of considering a range of potential design ideas simultaneously before selecting and refining one specific design approach. When applied before iterative design, parallel prototyping enables teams to more fully experiment with and investigate a wide range of opportunities in a design space. It can also help designers to avoid becoming fixated on a design, and avoid "hill climbing" toward a less superior result, which has been a long-standing criticism of the iterative design methodology.[2]

Parallel prototyping asks that designers quickly and independently create a range of low-fidelity prototypes, and then submit designs to testing by end users, or to heuristic evaluation by experts. The intention of these design evaluations is not to pick the "best" or "most preferred" design. Rather, the evaluations should help the designers to thoughtfully reflect and consider how people react to individual elements of the design, and which accomplish the intended goals of the project. The best qualities of all preceding designs can then be refined and merged to inform a superior, optimized design. Parallel prototyping affords other advantages when exploring potential solutions to a problem space. Parallel prototyping:

- **Encourages divergent explorations.**[3] Because a goal of parallel prototyping is to create multiple design options, the method frees designers to explore and get feedback on a wide range of options, as opposed to locking in on and refining only their first idea.

- **Shifts focus from the designer onto the design.**[4] Parallel prototyping provides a safe backdrop for giving and receiving constructive criticism. When multiple designs are being considered side by side, it is harder for the designer to feel defensive about any one particular design. When practiced repeatedly, it can help sensitive or novice designers learn to view their designs as separate from themselves.

- **Promotes team collaboration and builds rapport.**[5] Designers collaborating on parallel designs will often merge and refine others' concepts into their subsequent designs. This sort of idea sharing on a team goes a long way toward team building, and also minimizes internal competition among team members.

Use parallel prototyping when working with teams that have a tendency to "get stuck" on one design approach in the early exploration and concept generation phases. The method can be used to make design critiques more engaging and less stressful: design managers and educators will find that parallel prototyping helps critiques become more effective and designers less apprehensive, promoting a safe environment where divergent design ideas can be explored and discussed.

1. Dow, Steven P., Alana Glassco, Jonathan Kass, Melissa Schwarz, Daniel L. Schwartz, and Scott R. Klemmer. "Parallel Prototyping Leads to Better Design Results, More Divergence, and Increased Self-Efficacy." *ACM Transactions on Computer-Human Interaction* 17, no. 4 (2010).

2. Nielsen, Jakob. "Parallel & Iterative Design + Competitive Testing = High Usability," 2011, http://www.useit.com.

3. See note 1 above.

4. Dow, Steven P., Julie Fortuna, Dan Schwartz, Beth Altringer, Daniel L. Schwartz, and Scott R. Klemmer. "Prototyping Dynamics: Sharing Multiple Designs Improves Exploration, Group Rapport, and Results." *CHI 2011 Conference Proceedings*, 2011.

5. See note 3 above.

Further Reading

Dow, Steven P., Kate Heddleston, and Scott R. Klemmer. "The Efficacy of Prototyping Under Time Constraints." *Proceedings of ACM Conference on Creativity and Cognition*, 2009: 165-174.

Behavioral	Quantitative	**Innovative**	Exploratory	Participatory
Attitudinal	**Qualitative**	Adapted	**Generative**	Observational
		Traditional	**Evaluative**	Self reporting
				Expert review
				Design process

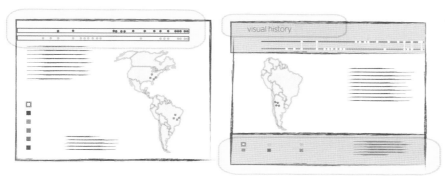

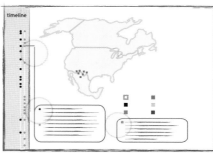

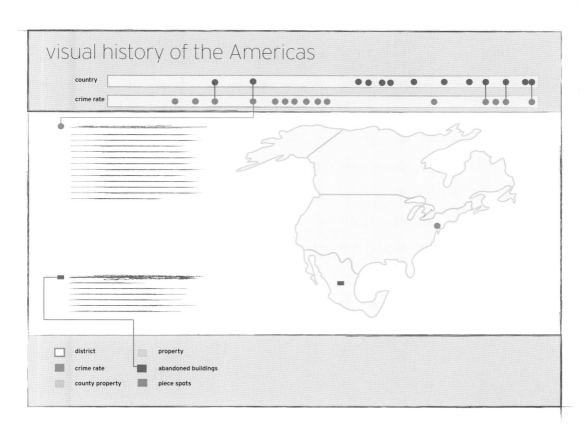

visual history of the Americas

country

crime rate

district   property

crime rate   abandoned buildings

county property   piece spots

By simultaneously designing and testing multiple design approaches and delaying the selection of any one specific direction, there is a better chance that the final design will represent the best qualities of all the design options. Above, the parallel prototypes at the top of the page show yellow highlights that tested best with participants. Each informs the design decisions made in the final interactive map.

See also 26. Design Charette • 66. Prototyping • 70. Research Through Design

59 Participant Observation

Participant observation is an immersive, ethnographic method for understanding situations and behaviors through the experience of membership participation in an activity, context, culture, or subculture.

Participant observation, or PO, is a foundational method of anthropology, adapted for design use.[1] Whereas anthropologists may immerse themselves as participants in a context or culture for extended periods of time, design researchers will typically have a more time-limited engagement. However, the intent is the same, for the designer-researcher to actively participate in the community, forming deep connections and empathy with the people and the things that are important to them, experiencing events in the same way as the people they are studying.

Systematic observation and recording are critical, documenting not only what is physically evident in the environment, but the behaviors, interactions, language, motivations, and perceptions of the participants.[2] To this end, participant observation is generally combined with several other ethnographic methods, including interviews.

John Zeisel discusses observations from the vantage point of the observer, identifying two levels of participation.[3] *Marginal participants* blend into an environment as natural observers of an activity or event. For example, researchers may ride the bus to watch transit commuters, or attend a soccer game to observe audience behaviors.

Full participants become complete members of a group, subculture, or culture, in extreme cases through infiltration or a covert role. This is not a typical role adopted by design researchers, because of ethical considerations, and the significant investment of time and risks involved in becoming, for example, a waitress to study restaurant behaviors, or the impossibility of becoming part of a medical staff to study a hospital environment. However, designers may take on a membership role in more limited capacities or for shorter durations to approximate full participation, or they may already occupy a role that allows for full participation. Researchers engaged in participant observation need to stay vigilant to retain some measure of objectivity, and to avoid undue influence on member behaviors.

1. Anthropologists as early as Malinowski (1928) and Mead (1930) conducted participant observations. For an excellent history see:

Dewalt, K. and B. Dewalt. *Participant Observation: A Guide for Fieldworkers*. Walnut Creek, CA: AltaMira Press, 2002.

2. "Researchers enter a setting and earn enough trust from the people in the environment to actively participate (as participant observers) in the community of practice. Their goal is to connect deeply with the content and issues that matter to that community and then document in regular, systematic ways, what is learned and observed."

From: Evenson, Shelley. "Directed Storytelling: Interpreting Experience for Design" in *Design Studies: Theory and Research in Graphic Design, A Reader*. New York: Princeton Architectural Press, 2006: 231-240.

3. Zeisel, John. *Inquiry by Design: Environment/Behavior/Neuroscience in Architecture, Interiors, Landscape, and Planning*. New York: Norton, 2006.

4. Moore, Pat with Charles Paul Conn. *Disguised*. Waco, TX: Word Books, 1985.

Further Reading

Robson, Colin. *Real World Research: A Resource for Social Scientists and Practitioner-Researchers*, 2nd ed., Oxford: Blackwell Publishers, 2002.

Behavioral	Quantitative	Innovative	Exploratory	Participatory
Attitudinal	Qualitative	Adapted	Generative	Observational
		Traditional	Evaluative	Self reporting
				Expert review
				Design process

Left: Marginal participant observation of transit riders for a service design project on "commutenity," promoting community and reinforcing positive behaviors among bus riders.

Courtesy of Amy Lew

Below: In an exceptional case of full participant observation, industrial designer Patricia Moore, at age 26, was prosthetically altered to approximate the abilities and appearance of women in their 80's, traversing more than 100 cities from 1979 to 1982 in an extensive empathy experiment.[4]

Photos by Bruce Byers Photography NYC, courtesy of Patti Moore

See also **27. Design Ethnography** • **42. Fly-on-the-Wall Observation** • **57. Observation**

60 Participatory Action Research (PAR)

PAR is a cyclical, collaborative research process that seeks to intentionally change the community or other aspects that are the focus of the inquiry.[1]

Participatory Action Research (PAR) is differentiated from many "objective" methods of research inquiry that seek only to describe, understand, and explain, in its explicit mission to actually change the community, parties, or policies under study. With an overtone of empowerment, emancipation, and activism, the approach has been popular in arenas such as education, feminist research, and social justice. PAR is also appropriate where involving practitioners directly in social research serves the purpose of bringing skills and experience to facilitate change, advocating for the creation of practitioner researchers in areas such as nursing and social work.[2]

The process of PAR is dynamic and cyclical in its sequence of planning, taking action, observing, evaluating (including self-evaluation), and critical reflection prior to planning the next cycle.[3] Robson outlines common stages of PAR as follows:[4]

1. Define the inquiry.
2. Describe the situation.
3. Collect evaluative data and analyze it.
4. Review the data and look for contradictions.
5. Tackle a contradiction by introducing change.
6. Monitor the change.
7. Analyze evaluative data about the change.
8. Review the change and decide what to do next.

PAR is defined by the collaborative relationship between researchers and those being researched. Specific research methods utilized within the approach are variable, but tend to be flexible, qualitative, and ethnographic, including traditional observations, participant observation, and interviews. While there is little evidence to date of PAR being formally employed in design research, the connections with participatory design and new movements in social impact by design suggest a natural affiliation and opportunities for an expanded relationship. For example, contextual, immersive, and collaborative methods of design including *contextual inquiry*, *design ethnography*, *participatory design*, *design workshops*, and *creative tool kits* would be powerful when aligned with PAR, corresponding naturally to an approach designed to address issues identified by the community at hand and inspiring action applied directly to problems.

PAR has been criticized for its weaknesses, most notably for its inherently political nature, the potential lack of systematic methods employed, and the shared power over research design and data collection that is necessary in the collaborative relationship. Caution must therefore be exercised when using PAR, in designing and conducting the inquiry, assumptions, and in communicating the project. However, the powerful change that can result from the PAR approach makes it worthy of serious evaluation and consideration by design.

1. First usage of the term "action research" is credited to Kurt Lewin in "Action Research and Minority Problems," which appeared in the *Journal of Social Issues* 2 (1946): 34-46.

2. Robson, Colin. *Real World Research: A Resource for Social Scientists and Practitioner-Researchers*, 2nd ed. Oxford: Blackwell Publishers, 2002.

3. McNiff, Jean. *Action Research for Professional Development*, 2002, http://www.jeanmcniff.com/ar-booklet.asp

4. See note 2 above.

Further Reading

Sommer, Robert, and Barbara Sommer. *A Practical Guide to Behavioral Research: Tools and Techniques*. New York: Oxford University Press, 2002.

A professional journal, manifesto, and blog is dedicated to (Participatory) Action Research at http://arj-journal.blogspot.com and http://arj.sagepub.com

Behavioral	Quantitative	Innovative	Exploratory	Participatory
Attitudinal	Qualitative	Adapted	Generative	Observational
		Traditional	Evaluative	Self reporting
				Expert review
				Design process

GET FIT WITH THE FITWITS:
CO-DESIGNING A COMMUNITY-WIDE OBESITY PREVENTION GAME

The challenge for this project required connecting with a local community to design an appropriate health literacy game.

Engaged players described three positive behavior changes: (a) a positive self-image through the game by succeeding in healthy behavior game challenges; (b) better physical and psychological well-being and continued healthy activities; and (c) positive reinforcement from friends and family. Participants took the message well beyond the original game, promoting Fitwits through new activities in other communities, at work and in summer camps, and raising funds for their own appropriated version. The design research team was in turn inspired to expand the program and run it in a school, where materials are now being integrated into teaching units on health.

Courtesy of Kristin Hughes

See also 11. Case Studies • 61. Participatory Design

61 Participatory Design

Participatory design is a human-centered approach advocating active user and stakeholder engagement throughout all phases of the research and design process, including co-design activities.

The origin of participatory design is generally credited to Scandinavian initiatives in the 1970s, first in Norway, where computer professionals worked closely with ironworker and metalworker union leaders and members on the integration of new technologies into the workplace.[1] Several subsequent projects in Scandinavia involved interdisciplinary research teams from computer science, sociology, economics, and engineering, collaborating with union leaders and members in repair shops, factories, and a department store, again on issues surrounding computer integration and its effect on workplace production and processes. The UTOPIA project of the late 1980s, involving graphics workers in the newspaper industry, sparked the introduction of innovative, experience-based methods such as role-playing scenarios using low-fidelity prototypes.[2]

Participatory design has since expanded in scope and methods, gaining widespread acceptance as an approach to practice in research and application across industrial design, architecture, urban design, interaction design, and communication design. Participatory design encompasses several methods, with the unifying philosophy that they all involve active consultation with users, clients, and other stakeholders in the design process, ideally through face-to-face contact in activity-based co-design engagements. Methods include cultural probes, diary studies, photo studies, collage, flexible modeling, and creative tool kits and design workshops. Participatory design respects the creative insight of participants to inspire and help guide the design process, and to respond to design outcomes. However, participant input is paired with design expertise, supporting the creative authority of designers to translate collaborations into design criteria, services, and artifacts.

Sanders, Brandt, and Binder have proposed a useful framework for organizing the various approaches, tools, techniques, and methods of current-day participatory design, consolidating several years of research in the area.[3] The framework is based on the *form* of participatory action that describes the method or technique (making, telling, enacting), and *purpose*, or why the tools and techniques are being used. Four dimensions of purpose are described as *probing* participants for self-discovery and reporting, *priming* participants for further participatory engagement, *understanding* current experience, and *generation* of future scenarios and concepts. *Context* further describes how and where participatory design might occur, based on group size and composition, face-to-face or online, venue, and stakeholder relationships between the designer-researchers and participants.

1. Kuhn, Sara, and Terry Winograd. "Participatory Design" in *Bringing Design to Software*, New York: Addison-Wesley, 1996.

2. Ehn, Pelle. "Scandinavian Design: On Participation and Skill" in *Usability: Turning Technologies into Tools*, New York: Oxford University Press (1992): 96-132.

3. Sanders, Elizabeth B.-N., Eva Brandt, and Thomas Binder. "A Framework for Organizing the Tools and Techniques of Participatory Design." *Participatory Design Conference (PDC) Proceedings*, 2010.

4. Baskinger, Mark, and Bruce Hanington. "Sustaining Autonomous Living for Older People Through Inclusive Strategies for Home Appliance Design" in *Designing Inclusive Futures*. London: Springer, 2008.

Baskinger, Mark. "Autonomy + the Aging Population: Designing Empowerment into Home Appliances." *Proceedings of Design and Semantics of Form and Movement (DeSForM)* (2007): 133-146.

Behavioral | Quantitative | Innovative | Exploratory | Participatory
Attitudinal | Qualitative | Adapted | Generative | Observational
| | Traditional | Evaluative | Self reporting
| | | | Expert review
| | | | Design process

Participatory design engages users in a wide range of activities throughout the exploratory, generative, and evaluative cycles of research and design. Here participants use creative toolkits for design input, and offer feedback on prototypes, for a project on appliance design for the aging population.[4]

See also 21. Creative Toolkits • 28. Design Workshops

62 Personal Inventories

Personal inventories allow the designer to see and understand the relevance of objects in a user's life from the participant's point of view, to inspire design themes and insight.[1]

By understanding the role that objects play in users' lives, design teams can be appropriately inspired to create responsive products and systems based on true needs and values.

Personal inventories are representative collections of artifacts selected by the participant for the designer-researcher, most commonly solicited through paired methods such as guided tours, contextual interviews, and photo and diary studies. Although the method can be used to understand the relationships people have with artifacts in the workplace, because of the personal nature of the inventory, studies are more typically conducted in the home. Smaller inventories may also be taken of backpacks, purses, or briefcases, or items carried during travel.

As an integral component of touchstone tours, participants are asked to talk about the things they own as they walk the researcher through their home or other environment, engaged in conversation. As an element of photo studies, participants document the objects of meaning to them, often with companion notations entered into a diary. Contextual interviews during tours or instructions for diary entries probe for the meaning of objects, through such questions as the role or specific purpose objects play in the participant's life; the history of their acquisition and ownership; aspects of their operation and use; their placement for storage, display, or transport; and how they might feel if the object were lost, discarded, or damaged.

The focus of personal inventories may be specifically targeted toward certain types of objects or products, but is more commonly driven by the participant, who is encouraged to identify any and all items of personal significance. In this way, the inventory is generally informative, but relies on the designer to extract insight about the user and their context relevant to the design inquiry. For example, in a study of sustainability and interaction design, personal inventories were used to understand the difference between objects that were cherished and those that were discarded.[2] Additional methods may be used to draw out meaning from participants. For example, in one study participants were asked to think aloud while card sorting their photographed objects along semantic differential scales indicating levels of attachment, perceptions of new versus old, emotional versus functional value, etc.[3]

1. The seminal work in documenting the personal meaning of artifacts in the home, often cited by designers, is:

Csíkszentmihályi, Mihaly, and Eugene Rochberg-Halton. *The Meaning of Things: Domestic Symbols and the Self.* Cambridge: Cambridge University Press, 1981.

The seminal work in design and origin of the term "personal inventories" is documented in:

Blevis, Eli, and Erik Stolterman. "Ensoulment and Sustainable Interaction Design" in *Proceedings of International Association of Design Research Societies Conference IASDR 2007.* Hong Kong: HKPT, 2007.

2. Odom, William, Eli Blevis, and Erik Stolterman. "Personal Inventories in the Context of Sustainability and Interaction Design." *Interactions* XV, no. 5 (September–October 2008): 17-20.

3. Odom, William, and James Pierce. "Improving with Age: Designing Enduring Interactive Products." *Proceedings of CHI,* ACM, 2009.

Behavioral	Quantitative	Innovative	Exploratory	Participatory
Attitudinal	Qualitative	Adapted	Generative	Observational
		Traditional	Evaluative	Self reporting
				Expert review
				Design process

Collected objects from personal inventories reveal much about the significance of participant-owned objects, but may rely on the designer to extract insight about the user and their context relevant to the particular design inquiry.

Courtesy of Will Odom

See also *04. Artifact Analysis* • *30. Diary Studies* • *89. Touchstone Tours*

63 Personas

Personas consolidate archetypal descriptions of user behavior patterns into representative profiles, to humanize design focus, test scenarios, and aid design communication.[1]

For user-centered design, you need to understand people. However, attempting to design for *everyone* results in unfocused or incoherent solutions, so some level of consolidation is needed. Surveys and quantitative methods tend to result in abstracted and dehumanized caricatures. Traditional market segments don't work because they describe demographic populations rather than aggregates of behavior. Crafted from information collected from real users through sound field research, personas provide an ideal solution by capturing common behaviors in meaningful and relatable profiles.[2] Their human description facilitates easy empathy and communication, while their distinctions create useful design targets for responsible design.

Once you have enough information collected to describe several users, look for behavior patterns and themes that constitute commonalities. To arrive at consolidated descriptions, it may be useful to employ affinity diagramming or similar methods. The similarities across users can then be clustered to begin forming synthesized, aggregate archetypes. Personas should be limited in number, for example, three to five for any given project, to maintain a manageable design focus and avoid targeting extreme outliers.

Personas are typically presented in page-length or shorter descriptions, providing a name for the person, a photograph (use stock photography to avoid connection to a real identity) or sketch, and a narrative story describing in detail key aspects of his or her life situation, goals, and behaviors relevant to the design inquiry. Supplementary images may be used to add a compelling impression of the persona lifestyle, including typical spaces, objects, and activities. Personas are then used as a lasting human reference by teams throughout all phases of the project. They are helpful in developing, discussing, and presenting product or system design in the definition and ideation phase. They are also used to check scenarios of use, highlighting positive experiences and potential breakpoints. In addition to personas being a useful working tool within the design team (including distributed teams), personas provide a persuasive human reference when communicating research summaries and scenarios to clients.

1. The seminal text that first introduced personas to the world of interaction design is:

Cooper, Alan. *The Inmates Are Running the Asylum: Why High-Tech Products Drive Us Crazy and How to Restore the Sanity.* Indianapolis, IN: Sams–Pearson Education, 2004.

Personas originated from Alan Cooper's need to synthesize and communicate design research, for software development. Cooper first utilized actual project managers and IT managers he met as loose models of users for whom he would target design. The method later evolved into fictional personas based on distinct behavior patterns that emerged from interviews. Each persona captured important differences in goals, tasks, and skill levels. From:

Cooper, Alan. "The Origin of Personas," August 2003, www.cooper.com/journal/2003/08/the_origin_of_personas.html

2. Personas may be entirely fictionalized, but this is not recommended unless part of an intentional approach. For example, Gaver et. al. propose a method of "design for extreme characters" (the drug dealer, the fictitious Pope) with exaggerated emotional attitudes, to expand creative possibilities in considering the aesthetics of interaction design. See:

Djajadiningrat, J., W. Gaver, and J. Frens. "Interaction Relabelling and Extreme Characters: Methods for Exploring Aesthetic Interactions." *Proceedings of Designing Interactive Systems DIS '00*, ACM, 2000: 66-71.

Further Reading

Goodwin, Kim. *Designing for the Digital Age: How to Create Human-Centered Products and Services.* Indianapolis, IN: Wiley, 2009.

Behavioral	Quantitative	**Innovative**	Exploratory	Participatory
Attitudinal	**Qualitative**	Adapted	**Generative**	Observational
		Traditional	Evaluative	Self reporting
				Expert review
				Design process

Above: Persona development using affinity diagramming from field research for a customer-centered project on the library experience.

Courtesy of MAYA Design

Right: Persona of a college student. The majority of information about the persona is visually illustrated to reflect her knowledge, activities and interests, influencers, and backstory.

Courtesy of Todd Zaki Warfel, Principal Designer, messagefirst | design studio

See also *72. Scenario Description Swimlanes • 73. Scenarios • 95. User Journey Maps*

64 Photo Studies

Photo studies invite the participant to photo-document aspects of his or her life and interactions, providing the designer with visual, self-reported insights into user behaviors and priorities.

Photo studies are an ideal way to have participants highlight details of their personal lives directly, providing visual samples of the important things in their world to inform and inspire design. Photo studies are common in exploratory research as a method for understanding the world of users, particularly when engaging in territory unfamiliar to the designer.

To initiate a photo study, participants are provided with a camera, or instructed how their own cameras are to be used for the purposes of the research. Participants are given general instructions on what to document through images, for example, to take pictures of each technology interaction during the day, or objects of significance, or items associated with scheduling appointments and meetings. They may also be instructed to take images of their surroundings when they are feeling a particular way (energized, sad, overwhelmed), or, in rare circumstances, of human interactions. When documenting human interactions, caution needs to be exercised in requesting photos of uncomfortable situations such as work encounters, or photographing the personal details of others.

Photo studies are most often used as a complementary component of other methods. For example, diary studies may include a photographic requirement, whereby pictures are taken by participants to supplement journal entries about behaviors or encounters during a specified time period. Diaries or journals may in turn be a significant part of the experience sampling method.

Like many creative methods, participants are more likely to enthusiastically engage in requests to complete a photo study of their personal lives than they are to traditional means of behavior survey. Furthermore, photo studies provide visual collateral for designers to work with, and particularly when contextualized with journals or other written material, can lead to unique discoveries about users, their behaviors, and priorities.

To synthesize findings from photo studies, the designer may rely solely on the photographs and simple notes provided by the participant. However, it is more common, and recommended, to have the participant explain his or her photos in follow-up interviews, possibly to include sorting or collage of the images or detailing them along a time line or other axis, such as positive-negative interactions. Because the output of photo studies is primarily used for exploratory purposes, the research is summarized as visual support for understanding and inspiration, not for specific meaning through formal analysis. However, patterns and themes might emerge across an inventory of several photos from multiple participants, providing insight for design implications.

Behavioral	Quantitative	**Innovative**	**Exploratory**	Participatory
Attitudinal	**Qualitative**	Adapted	Generative	Observational
		Traditional	Evaluative	**Self reporting**
				Expert review
				Design process

Collected photos from a crowdsourced photo study on energy use reveal a diverse range of interpretations on the subject matter for design consideration.

Courtesy of frog, frogmob.frogdesign.com

See also 24. Cultural Probes • 30. Diary Studies • 37. Experience Sampling Method

65 Picture Cards

Picture cards contain images and words that help people think about and tell true stories of their life experiences, grounded in context and detail.[1]

Picture cards are an artifact-based interview method, providing an anchor around which participant conversations can take place. As with guided tours, people are generally put at ease when interviews are facilitated through concrete, visual reference points. Picture cards as a methodology stem from activity theory, which holds that, "the human mind is the product of our interaction with people and artifacts in the context of everyday activity."[2]

Picture cards are images provided to research participants to aid in their recall of experience. Cards are created with images and caption text relevant to the research inquiry, but connected to the personal accounts of participant lives. Card sets should account for current and future product and service experiences, and include blank cards for details that might emerge during research sessions. Card sets may contain upward of 100 images, but will vary depending on the particular research inquiry. The method should be used flexibly, adding, subtracting, and editing picture cards in pretesting prior to field use, and even between research sessions.

In a picture card session, participants will be instructed to recall a story about an experience, using the cards to support memories and evoke conversation. The session may begin with a sorting task, asking for cards that represent products or services that the participant uses to be identified and grouped. Examples may then be pulled from the sorted sets, asking the person to tell stories of experience, prompted with questions by the researcher under themes such as time of use, location, relationships, life events, mental states, and other resources associated with the product or service. The cards can be used for sorting and "sketching" future scenarios, laid out as a story unfolds.

Picture cards are used in exploratory research to help understand user communities, their experiences and desires. The method is commonly paired with other forms of research, such as guided tours of the home or work environment, or contextual observations. The cards are often employed near the end of the research protocol to ground the stories in immediate experiences.

Picture cards are ideal for engaging couples and families, acting as participatory prompts to inspire the telling of human stories, with participants reminding each other of missing details, habits, and history. The powerful essence of the picture card method lies in the stories told, allowing people to see their life experiences in aggregate, revealing complexity and patterns to themselves and to the researcher, and facilitating meta conversations.

1. The Picture Cards method was developed by and is actively used by Adaptive Path, www.adaptivepath.com.

2. Kaptelinin, Victor, and Bonnie A. Nardi. *Acting with Technology: Activity Theory and Interaction Design.* Cambridge, MA: The MIT Press, 2006.

Behavioral	Quantitative	Innovative	Exploratory	Participatory
Attitudinal	**Qualitative**	Adapted	Generative	Observational
		Traditional	Evaluative	**Self reporting**
				Expert review
				Design process

The power of the picture cards method lies in the artifact-centered nature of the interview. Cards are sorted by participants and used to guide storytelling of past experiences and the sketching of future scenarios.

Above and left: Participants arrange picture cards as they recall and review stories of experience.

Courtesy of Adaptive Path

See also *31. Directed Storytelling • 48. Interviews • 89. Touchstone Tours*

66 Prototyping

Prototyping is the tangible creation of artifacts at various levels of resolution, for development and testing of ideas within design teams and with clients and users.

A prototype, much like a picture, is worth a thousand words. The physical realization of product or interface concepts is a critical feature of the design process, representing the creative translation of research and ideation into tangible form, for essential testing of concepts by the designer, design team, clients, and potential users.

Design prototypes are defined by their level of fidelity, or resolved finish. Low-fidelity prototyping is common throughout early ideation processes in all design disciplines, appearing as concept sketches, storyboards, or sketch models. These prototypes serve an internal development purpose, as a checkpoint for the designer or team. However, low-fidelity prototypes are an excellent tool for the early testing of ideas with clients and users in generative research, so that the product is seen as a concept proposed for constructive review and timely feedback for iterative changes.

A common method of low-fidelity prototyping in interface and software design is paper prototyping. Users are presented with pages representing interface screens. In completing a task or working toward a goal, the participant indicates what he or she would do on each screen page, while the researcher swaps subsequent pages to simulate the interface response. Areas of difficulty or positive reactions are documented, sometimes directly on the paper prototype with annotations or codes.

In graphic design, the "comp" serves as a low-fidelity prototype, presenting a mocked-up version of a proposed printed piece, usually for client review. In industrial design, low-fidelity prototypes may appear as sketch models intended for iterative design review, or as proof of concept models to test aspects of form and scale.

High-fidelity prototypes are more refined, often representing the appearance of the final product in look and feel, and sometimes even basic functionality. These are useful in later phase evaluation testing for feedback from clients and users, who can now provide a response based on aesthetics, form, interaction, and usability. Examples of high-fidelity industrial design prototypes include sophisticated models presented in computer-aided design (CAD) or physical form, or working models with some level of interactive functionality. In software design, high-fidelity usually implies an interactive prototype capable of providing a real user experience for feedback.

If low- and high-fidelity prototypes are end points on a continuum, it stands to reason that there are many variations of prototyping in between. For example, test rigs are frequently used to exhibit and test the functionality of machines prior to aesthetic form development. In interface design, screen renderings may be used for documentation and presentation, without any interactive functionality.

Further Reading

Various perspectives are offered on prototyping, depending in part on design discipline. See for example:

Houde, S., and C. Hill. "What Do Prototypes Prototype?" in *Handbook of Human-Computer Interaction*, 2nd ed. Amsterdam: Elsevier Science B. V, 1997.

Interactions. The Art of Prototyping, special section edited by Michael Arent. vol. 13, no. 1, January/February, ACM, 2006.

Lidwell, William, Kritina Holden, and Jill Butler. *Universal Principles of Design: 125 Ways to Enhance Usability, Influence Perception, Increase Appeal, Make Better Design Decisions, and Teach through Design*, 2nd ed. Beverly, MA: Rockport Publishers, 2010.

Warfel, Todd Zaki. *Prototyping: A Practitioner's Guide*. Brooklyn, N.Y.: Rosenfeld Media, 2009.

Behavioral	Quantitative	Innovative	Exploratory	Participatory
Attitudinal	**Qualitative**	Adapted	**Generative**	Observational
		Traditional	**Evaluative**	Self reporting
				Expert review
				Design process

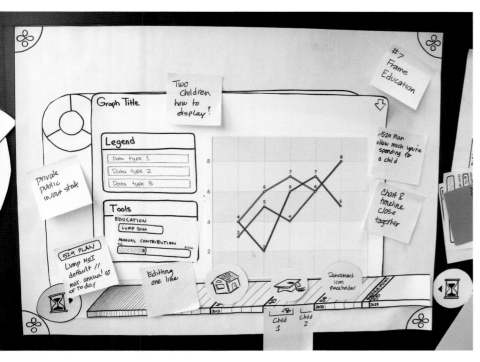

Left: Low-fidelity prototypes of interface behaviors are used to build consensus and understanding among project team members and clients.

Courtesy of POP

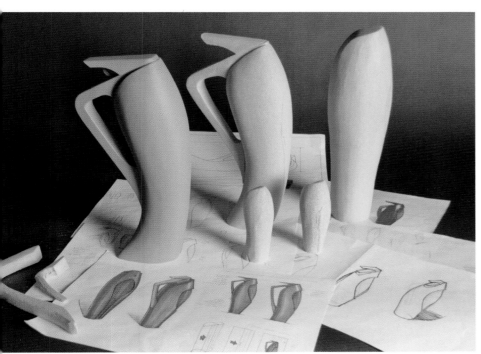

Left: Industrial design prototypes are used for iterative form development, gauging user response, and communication of design concepts.

Courtesy of Lilian Kong

See also 36. Experience Prototyping • 70. Research Through Design • 82. Storyboards

67 Questionnaires

Questionnaires are survey instruments designed for collecting self-report information from people about their characteristics, thoughts, feelings, perceptions, behaviors, or attitudes, typically in written form.

Questionnaires are one of the primary tools used to collect survey information, the other being interviews.

Questionnaires are simple to produce and administer, but careful attention should be paid to question wording and response options, sequencing, length, layout, and design. Software and online services are excellent resources for efficient and effective questionnaire construction and distribution, but are no substitute for good judgment in wording and design. In fact, among several factors in securing a good response rate are the appearance, clarity, instructions, arrangement, design and layout of questionnaires.[1]

The way a question is constructed will play a key role in the type of response and analysis. For example, open-ended questions provide opportunity for depth of response, whereas closed-ended questions are easier to numerically analyze and communicate. Asking participants to rank order their choices or to divide a constant sum (for example, 100) among a set number of options, will give a better indication of preferences than a single checked response. To maintain question neutrality while also gaining an indication of strength of response, Likert scale questions are highly recommended. For example, rather than asking if participants merely agree with a statement or not, providing a five-point range from strongly disagree to strongly agree will give them the option of scaling their responses along a continuum of choices to indicate the strength of their agreement, or disagreement.

Questionnaires may be used in isolation, but are more commonly triangulated with other methods such as observation, which supplement the data with personal insights that may not be evident in written responses, and may verify or challenge self-reported behaviors.[2] Questionnaires can be used as an integral component of research in various phases of research for different purposes, for example, imbedded in a journal as part of a diary study, or as a self-reporting element within product evaluation.

1. Robson, Colin. *Real World Research: A Resource for Social Scientists and Practitioner-Researchers*, 2nd ed. Oxford: Blackwell, 2002.

2. Questionnaires are efficient tools for collecting large quantities of data, but are subject to the weaknesses of self-reporting, and should therefore be complemented with other methods.

"As Agnew and Pyke (1982) put it, 'On a questionnaire, we only have to move the pencil a few inches to shift our scores from being a bigot to being a humanitarian...'" From:

Robson, Colin. *Real World Research: A Resource for Social Scientists and Practitioner-Researchers*, 2nd ed. Oxford: Blackwell, 2002: 310.

Further Reading

Bradburn, Norman, Seymour Sudman, and Brian Wansink. *Asking Questions: The Definitive Guide to Questionnaire Design—For Market Research, Political Polls, and Social and Health Questionnaires* (Research Methods for the Social Sciences). San Francisco, CA: Jossey-Bass, 2004.

Behavioral	Quantitative	Innovative	Exploratory	Participatory
Attitudinal	Qualitative	Adapted	Generative	Observational
		Traditional	Evaluative	Self reporting
				Expert review
				Design process

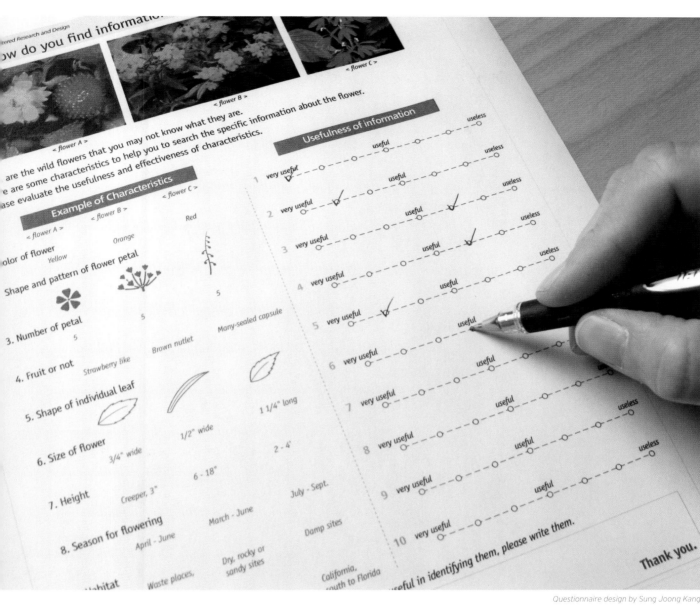

Questionnaire design by Sung Joong Kang

See also 48. Interviews • 75. Semantic Differential • 83. Surveys

68 Rapid Iterative Testing & Evaluation (RITE)

RITE is a powerful formative usability inspection method that helps teams identify and remove major problems in an interface early in the design process before costly prototypes are built.

Rapid Iterative Testing and Evaluation (RITE) is a rigorous method that can be used to evaluate and identify interface problems, quickly fix them, and then empirically verify the efficacy of the fixes,[1] using a rapid test-fix-test-fix approach. Formative usability testing methods such as RITE are used to gain exploratory insights into the user behavior as it relates to the overall design direction, with the intention of quickly iterating and fixing problems, as opposed to summative goals, which seek to find and measure usability issues.[2] For RITE, this distinction is important, as the power of the method depends on the *early* identification of the big problems that block people from completing a task, and on uncovering issues that fail to meet one of the overarching goals of the design. Other ways RITE as a formative method differs from traditional summative usability tests include the following:

- RITE can be used early in the design process as a *guide* through the design solution space, rather than trailing behind development to identify usability problems in later phases.

- Prototypes are changed as soon as problems are identified and the team agrees to a solution —usually within a few hours of the session. The fix is then retested with more participants.

- No usability reports are written, as an updated prototype serves as the new design direction.

- The number of scheduled tests (and by extension, the number of participants you have to schedule) continues after each design change until there is a consecutive string of successful tests with no failures.

- It is preferred that observers and facilitators have domain expertise over test facilitation expertise. Domain knowledge can help observers prioritize fixes based on their judgment of what is truly a problem versus what is an artifact of a particular participant.

RITE can be scheduled as soon as you have a low-fidelity prototype to test. When a team adopts the process, RITE has the power to promote a shared understanding about the ways in which end users cognitively process an interface, how they go about solving problems, and successfully completing tasks. It is an effective and reliable method that helps teams to immediately identify and remove the biggest issues blocking task completion early in the process, before time and resources are spent producing a high-fidelity prototype.

1. In 2002, researchers from Microsoft Games documented the RITE method while designing and testing Age of Empires II. They presented the method and the case study at the 2002 UPA Conference. See:

Medlock, Michael C., Dennis Wixon, Mark Terrano, Ramon L. Romero, and Bill Fulton. "Using the RITE Method to Improve Products: A Definition and a Case Study." *UPA Conference Proceedings*, 2002.

2. Schrag, John. "Using Formative Usability Testing as a Fast UI Design Tool." *UPA Conference Proceedings*, 2006.

3. See note 2 above.

Further Reading

Courage, Catherine, and Kathy Baxter. *Understanding Your Users: A Practical Guide to User Requirements Methods, Tools, and Techniques.* San Francisco, CA: Morgan Kaufmann, 2005.

Sawyer, Paul, Alicia Flanders, and Dennis Wixon. "Making a Difference—The Impact of Inspections." *CHI Conference Proceedings*, 1996.

Behavioral	Quantitative	Innovative	Exploratory	Participatory
Attitudinal	Qualitative	Adapted	Generative	Observational
		Traditional	Evaluative	Self reporting
				Expert review
				Design process

AN EXAMPLE TEST CYCLE USING THE RITE METHOD[3]

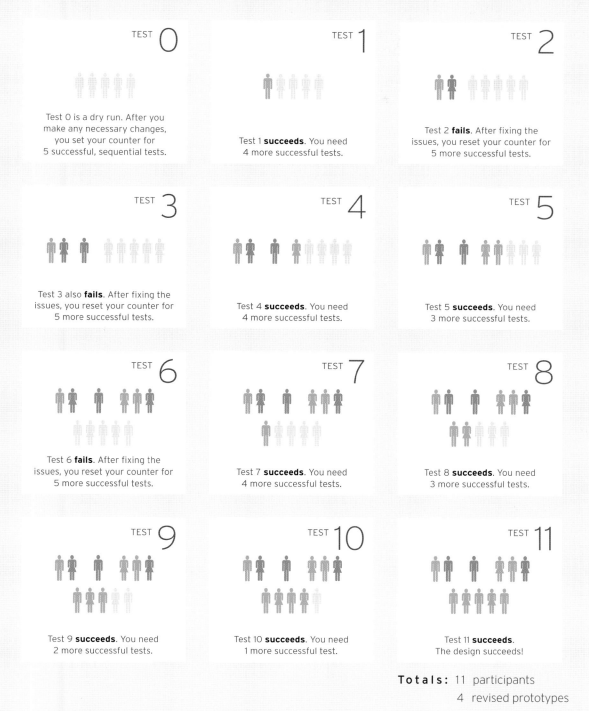

TEST 0

Test 0 is a dry run. After you make any necessary changes, you set your counter for 5 successful, sequential tests.

TEST 1

Test 1 **succeeds**. You need 4 more successful tests.

TEST 2

Test 2 **fails**. After fixing the issues, you reset your counter for 5 more successful tests.

TEST 3

Test 3 also **fails**. After fixing the issues, you reset your counter for 5 more successful tests.

TEST 4

Test 4 **succeeds**. You need 4 more successful tests.

TEST 5

Test 5 **succeeds**. You need 3 more successful tests.

TEST 6

Test 6 **fails**. After fixing the issues, you reset your counter for 5 more successful tests.

TEST 7

Test 7 **succeeds**. You need 4 more successful tests.

TEST 8

Test 8 **succeeds**. You need 3 more successful tests.

TEST 9

Test 9 **succeeds**. You need 2 more successful tests.

TEST 10

Test 10 **succeeds**. You need 1 more successful test.

TEST 11

Test 11 **succeeds**. The design succeeds!

Totals: 11 participants
4 revised prototypes

See also 66. Prototyping • 87. Think-aloud Protocol • 94. Usability Testing

69 Remote Moderated Research

Remotely observing users completing tasks on their own electronic devices can reveal rich insights into contexts of use that cannot be replicated in a controlled lab environment.

Remote moderated research is a method adapted from traditional usability testing techniques, but relies on screen-sharing software in lieu of the usability lab equipment to conduct it. There is still live interaction between the researcher and participants in remote moderated tests, and anything from websites to prototypes, screen mock-ups, and sketches can be tested and evaluated. However, a key differentiator and benefit of the method is that it exposes rich, qualitative data about a participant's native computer and possibly his or her physical environment, which usability tests that take place in a controlled lab setting do not.

Depending on your needs and time line, participants for remote moderated testing can be recruited using traditional means, or "live recruited" (see *Time Aware Research*). Live recruiting participants is particularly powerful, as the participant can be intercepted as he or she begins a process, and the research session can be initiated immediately upon his or her consent.[1] This flexibility allows the research team to observe behavior in a task that the participant has selected, as opposed to the team assigning a task or set of tasks that may not carry a sense of urgency or importance to the user.

Once intercepted, observing how people complete tasks that they've initiated can be insightful. For instance, if your interface requires some organization of personal media (e.g., pictures, videos, or music), asking users to work with their own files can provide deeper insight into the organizing principles, tools, and workarounds people devise to create meaning and simplify access rather than assigning them to organize stock photos or other files to which they are not attached.

Unlike traditional usability testing, which requires that participants travel to the usability lab, remote moderated research opens up the opportunity to work with participants who are unable to travel because of geography or other limitations. As long as the participants have an Internet connection and a computer, under most circumstances the test can be successfully administered.[2]

Remote moderated research is not necessarily a cheaper option to the traditional usability test, nor is it likely that it will be completed in less time. Although you may be able to save on lab equipment costs, travel expenses, and even cut some costs related to recruiting, there are still the costs associated with participant incentives, and use of moderator and analyst time.[3] Use remote moderated research when the benefits of accessing a geographically diverse group of participants, being able to live recruit participants, and studying people in their native environments outweigh the costs and time constraints.

1. Bolt, Nate, and Tony Tulathimutte. *Remote Research: Real Users, Real Time, Real Research*. San Francisco, CA: Rosenfeld Media, 2010.

2. See note 1 above.

3. See note 1 above.

Further Reading

Tullis, Tom, and Bill Albert. *Measuring the User Experience*. San Francisco, CA: Morgan Kaufmann, 2008.

Tullis, Tom, Donna Tedesco, and William Albert. *Beyond the Usability Lab: Conducting Large-Scale User Experience Studies*. San Francisco, CA: Morgan Kaufmann, 2010.

If you are recording sessions, it is imperative that you obtain consent from the participant, and disclose the ways in which the recording will be used. If you are recording a phone conversation separately from the screen capture software, certain state regulations may apply. Refer to the "Privacy and Consent" chapter in *Remote Research* for more information, and consult your legal team before you record any remote research sessions.

Behavioral	Quantitative	Innovative	Exploratory	Participatory
Attitudinal	Qualitative	Adapted	Generative	Observational
		Traditional	Evaluative	Self reporting
				Expert review
				Design process

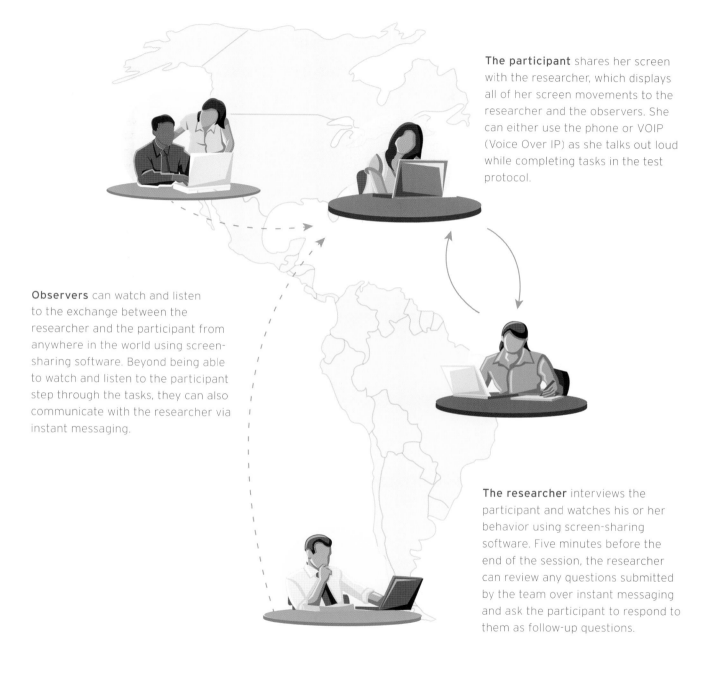

The participant shares her screen with the researcher, which displays all of her screen movements to the researcher and the observers. She can either use the phone or VOIP (Voice Over IP) as she talks out loud while completing tasks in the test protocol.

Observers can watch and listen to the exchange between the researcher and the participant from anywhere in the world using screen-sharing software. Beyond being able to watch and listen to the participant step through the tasks, they can also communicate with the researcher via instant messaging.

The researcher interviews the participant and watches his or her behavior using screen-sharing software. Five minutes before the end of the session, the researcher can review any questions submitted by the team over instant messaging and ask the participant to respond to them as follow-up questions.

70 Research Through Design

Research through design recognizes the design process as a legitimate research activity, examining the tools and processes of design thinking and making within the design project, bridging theory and building knowledge to enhance design practices.[1]

Frayling identifies three types of design research: research into design, research through design, and research for design.[2] Research *into* design is the most common form, encompassing research activity which studies design, or constitutes research about design, such as historical, aesthetic, perceptual, or theoretical research. Research *for* design is controversial, as it is really the reference material that informs and is embodied in the designed artifact, bringing into question whether this accurately constitutes "research." Research *through* design is constituted by the design process itself, including materials research, development work, and the critical act of recording and communicating the steps, experiments, and iterations of design.

As an approach to interaction design, research through design integrates models and theories with technical knowledge in the design process.[3] Designers first look at secondary design research, then combine it with their own up-front exploratory research, using methods such as design ethnography, contextual inquiry, observation, interviews, experience sampling methods, and diary and photo studies. Through a process of ideation, experimentation, and critique, designers then reframe the problem to arrive at the "right" solution. Of the artifacts that emerge from the design process, including sketches, drawings, models, and prototypes, the most critical is documentation, which contextualizes and communicates design action.

In a similar perspective, "design (as) research" is explicitly contrasted to human-centered design and usability testing, suggesting that the act and material of design and making, *rather* than observing or interviewing, constitutes the means of investigation and generation of new knowledge.[4] Differences aside, the intent of design (as) research runs parallel to design *through* research, because designers who conduct their research through creative, critically reflective practice may at once be responding to a design brief and a set of larger questions, utilizing their body of work to experiment and interrogate their ideas, test hypotheses, and pose new questions, documenting and communicating their work to advance design scholarship and enhance the inventory of design resources.

1. This recognition of design as research is articulated by Anne Burdick in her introduction to a selection of seven essays on the topic:

"Design requires a space—the research lab—for design risk-taking, speculation, and discovery, not only for specific applications but also to expand our knowledge of design itself." From:

Burdick, Anne. "Design (As) Research" in *Design Research: Methods and Perspectives.* Brenda Laurel, ed. Cambridge, MA: MIT Press, 2003: 82.

2. Frayling, Christopher. "Research in Art and Design." *Royal College of Art Research Papers* 1, no. 1 (1993): 1-5.

3. Zimmerman, John, Jodi Forlizzi, and Shelley Evenson. "Research Through Design as a Method for Interaction Design Research in HCI." *Proceedings of CHI,* ACM, 2007.

4. Burdick, Anne. "Design (As) Research" in *Design Research: Methods and Perspectives.* Brenda Laurel, ed. Cambridge, MA: MIT Press, 2003: 82.

5. Baskinger, Mark. "Playing in the Sandbox: The Role of Experimentation in Designing," *UX Magazine,* 2010, http://www.uxmag.com/design/playing-in-the-sandbox.

Baskinger, Mark and Mark Gross. "Tangible Interaction = Form + Computation." *Interactions* xvii, no. 1. ACM, January-February, 2010.

Behavioral	Quantitative	Innovative	Exploratory	Participatory
Attitudinal	Qualitative	Adapted	Generative	Observational
		Traditional	Evaluative	Self reporting
				Expert review
				Design process

INVESTIGATING FORM THROUGH MAKING

These form studies were created by the designer-researcher
from a variety of media ranging from rib bones to 3D plaster
prints as a method of research through design. Using
computer modeling and hand shaping, each piece embodies
an inquiry into materials, surfaces, volumes, and edges,
informing research and teaching in the generation of form
and experimental form.[5]

Courtesy of Mark Baskinger © 2011

See also 11. Case Studies • 35. Evidence-based Design • 66. Prototyping

71 Role-playing

Acting the role of the user in realistic scenarios can forge a deep sense of empathy and highlight challenges, presenting opportunities that can be met by design.

Role-playing consists of exercises whereby the designer takes on the role of the user, assuming the routines and behaviors that he or she might experience in actual scenarios of use. It is a relatively low-cost, low-investment method; however, a certain amount of work is necessary to make the role-play credibly connected to the real lives of users.

Members of the design team have to be willing to participate and play along realistically. On the other hand, caution sometimes needs to be exercised, as people may become so immersed in the role that social exchanges can lead to hurtful or upsetting actions, words, and responses. In fact, the criticisms of role-playing and simulation highlight the need for finding an appropriate balance: the exercises are critiqued for being not realistic enough, and for being too realistic, depending on the situation.[1]

The setup for role-playing is typically easy, and may need nothing more than the people in the room. If more sophisticated environmental props are deemed necessary, then simulation exercises should be considered instead. If more elaborate acting targeted toward creative concept generation is called for, then bodystorming methods should be conducted instead. The role-play or acting out of user scenarios is usually guided at least by describing a general situation or suggestions for actions to be performed, tasks to be accomplished, or goals to be reached. The players then begin acting their various roles, including those of the user and supporting stakeholders for the situation. Because role-playing attempts to approximate real-life situations, improvisation is expected and encouraged.

Role-playing is difficult to document by the actors involved, so it is useful to have other team members record the sessions using photos and notes or video. To make sense of what occurred during the exercise, and to assess genuine feelings that may have resulted from the session, a thorough review of role-playing after the fact is critical.

Mock activities through role-playing are particularly useful when direct observation is not feasible or ethical, for example, for personally sensitive situations or where access to the users is restricted. However, wherever possible, role-playing should still be built upon realistic scenarios and user behaviors, either through collecting enough information to guide the exercise, or at least by comparison to real users and situations later, through other research means such as interviews, contextual observations, or secondary research.

1. Sommer, Robert, and Barbara Sommer. *A Practical Guide to Behavioral Research: Tools and Techniques.* New York: Oxford University Press, 2002.

Further Reading

Burnette, Charles. "A Role-Oriented Approach to Problem-Solving" in S.A. Olsen, *Group Planning and Problem Solving Methods in Engineering Management*, New York: John Wiley and Sons, 1982.

Behavioral	Quantitative	Innovative	Exploratory	Participatory
Attitudinal	Qualitative	Adapted	Generative	Observational
		Traditional	Evaluative	Self reporting
				Expert review
				Design process

Members of design teams engaged in role-playing have to be willing and realistic participants. In this scene, designers are enthusiastically role-playing services for parents with young children.

Courtesy of Elizabeth Gerber

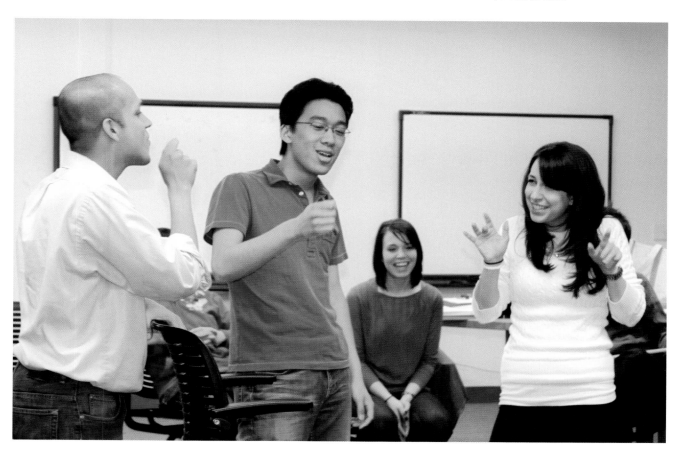

See also 07. Bodystorming • 36. Experience Prototyping • 77. Simulation Exercises

72 Scenario Description Swimlanes

Scenario description swimlanes are deliverables that visualize the activities of multiple actors in a flow of events and prove that a holistic perspective is greater than the sum of its parts.[1]

Scenario description swimlanes can benefit any project where several processes or actors have to come together to shape the outcome of the same flow of events. Its direct, visual nature provides a bird's-eye view of all of the moving parts within a story, and serves to get everyone on a project team on the same page, regardless of individual technical abilities. Because swimlanes represent multiple points of view, it is a powerful conversation starter and reminder that the success of the system depends on multiple components working together.

Within a given project, multiple scenario description swimlanes should be created, each focused on its own specific user story. It is important to represent each story independently, as each story will have each of the following elements in its own "swimlane":

Storyboard lane: The top lane is the most visually powerful element of the document, and captures the events in a user story in a visual way. It is this top lane that draws the most attention from executives and stakeholders, and can be used to facilitate discussions about the user experience without getting too technical. Comics, photographs, illustrations, or sketches can be used to communicate the story.

User Experience lane: Using a flowchart of boxes and arrows, this lane depicts the story shown in the storyboard lane with more detail and insight into the process of the user experience.

Business Process lane: The business logic that supports the user story and user experience is flowcharted in the third lane. It provides the information supplied by business analysts in terms of required business processes that facilitate the steps of the user experience.

Tools and Systems lane: The back-end technology that is involved to support the user actions and business goals is documented here, and is provided by technical team members such as engineers and database administrators.

Scenario description swimlanes are best used for application-based products or process reengineering projects versus marketing/content-heavy projects. The information used to build the deliverable comes from workshops and interviews with the different groups that are represented in the swimlanes above. By visually connecting the goals and requirements of different actors into an overarching user story, scenario description swimlanes serve to remind us how and why we are solving a specific problem at a very high-level "macro" perspective as well as a detailed "micro" view.

1. Swimlanes are an activity diagram of the Unified Modeling Language (UML), which seeks to show activities occurring at the same time but that are performed by different actors. Yvonne Shek at nForm adapted the UML activity in 2007, and created the scenario description swimlanes. In 2008, nForm submitted the deliverable to the IA Summit's *Wall of Deliverables*, where it won the People's Choice award. It has also been integrated into the EightShapes Unify collection of deliverables: http://unify.eightshapes.com

Behavioral	Quantitative	Innovative	Exploratory	Participatory
Attitudinal	Qualitative	Adapted	Generative	Observational
		Traditional	Evaluative	Self reporting
				Expert review
				Design process

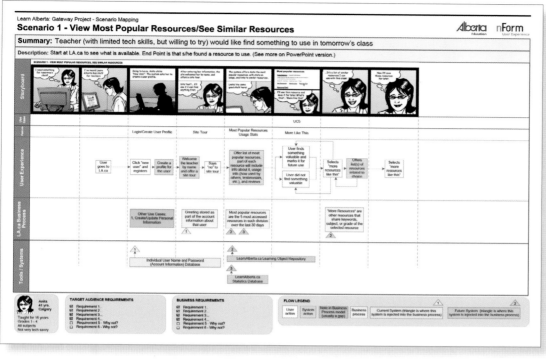

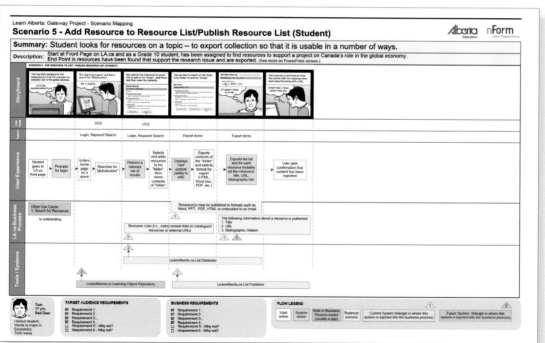

Courtesy of nForm User Experience Consulting, Inc.

See also 63. Personas • 73. Scenarios • 80. Stakeholder Maps

73 Scenarios

A scenario is a narrative that explores the future use of a product from a user's point of view, helping design teams reason about its place in a person's day-to-day life.

A scenario is a believable narrative, usually set in the future, of a person's experience as he or she engages with a product or a service. Ultimately, the purpose of writing scenarios is to make design ideas explicit and concrete, so that the design team can empathetically envision the future ways in which a product is likely to be used. When referred back to throughout the development process, scenarios serve as an anchor for the team to revisit the product's future use.[1] In this way, scenarios help teams avoid the tendency to design toward technical requirements, and instead focus efforts on building culturally meaningful artifacts that augment actual day-to-day human activity.

Scenarios are flexible, and take on many variations. Written like a story with few visuals, it is generally agreed that scenarios should be written from a *persona's* point of view, and focus more on what technology enables than the details of the technology itself. Each persona should get at least one scenario that explores the baseline, status-quo situation for that persona, but writing realistic scenarios about high-stress situations where conditions are less than optimal is also recommended. Once framed by a specific persona's point of view, scenarios can be written to follow a traditional story arc. The action begins with a trigger event, which sets the scene and preconditions, and ends with the resolution of a task by using an intervening technology that assists (and hopefully delights) the persona. Scenarios, therefore, serve to bring personas to life; both deliverables reinforce the value of the other.

Like personas, scenarios and storyboards also work well together, and both serve to communicate the user's point of view. Scenarios inform and guide the production of highly visual storyboards, and in this way, the two supplement each other.

Writing successful scenarios asks that we tap into our capacity for human empathy and to write stories about a superior, future state that ultimately delights people. Scenarios can be used successfully on projects with even the tightest budgets, and although they are most reliable when informed by research and research-backed personas, they can be written based on the design team's understanding of their target users. Scenarios are a widely used strategic planning tool,[2] and are a powerful method to align teams to a shared product vision and goal—whether it is a few months, or a few years, away.

1. Carroll, John M. *Scenario Based Design: Envisioning Work and Technology in System Development.* New York: Wiley, 1995.

2. Schwartz, Peter. *The Art of the Long View: Planning for the Future in an Uncertain World.* New York: Currency Doubleday, 1996.

Further Reading

Carroll, John M. *Making Use: Scenario-Based Design of Human Computer Interactions.* Cambridge, MA: MIT Press, 2000.

Goodwin, Kim. *Design in the Digital Age: How to Create Human-Centered Products and Services.* Indianapolis, IN: Wiley & Sons, 2009.

Behavioral	Quantitative	Innovative	Exploratory	Participatory
Attitudinal	Qualitative	Adapted	Generative	Observational
		Traditional	Evaluative	Self reporting
				Expert review
				Design process

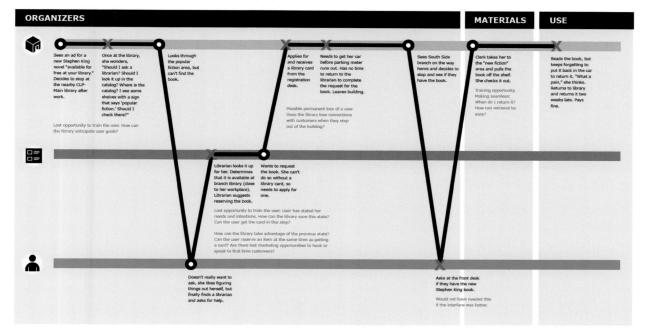

In the following pages, we have taken four personas and developed goal-oriented scenarios to illustrate the current experience. At each key interaction red crosses depict barriers to a successful experience.

Non-user
Naomi

Primary goal
Wants bestseller

Secondary goals
Check out CDs or DVDs
Get answers about health or family history

Description
Naomi is 39 and married with two children. She works full time as the Director of Sales for PhilTek Systems in Oakland. She's either traveling or at the office late into the night. She lives with her family in a renovated loft on the South Side. She often orders books and DVDs online using Amazon or Netflix, which are conveniently accessible when she's on the go.

Library experience
Naomi has never been to the library as an adult and thinks of it only as a musty institution from her childhood. She thinks it is unlikely that they have anything "fresh."

Frequency of visit: Never
Help-seeking: Negative
Gender: Female
Age: 20s–40s

ORGANIZERS | **MATERIALS** | **USE**

Sees an ad for a new Stephen King novel "available for free at your library." Decides to stop at the nearby CLP-Main library after work.

Lost opportunity to train the user. How can the library anticipate user goals?

Once at the library, she wonders, "Should I ask a librarian? Should I look it up in the catalog? Where is the catalog? I see some shelves with a sign that says 'popular fiction.' Should I check there?"

Looks through the popular fiction area, but can't find the book.

Applies for and receives a library card from the registration desk.

Needs to get her car before parking meter runs out. Has no time to return to the librarian to complete the request for the book. Leaves building.

Possible permanent loss of a user. Does the library lose connections with customers when they step out of the building?

Sees South Side branch on the way home and decides to stop and see if they have the book.

Clerk takes her to the "new fiction" area and pulls the book off the shelf. She checks out.

Training opportunity. Making seamless: When do I return it? How can retrieval be easy?

Reads the book, but keeps forgetting to put it back in the car to return it. "What a pain," she thinks. Returns to library and returns it two weeks late. Pays fine.

Librarian looks it up for her. Determines that it is available at branch library (close to her workplace). Librarian suggests reserving the book.

Lost opportunity to train the user. User has stated her needs and intentions. How can the library save this state? Can the user get the card in this step?

How can the library take advantage of the previous state? Can the user reserve an item at the same time as getting a card? Are there lost marketing opportunities to hook or speak to first-time customers?

Wants to request the book. She can't do so without a library card, so needs to apply for one.

Doesn't really want to ask, she likes figuring things out herself, but finally finds a librarian and asks for help.

Asks at the front desk if they have the new Stephen King book.

Would not have needed this if the interface was better.

SEEING · THINKING · HEARING · FEELING

Above: A scenario for a customer-centered project on the library experience.

Courtesy of MAYA Design

Left: "Seeing, Thinking, Hearing, Feeling" framework that designers can use when thinking about and constructing scenarios.

Courtesy of XPLANE | Dachis Group © 2011

RESEARCH METHOD

74 Secondary Research

Secondary research consists of information collected and synthesized from existing data, rather than original material sourced through primary research with participants.

While human-centered design generally implies primary research with users, secondary research can also be a critical component of the project, establishing what has already been done and what hasn't, gathering comparison data, and helping to suggest a research direction or methods that should be used in the current study. Secondary research is sometimes referred to as desk research, in contrast to primary research conducted as fieldwork, or empirical research. Secondary research is valuable as a relatively low-cost method, although it can be time consuming.

Sources of secondary research may include books, research papers, journal articles, and conference papers, as well as records and statistics from government, nongovernmental organizations (NGOs), or any number of other sources or archives. For designers, useful material to be sourced can also include precedent projects, products or case studies documented in various ways, photographs, maps, diagrams, and other visual support records. The Internet has expedited the process of secondary research and access to online databases, but caution needs to be exercised in establishing the credibility of sources.

Secondary research is traditionally summarized in systematic reviews, or literature reviews, with full citations of sources. While these reviews are most commonly communicated in written reports, in design, secondary research can also be collected into visual summaries for shared viewing, sorting, synthesis, and the crafting of narratives. Recently, blogs have become common repositories for collecting secondary research, facilitating the organization of text, visual references, and source links, in a format convenient for sharing.

Secondary research is an excellent method for establishing definitional boundaries of the design project, because it identifies what precedents exist and where there may yet be opportunity gaps. As a component of exploratory research, secondary research will contribute an essential component of groundwork to aid in the understanding of the design research and user territory under investigation.

Further Reading

Booth, Wayne C., Gregory G. Colomb, and Joseph M. Williams. *The Craft of Research*, 3rd ed. Chicago, IL: The University of Chicago Press, 2008.

Behavioral	Quantitative	Innovative	Exploratory	Participatory
Attitudinal	Qualitative	Adapted	Generative	Observational
		Traditional	Evaluative	Self reporting
				Expert review
				Design process

FirstSearch

WorldCat Advanced Search

- Enter search terms in one or more boxes and click on **Search**.
- WorldCat Hot Topics: [Select a topic to search: ▼] ❓

| Home | Databases | **Searching** |

| Basic Search | Advanced Search | Expert Search | Previous Searches | Go to page ▼ |

🔳 📖 ❓
Subjects News Help

Current database: **WorldCat**

[Search] [Clear]

Search in database: [WorldCat ▼] ⓘ (Updated: 2011-08-19)
OCLC catalog of books and other materials in libraries worldwide

Search for: [design research] [Keyword ▼] 🔲

[and ▼] [   ] [Keyword ▼] 🔲

[and ▼] [   ] [Keyword ▼] 🔲

Year [   ] (format: YYYY-YYYY)
Limit to: Language [No Limit ▼] Show all languages ...
Number of Libraries [All ▼] ❓

Limit type to:
match any of the following

- ☐ ◆ Books
- ☐ 📖 Serial Publications
- ☐ 📄 Articles
- ☐ 📷 Visual Materials
- ☐ 🔊 Sound Recordings
- ☐ 🎵 Musical Scores
- ☐ 💾 Computer Files
- ☐ 📑 Archival Materials
- ☐ 🗺 Maps
- ☐ 🌐 Internet Resources
- ☐ 📲 Continually Updated Resources ❓

Subtype limits [Any Audience ▼] [Any Content ▼] [Any Format ▼] ❓

Limit availability to:
match any of the following
☐ 🔖 Items in my library (PMC, CARNEGIE MELLON UNIV) ❓
Library Code [   ] Find codes ...

Rank by: [Number of Libraries ▼] ❓

[Search] [Clear]

English I Español I Français I عربي I 日本語 I 한국어 I 中文 (繁體)

The Worldcat database allows users to search the collections and services of more than 10,000 libraries worldwide, including the option to select specific media types.

See also 11. Case Studies • 53. Literature Reviews • 92. Unobtrusive Measures

75 Semantic Differential

Semantic differentials can help reveal "felt" meanings that are a direct product of one's experiences, culture, and dearly held beliefs.[1]

The semantic differential scale is a linguistic tool designed to measure people's attitudes toward a topic, event, object, or activity, so that its deeper connotative meaning can be ascertained. Although used in marketing surveys to evaluate products and services, its original intention was to measure social attitudes by exposing the outer limits of a semantic space. Its recent popularity is probably due to its straightforward format: the respondent is asked to indicate where on a continuum a concept is best described. For instance, given the concept of "Art:"

Negative   __-_-_-_-_- X -__   Positive
Pleasant   __-X -_-_-_-_-   Unpleasant
Worthless   _-_-_-_-_-_- X   Valuable

Much care must go into the design of an effective semantic differential in order to yield useful results. Each of these components should be considered before conducting a semantic differential:[2]

Concepts The stimuli of the semantic differential, concepts can be a topic, event, object, or activity. Concepts should be carefully chosen based on research objectives, and should be meaningful to respondents.

Bipolar Word Pairs Usually, pairs of antonyms are selected as the polar ends of a semantic differential scale. They can be complementary antonyms (e.g., *pleasant–unpleasant*) or more nuanced, gradable antonyms (e.g., the opposite of *friendly* isn't necessarily *unfriendly*; *shy* or *guarded* could be a more meaningful opposite). Poles should be randomized so that negative and positive connotations don't consistently fall on the same side.

Survey Scale It is common to see six- and seven-point scales, but the seven-point scale is preferred because it provides a neutral midpoint. A neutral answer could indicate apathy, indecisiveness, or that the concept is socially irrelevant, all of which are meaningful judgments. The distance the rating is from the midpoint reflects the *intensity* of the judgment.

Dimensions for Classification All bipolar word pairs belong to a dimension of classification. Osgood et al. recommend three dimensions to classify concepts: evaluation (e.g., *valuable–worthless*), potency (e.g., *strong–weak, heavy–light*), and activity (e.g., *active–passive, excitable–calm*).[3]

After multiple concepts are assessed against the same dimensions, the semantic differential between concepts can be mapped. The differences in where concepts are mapped in a semantic space reflect their differences in connotative meaning.

1. The Semantic Differential Scale (SDS) was pioneered in 1957 by Charles Osgood, George Suci, and Percy Tannenbaum. The methodology and theory were documented in their book *The Measurement of Meaning*, and has since been used extensively in language attitude studies. See:

Osgood, Charles, George Suci, and Percy Tannenbaum. *The Measurement of Meaning*. Urbana, IL: University of Illinois Press, 1957.

2. Al-Hindawe, Jayne. "Considerations when Constructing a Semantic Differential Scale." Dissertation: Linguistics Program at La Trobe University, 1996.

3. See note 1 above.

4. Bartneck, C. "Who Like Androids More: Japanese or US Americans?" *Proceedings of the 17th IEEE International Symposium on Robot and Human Interactive Communication*, 2008.

Further Reading

Williams, Frederick. "The Identification of Linguistic Attitudes." *International Journal of the Sociology of Language* 3, no. 1 (1974): 21-32.

Behavioral	**Quantitative**	Innovative	**Exploratory**	Participatory
Attitudinal	Qualitative	**Adapted**	Generative	Observational
		Traditional	Evaluative	**Self reporting**
				Expert review
				Design process

Please rate this **human** on the adjective scales below.

		1 2 3 4 5 6 7
1=Awful	7=Nice	○○○○○○○
1=Machinelike	7=Humanlike	○○○○○○○
1=Artificial	7=Lifelike	○○○○○○○
1=Unpleasant	7=Pleasant	○○○○○○○
1=Fake	7=Natural	○○○○○○○
1=Unfriendly	7=Friendly	○○○○○○○
1=Unconscious	7=Conscious	○○○○○○○
1=Unkind	7=Kind	○○○○○○○

Please rate this **human** on the adjective scales below.

		1 2 3 4 5 6 7
1=Awful	7=Nice	○○○○○○○
1=Machinelike	7=Humanlike	○○○○○○○
1=Artificial	7=Lifelike	○○○○○○○
1=Unpleasant	7=Pleasant	○○○○○○○
1=Fake	7=Natural	○○○○○○○
1=Unfriendly	7=Friendly	○○○○○○○
1=Unconscious	7=Conscious	○○○○○○○
1=Unkind	7=Kind	○○○○○○○

Semantic differential scales are particularly powerful when eliciting cross-cultural attitudes and perceptions to the same stimuli. In Christoph Bartneck's research study "Who like Androids More: Americans or Japanese," eight semantic differential scales were used to investigate the degree to which a person's cultural background influences one's perception of a robot's anthropomorphism and likeability.[4] The experiment used static pictures of 18 different robots (like the iCat and Geminoid HI-1, above) as the stimuli for the study.

Courtesy of Christoph Bartneck

See also 52. Laddering • 67. Questionnaires • 83. Surveys

76 Shadowing

Shadowing provides key insight into a participant's activities and decision patterns as the researcher follows him or her closely throughout his or her daily routines.

Shadowing is an observational method that involves tracking someone in his or her role to experience the situations of his or her daily life or work in parallel with him or her, collecting insights through the detailed nuance of firsthand, real-time exposure. Where possible, shadowing observations should be well documented, with photographs, detailed notes and sketches, or audio.

As it is primarily intended to help the designer-researcher gain a true sense of the user's actions, decision patterns, and routines, shadowing is an exploratory research method, contributing to a baseline familiarity of the user group and possibly suggesting early design implications. Ideally, several team members will complete shadowing exercises across representative users, to begin crafting a general picture of patterns that describe the population being studied.

Variations on shadowing include ride-alongs—joining professionals such as police officers or Emergency Medical Services (EMS) personnel on their shift work. Obviously in shadowing certain professions or roles, special clearances may be necessary, and the risks and dangers associated with the research need to be carefully weighed against the value of the outcomes. Even in simple shadowing of typical work roles or people in their daily lives, cooperation needs to be obtained, and a respectful distance maintained to avoid interruption to natural routines, or participant behavior change as a result of being observed. However, as long as these stipulations are kept in mind, shadowing may involve interactions with the person being shadowed, asking pertinent questions or engaging in conversation.

Shadowing is not intended to be a covert research method used to follow people without their knowledge or consent. However, subtle instances of covert shadowing observations might be completed of people in public spaces, for example, following students during class changes to determine common pathways on a college campus, or tracing shoppers in a mall to observe activity patterns.

Behavioral	Quantitative	Innovative	Exploratory	Participatory
Attitudinal	Qualitative	Adapted	Generative	Observational
		Traditional	Evaluative	Self reporting
				Expert review
				Design process

SERVICE DESIGN FOR GROCERY SHOPPING

In this shadowing research, participating grocery shoppers were observed, asked about their decisions, and photographed during a typical shopping trip, revealing patterns to inform a study of the relationship between food providers and consumers in creating sustainable healthy food communities.

Courtesy of Sarah Calandro © 2011

See also 06. Behavioral Mapping • 42. Fly-on-the-Wall Observation • 89. Touchstone Tours

77 Simulation Exercises

Simulation exercises are deep approximations of human or environmental conditions, designed to forge an immersive, empathic sense of real-life user experiences.

Simulation exercises have an established history across various professions. Flight simulators have long been used for military, aircraft, and NASA training, and driving simulators have been used for driver's education. Virtual worlds simulate real-world conditions, placing people in situations that test their response time, decision making, or interactions. Students of medicine and physical or occupational therapy commonly spend time in wheelchairs or blindfolded, to empathically experience the patients' world of restricted mobility or visual impairment. The intent of simulation exercises for design research teams is to likewise form a tangible sense of user empathy, influencing design sensitivity and decisions through direct, although simulated, experience.

Simulation exercises for designers might approximate the limitations or disabilities that are experienced by people with physical disabilities, brain injuries, or age-related sense and cognition deficits. Human factors engineers at the Ford Motor Company developed a "Third Age Suit" that restricted mobility and senses, simulating the deteriorated agility that is associated with aging, to increase the sensitivity of designers and engineers in producing the Ford Focus automobile.[1] Similarly, researchers at the MIT AgeLab have developed a suit and helmet system that simulates physical conditions of the elderly, to inspire empathy and innovation in design and marketing.[2]

Low-tech versions of simulation can also achieve the desired results of empathetic sensitivity among designers. In "geriatric sensitivity training" sessions, for example, participants wear glasses simulating yellowing of the cornea, macular degeneration, cataracts, or stroke, while attempting to perform everyday tasks such as reading and eating. Latex gloves reduce tactile sensitivity while threading a needle; and an "unfair hearing test" simulates audio as people with hearing deficits might experience it. Designers then translate these experiences into implications for design.[3]

Designers are involved in the creation of simulated environments, whether through digital games and virtual reality, or physical space and artifacts. Patricia Moore of Moore Design Associates has designed several simulated environments for rehabilitation facilities, with mock communities that include various street surfaces, signage, grocery stores, ATMs, home spaces and appliances. These simulation environments are used in training therapies for conditions ranging from balance disorders, to post-traumatic stress disorder and depression, to brain injuries, allowing patients to make progress toward independence in safe conditions.[4]

1. "Third-Age Suit Helps Ford to Understand Mature Drivers," http://media.ford.com/article_display.cfm?article_id=624

2. Singer, Natasha. "In a Graying Population, Business Opportunity." *The New York Times*, February 5, 2011, http://www.nytimes.com/2011/02/06/business/06aging.html

See also:
http://agelab.mit.edu

3. Hanington, Bruce. "Factoring the Human in Design Education" in *Proceedings of the international Conference on Affective Human Factors Design* (CAHD). Asean Academic Press, 2001.

4. Kaplan, Melanie D. G. "At the VA, Preparing Brain-injured Veterans for the Real World." *Smartplanet*, Feb. 2, 2011, http://www.smartplanet.com/people/blog/pure-genius/at-the-va-preparing-brain-injured-veterans-for-the-real-world/5451

5. See note 2 above.

Further Reading

Sommer, Robert, and Barbara Sommer. *A Practical Guide to Behavioral Research: Tools and Techniques*. New York: Oxford University Press, 2002.

Behavioral	Quantitative	Innovative	Exploratory	Participatory
Attitudinal	**Qualitative**	Adapted	**Generative**	Observational
		Traditional	Evaluative	Self reporting
				Expert review
				Design process

Left: Researchers perform everyday tasks wearing the "Age Gain Now Empathy System" (AGNES), developed in the MIT AgeLab. Calibrated to simulate the dexterity, mobility, strength, and balance of a 74-year-old, AGNES is a suit and helmet that constrains the neck and spine, yellows vision, restricts bending, throws off center of gravity, and reduces tactile sensitivity. Simulations are intended to encourage designers and marketers to innovate as they address real needs, in this case, the needs of the elderly.[5]

Courtesy of Nathan Fried-Lipski / MIT AgeLab

Below: Low-tech simulations expose designers to age-related deficits, such as deteriorated vision and mobility, for empathic translation into design criteria.

See also 07. Bodystorming • 36. Experience Prototyping • 71. Role-playing

78 Site Search Analytics

Analyzing the words and phrases entered into a site search gives organizations insight into what people are looking for, which is an opportunity to evaluate how well site content meets those needs.

If you provide search functionality as part of your website or digital application, you may be sitting on a gold mine of semantically rich data that reveals what your users are searching for online. Site Search Analytics (SSA) is the process for reporting and analyzing the queries submitted as search criteria. Whereas the industries converging around *Search Engine Optimization* (SEO) or *Search Engine Marketing* (SEM) are concerned with attracting and driving potential customers to your site, site search analytics is focused on understanding the people who are already on your site, and making sure that they can find the information they need.[1] When accomplished, site search analytics can bolster customer retention and conversion rates, not to mention customer satisfaction levels.

Site search analytics data lends itself to qualitative and quantitative analysis—which makes it a prime starting point for qualitative and quantitative researchers within an organization to work together. For qualitative researchers, understanding user intent and what information people want from your site can help you evaluate and improve the quality of the site search results. For those who prefer quantitative data, most search data will immediately reveal a Zipf distribution—a small number of search terms that represent the overwhelming statistical majority of all search activity within a given time frame.[2] A Zipf distribution pinpoints exactly which search terms should be optimized for greatest impact. More often than not, this data can be acted on quickly, and both the qualitative and quantitative experts at your organization can agree on the results.

If you are in the early phases of the design process, include specifications for search analytics extraction and reporting in the Product Requirements Documents (PRDs), which can save energy and developer time later. If you are in a digital application's "Launch & Monitor" phase, make your case by relating site search performance metrics to your organization's existing Key Performance Indicators (KPIs). For instance, search metrics like *% queries that retrieve zero results*, *% queries where users click on a search result*, *% queries that are followed by site exit* (also known as search bounce rate or search exit rate)[3] are likely to make stakeholders sit up and take note as to whether a digital application is meeting end users' needs.

The search metrics that are revealed by site search analytics can help you monitor, evaluate, and improve your digital application's overall performance, and continuously align user-centered activity and data to measurable business goals.

1. Rosenfeld, Louis. *Search Analytics for Your Site: Conversations With Your Customers.* Brooklyn, N.Y.: Rosenfeld Media, 2011.

2. See note 1 above.

3. See note 1 above.

Behavioral	Quantitative	Innovative	Exploratory	Participatory
Attitudinal	Qualitative	Adapted	Generative	Observational
		Traditional	Evaluative	Self reporting
				Expert review
				Design process

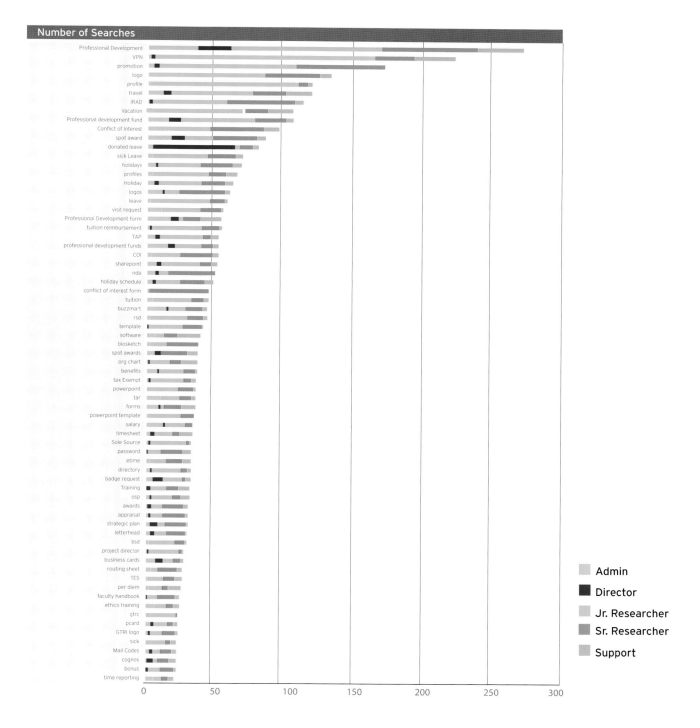

Number of Searches

Professional Development
VPN
promotion
logo
profile
travel
IRAD
Vacation
Professional development fund
Conflict of Interest
spot award
donated leave
sick Leave
holidays
profiles
Holiday
logos
leave
visit request
Professional Development form
tuition reimbursement
TAP
professional development funds
COI
sharepoint
nda
holiday schedule
conflict of interest form
tuition
buzzmart
rsd
template
software
biosketch
spot awards
org chart
benefits
tax Exempt
powerpoint
tar
forms
powerpoint template
salary
timesheet
Sole Source
password
etime
directory
badge request
Training
osp
awards
appraisal
strategic plan
letterhead
bsd
project director
business cards
routing sheet
TES
per diem
faculty handbook
ethics training
gtrc
pcard
GTRI logo
sick
Mail Codes
cognos
bonus
time reporting

Legend:
- Admin
- Director
- Jr. Researcher
- Sr. Researcher
- Support

x-axis: 0, 50, 100, 150, 200, 250, 300

Design Phase: ① ② ③ ④ ⑤

An example of a typical site search analytics Zipf distribution, where a small number of search terms represent the most popular searches.

Courtesy of Josh Cothran, Georgia Tech Research Institute.

See also *18. Content Inventory & Audit* • *51. Key Performance Indicators* • *97. Web Analytics*

79 Speed Dating

When people compare multiple design concepts in quick succession, design teams can learn how people react to new technology while also taking into account existing contextual and social factors.

Speed dating as a research method is inspired by the framework of its dating-scene namesake, but instead of people, researchers rapidly "speed date" design opportunities with potential users. The power of speed dating lies in exposing people to future design ideas via storyboards and simulated environments before any expensive technical prototypes are built. An overview of the speed dating process is as follows:[1]

Conduct contextual field research. Use methods such as interviews, role-playing, artifact analysis, directed storytelling, diary studies, and cultural probes to understand the people for whom you are designing.[2] Analysis efforts should focus on aligning the observed and verbalized needs of the participants, so the team can identify opportunities where people demonstrate and articulate a need.

Create storyboards for each scenario. Design storyboards to elicit an emotional, empathic reaction to the characters so that participants can easily identify with them. Focus scenarios on the specific needs uncovered by research, and show how each potential design would address the need. As with traditional scenarios, the details of the technology itself should be downplayed.

"Speed date" storyboards in a session. Each storyboard should be presented to a group of people in serial fashion, and then followed by a focus question to help design teams understand what is in the users' minds. At the end of the session, users rank how accurately the storyboards represent their needs, as well as the effectiveness of the proposed technology/solution under evaluation.

Reflect and discuss. Refocus conversations on the needs that were expressed in both the field research and the storyboard sessions. Instead of spending time ranking and prioritizing existing concepts, the team should use this time to articulate misunderstandings, refine scenarios, and consider new design opportunities.

Construct a simulated environment. User enactments in a simulated space allow people to act out a role from the revised scenarios. Over the course of several acted-out scenarios, the team can observe users dealing with specific problems in context to how they could play out in real life.

Use speed dating when exploring environments and social contexts that are not readily available (e.g., homes with ubiquitous computing).[3] The method can uncover risk factors across a series of related enactments, and focus design teams' efforts on understanding user needs before spending time and effort vetting and building expensive technological solutions.

1. Researchers Scott Davidoff, Min Kyung Lee, Anind K. Dey, and John Zimmerman at the Carnegie Mellon Human Computer Interaction Institute and School of Design first developed the speed dating method in 2007 while exploring opportunities for ubiquitous computing in smart homes. During their study, they used speed dating to explore over 100 concepts and prototype 27 variations over two weeks. The results helped them to pinpoint "showstopper" issues before costly technical prototypes were built, and also uncovered that certain user needs they once considered noncritical turned out to be promising new opportunities for innovation. See:

Davidoff, Scott, Min Kyung Lee, Anind K. Dey, and John Zimmerman. "Rapidly Exploring Application Design Through Speed Dating." *Proceedings of 9th International Conference on Ubiquitous Computing UbiComp '07*, 2007.

2. Davidoff, Scott, Min Kyung Lee, Charles Yiu, John Zimmerman, and Anind K. Dey. "Principles of Smart Home Control." *Proceedings of UbiComp '06*, 2006.

3. See note 1 above.

4. Odom, Will, John Zimmerman, and Jodi Forlizzi. "Teenagers and Their Virtual Possessions: Design Opportunities and Issues" *Proceedings of SIGCHI Conference on Human Factors in Computing Systems*, 2011.

Behavioral	Quantitative	**Innovative**	**Exploratory**	Participatory
Attitudinal	**Qualitative**	Adapted	**Generative**	**Observational**
		Traditional	Evaluative	**Self reporting**
				Expert review
				Design process

ENACTMENT ONE: THE PARENT BUTTON

What kinds of and how much virtual information can be comfortably displayed for parents to see?

ENACTMENT TWO: MULTIPLE SELF-PRESENTATIONS

How would your different online personas look if they were all visible in one place?

ENACTMENT THREE: BEDROOM QUILT

What are the boundaries and values of having personal information wrapped around you while you were sleeping?

Courtesy of Will Odom

Speed dating allows for structured engagements across multiple scenarios. The method creates new understanding about the potential design opportunities that should be more fully considered, as well as the problem areas that should be avoided, within the design space. Above, researchers designed and constructed a teenager's bedroom environment to explore several enactments regarding how teenagers interact with their virtual possessions in their bedrooms.[4] By acting out each scenario, design teams can understand the overlaps between scenarios, and what makes a type of product presence or intervention acceptable (or not) or desirable (or not).

See also 36. Experience Prototyping • 73. Scenarios • 82. Storyboards

80 Stakeholder Maps

Stakeholder maps help to visually consolidate and communicate the key constituents of a design project, setting the stage for user-centered research and design development.

As the design process begins, in the planning, scoping, and definition phase, it is particularly critical to identify who all the key constituents are that might have a stake in design outcomes. Stakeholder maps serve this purpose, as a visual reference point for the design team in planning for user research activities, and guiding appropriate communication with stakeholders throughout the project development process.

Stakeholder maps are often first created speculatively, with the team brainstorming any and all people who may have a vested interest in the design territory defining the project. At this point it is important to be exhaustive. As well as identifying end users, it is critical to include people who will benefit from the project, those who hold power, those who may be adversely affected, and even those who may thwart or sabotage designed outcomes or services.

Stakeholders can be identified by general roles (students, delivery drivers, nurses), specific roles (CEO, project manager, chief of surgery), or by actual people (Robert, office manager; Linda, resident physician). The initial process can be simply done as roles posted on a whiteboard, cards, notes or paper, and consolidated as a list or sketch. The sketch then evolves into a more organized structure, defining possible hierarchies, and key relationships between roles or people. These relationships can be visualized through scale, line, and proximity, striving for sense-making and clarity of communication for the team.

From the speculative version, iterations of the stakeholder map evolve as actual constituents and their working processes and relationships are more clearly identified and defined. Gradually as the sketch is developed and consensus is reached, it will typically be visualized as a comprehensive diagram. However, stakeholder maps can take on a variety of forms, casual or formal, with a mix of text, photos, and graphics. There is no one right way of expressing the stakeholder map, so long as it serves the purposes of identifying key players and their relationships to the design team.

Behavioral	Quantitative	Innovative	**Exploratory**	Participatory
Attitudinal	**Qualitative**	**Adapted**	Generative	Observational
		Traditional	Evaluative	Self reporting
				Expert review
				Design process

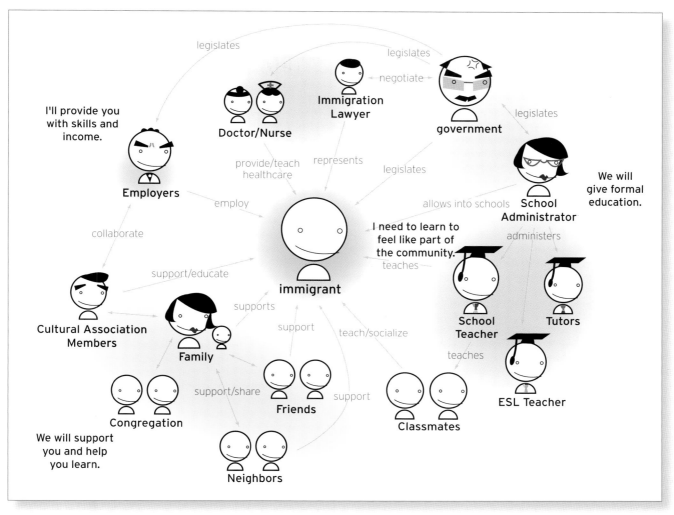

legislates

legislates

negotiate

Immigration
Lawyer

government

legislates

I'll provide you
with skills and
income.

We will
give formal
education.

Doctor/Nurse

Employers

provide/teach
healthcare

represents

legislates

allows into schools

School
Administrator

employ

I need to learn to
feel like part of
the community.

administers

collaborate

support/educate

teaches

School
Teacher

Tutors

Cultural Association
Members

immigrant

supports

support

teach/socialize

Family

teaches

We will support
you and help
you learn.

support/share

Friends

support

ESL Teacher

Congregation

Classmates

Neighbors

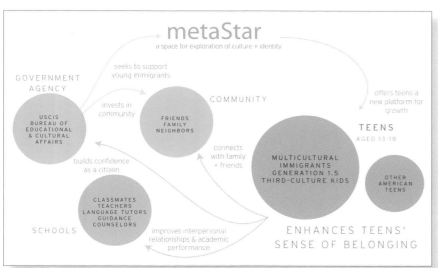

Stakeholder maps consolidating
key players and roles for the design
of "Metastar," a social networking
application for teenage immigrants
during cultural transitions into a new
life in the United States.

*Courtesy of Kim Dowd, Norman Lau, Gretchen Mendoza,
and Hyori Suri Park*

See also 81. Stakeholder Walkthrough • 85. Territory Maps

81 Stakeholder Walkthrough

Stakeholder walkthroughs bring end users, stakeholders, and the design team together to evaluate early prototypes, providing actionable recommendations for improvements and building empathy.[1]

The stakeholder walkthrough brings representative end users, the interdisciplinary development team, and project stakeholders together in a conference room setting to step through and evaluate a task-based scenario from the end user's perspective. It is a group usability inspection method that provides a forum in which to identify and consider usability problems early in the prototyping process, and it requires a diverse range of skills and perspectives to successfully do so. It is a great way of getting stakeholders and the development team to hear representative users think aloud as they process an interface to complete tasks.

All walkthrough attendees should be informed prior to the session that the end users invited to the meeting are the *primary participants* in the evaluation. When this expectation is not set beforehand, tensions can build if someone ends up feeling under-represented or less important (particularly stakeholders, who may be accustomed to directing meetings). Attendees should also be informed that they are going to be asked to take the end user's perspective as they provide feedback regarding the tasks and scenarios, as opposed to defending a system or design/development view.

If these meeting parameters create pushback, remind stakeholders and the development team that listening to how people use the interface to accomplish tasks will give them early insight into future satisfaction ratings, and also domain insight and business logic requirements (it is not uncommon for the development team to gain the most information from stakeholder walkthroughs). Also, remind the interdisciplinary team that although the users invited to the session will take the lead in the detection of usability problems, the whole team works together to come up with solutions to the problem. In this way, everyone has a voice in the process, and the discussion stays focused on usability problem detection and brainstorming solutions.

Team walkthroughs can be more costly than individual techniques, but they also have been shown to be more effective.[2] As the walkthrough plays out, the varied perspectives will create synergies that could not be achieved during individual inspections of the interface. Over time, recurring attendance in stakeholder walkthroughs will sharpen the team's empathic response to their end user's frustrations, challenges, and perspectives–an investment that will not only shape the user-centered culture of the company, but also improve the products that are built.

1. The stakeholder walkthrough is an adaptation of the pluralistic walkthrough, which was originally designed to include representative end users, usability experts, and system designers (and did not necessarily include stakeholders). Randolph G. Bias introduced the Pluralistic Walkthrough in the early 1990s, and the method is now widely acknowledged as one of the industry's *usability inspection* methods. See:

Bias, Randolph G. "The Pluralistic Usability Walkthrough: Coordinated Empathies" in *Usability Inspection Methods*. New York: John Wiley & Sons, 1994.

2. Karat, Claire-Marie, Robert Campbell, and Tarra Fiegel. "Comparison of Empirical Testing and Walkthrough Methods in User Interface Evaluation." *Proceedings of the SIGCHI Conference on Human Factors in Computing Systems*, 1992.

Further Reading

Bias, Randolph G. "Walkthroughs: Efficient Collaborative Testing." *IEEE Software* 8, no. 5 (1991): 94-95.

Behavioral	Quantitative	Innovative	Exploratory	Participatory
Attitudinal	**Qualitative**	**Adapted**	Generative	Observational
		Traditional	**Evaluative**	Self reporting
				Expert review
				Design process

Scheduling stakeholder walkthroughs early in the design process sharpens the team's focus on early user-centered task analysis. The combined perspectives of representative end users, stakeholders, developers, and members of the design and research team will create synergies that could not be achieved during individual, expert inspections of the interface.

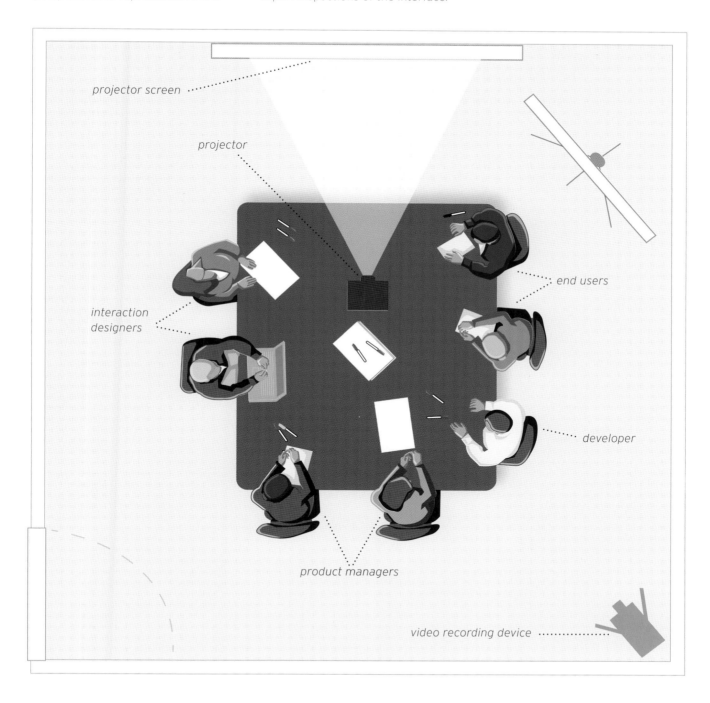

projector screen

projector

interaction designers

end users

developer

product managers

video recording device

See also *26. Design Charette* • *80. Stakeholder Maps* • *94. Usabilty Testing*

82 Storyboards

Storyboards provide a visual narrative that generates empathy and communicates the context in which a technology or form factor will be used.

Storyboarding can help visually capture the important social, environmental, and technical factors that shape the context of how, where, and why people engage with products. By illustrating contextually rich narratives, storyboards can be used to build empathy for end users, reframe multichannel touch points, and consider design alternatives in the early phases of the design process.

Experts approach storyboards by harnessing five design practices common to visual storytelling.[1]

1. *Degree of artistic or photo-realistic detail:* A misconception is that storyboards should be left to designers with artistic capabilities. However, simple, abstract drawings of stick figures are oftentimes more effective at focusing the attention of the storyboard audience on a specific detail or message.[2] Refine drawings so that they show enough context, but not so much that details begin to distract from the purpose that the storyboard is designed to communicate.

2. *Text-based narration or explanations:* Use text to supplement the visuals in a storyboard when it would otherwise take too much effort to illustrate a concept or idea. Text is usually added to storyboards as word or thought balloons, captions, or background signs.

3. *Emphasis on people, products, or both:* To elicit an emotional impact from the storyboard audience, illustrate characters in emotionally charged situations. If on the other hand the goal is to elicit technical or evaluative feedback regarding the concept, leaving characters out of the panels can focus attention on the details of the design.

4. *The right number of storyboard panels:* Storyboarding experts tend to use between three to six panels to communicate an idea. Each storyboard should be focused on one salient concept or idea; if more than one concept needs to be communicated, consider creating multiple storyboards that each focus on a different factor.

5. *Depicting the passage of time:* Time as a design element should be used to show large time lapses in a scene. Clocks, calendars, zoom-ins of wristwatches, or the movement of the sun in the background can be added to explicitly show the passage of time.

Construct the story and the storyboard panels depending on what information will resonate with the target audience. For instance, when designing for stakeholders, illustrate the range of potential design opportunities. For developers and programmers, illustrate a scene and a context in which the product or form factor will be most likely used. For visual designers, draw close-up details of the interface, and for users, show empathic scenes to determine if the situation is realistic and meaningful.[3]

1. Truong, Khai N., Gillian R. Hayes, and Gregory D. Abowd. "Storyboarding: An Empirical Determination of Best Practices and Effective Guidelines." *Proceedings of DIS 2006*, 2006.

2. McLoud, Scott. *Understanding Comics: The Invisible Art.* New York: Harper Paperbacks, 1994.

3. Vertelney, Laurie, and Gayle Curtis. "Storyboards and Sketch Prototypes for Rapid Interface Visualization." *CHI Tutorial*, ACM Press, 1990.

Further Reading

Cooper, Alan, Robert Reimann, and David Cronin. *About Face 3: The Essentials of Interaction Design.* Indianapolis, IN: Wiley & Sons, 2007.

Goodwin, Kim. *Designing for the Digital Age: How to Create Human-Centered Products and Services.* Indianapolis, IN: Wiley & Sons, 2009.

Landay, James A., and Brad A. Myers. "Sketching Storyboards to Illustrate Interface Behavior." *Conference Companion of ACM Conference on Human Factors in Computing Systems*, 1996.

Storyboards have been used by film and television preproduction for many decades, and their best practices are well understood and documented. See *The Art of the Storyboard, Second Edition: A Filmmaker's Introduction* by John Hart, Oxford: Focal Press, 2007.

Behavioral	Quantitative	Innovative	Exploratory	Participatory
Attitudinal	Qualitative	Adapted	Generative	Observational
		Traditional	Evaluative	Self reporting
				Expert review
				Design process

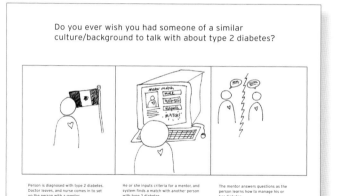

Do you ever wish you had someone of a similar culture/background to talk with about type 2 diabetes?

Person is diagnosed with type 2 diabetes. Doctor leaves, and nurse comes in to set up the person with a mentor.

He or she inputs criteria for a mentor, and system finds a match with another person with type 2 diabetes.

The mentor answers questions as the person learns how to manage his or her diabetes.

Do you ever wish you had someone to help your spouse/family to understand what you are dealing with and how best to support you?

Family doesn't know how they can help their loved one with their type 2 diabetes.

Trained caregiver answers the family's questions and provides helpful tips to be supportive.

Family is active in providing care for their loved one.

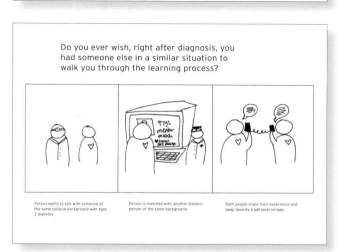

Do you ever wish, right after diagnosis, you had someone else in a similar situation to walk you through the learning process?

Person wants to talk with someone of the same cultural background with type 2 diabetes.

Person is matched with another diabetic person of the same background.

Both people share their experience and swap favorite traditional recipes.

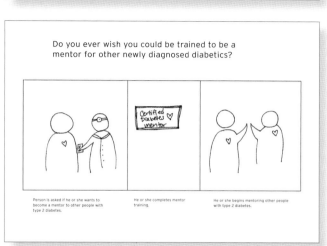

Do you ever wish you could be trained to be a mentor for other newly diagnosed diabetics?

Person is asked if he or she wants to become a mentor to other people with type 2 diabetes.

He or she completes mentor training.

He or she begins mentoring other people with type 2 diabetes.

Storyboards shape social, environmental, and temporal factors into a compelling narrative and help design teams to more carefully consider how products and services could improve people's lives. The storyboards shown here explore the idea of a peer mentoring service designed to help people who have been recently diagnosed with type 2 diabetes.

Courtesy of Lauren Chapman

See also 63. Personas • 71. Role-playing • 79. Speed Dating

83 Surveys

Surveys are a method of collecting self-reported information from people about their characteristics, thoughts, feelings, perceptions, behaviors, or attitudes.

Surveys are a common method for collecting information from people, typically from large samples of respondents. They are an efficient tool for collecting a lot of data in a short time frame, typically with little cost, and are versatile in the type of information that can be collected. With large enough samples, results can be analyzed statistically.

While the term describes a broad approach, there are two dominant techniques for survey data collection within the method—*questionnaires*, either self-completed or read to participants and completed by the researcher; and structured *interviews*, conducted in person, by phone, or through various communication technologies.

Like any self-report instrument, surveys may not be an accurate reflection of true thoughts, feelings, perceptions, or even behaviors. This argues for the careful design and administration of surveys, and the use of complementary observations or other methods. For example, it is common to survey a wide base of constituents using questionnaires to gain a lot of information, and pair this with a smaller set of in-depth observations, contextual inquiries, or participatory design sessions.

There are various types of survey questions for interviews or questionnaires:[1]

- Closed—forced choice, structured with limited response options
- Open—broad with no set response to encourage discussion or longer answers
- General—focused on big picture, broad spectrum issues
- Specific—focused on details particular to the situation
- Factual—with responses that can be verified by observation or supporting information
- Hypothetical—asks participant to speculate about behaviors or actions
- Judgmental—asks participant for his or her opinion, what he or she thinks about things
- Comparative—asks for a judgment on two or more alternatives
- Neutral—no value words used, remains objective
- Leading—to be avoided, suggests a correct or expected answer
- Blaming—to be avoided, suggests participant is wrong or at fault
- Request for suggestions—invites participant to suggest new ideas, opinions
- Request for questions—invites participant to suggest questions you have overlooked

The form of questions should be based on the inquiry, time constraints, and preferred response format.

1. Hackos, JoAnn T., and Janice C. Redish. *User and Task Analysis for Interface Design.* New York: Wiley, 1998.

Behavioral	Quantitative	Innovative	Exploratory	Participatory
Attitudinal	Qualitative	Adapted	Generative	Observational
		Traditional	Evaluative	Self reporting
				Expert review
				Design process

The "Produce Proposal Wall" provides a method of survey that allows customers to communicate what fresh fruits and vegetables they want available in the store, while fostering dialogue between grocery store owners and shoppers, and building a community around the topic.

Courtesy of Sarah Calandro © 2011

84 Task Analysis

Task analysis breaks down the constituent elements of a user's work flow, including actions and interactions, system response, and environmental context.

Traditional task analysis holds a scientific view of human interactions within systems, isolating key elements of human behavior, product or system behaviors and responses to human actions, the provision of system feedback, and the context in which tasks occur. Such analyses are usually expressed formally in flowcharts or other structured visuals, indicating tasks and subtasks, key decision points, and human-system response cycles. This analytic process stems from time and motion studies in industrial engineering, scientific management, and early human factors.[1]

While this level of formal task analysis can play a critical role in understanding user behaviors in context, designers will more typically employ a broader definition of the method, incorporating a blend of qualitative and quantitative approaches to gain insight into user and task processes.[2] *Task* in this sense is not isolated to mean completion of a specific job, but rather encompasses a broad definition of any physical actions and mental processes as activities used to achieve goals, and information flows within the system environment. Task analysis is useful for all design disciplines, with relevant applications ranging from navigation of print documents and software device interactions to wayfinding in the built environment.

Task analysis is similar to contextual inquiry, because they employ many of the same methods, including observation and interviews. However, the difference is in focus, with contextual inquiry being more inclusive of general aspects of user behavior, decision making and interactions within the wider context, and task analysis concentrating solely on the task at hand. Interviews and observations specifically target user options, tools available, and choices made; decision points; identification of common mistakes and corrections; process inputs and outputs; frequency and importance of the tasks; and risks of failure.[3]

Task analysis can be deciphered using task decomposition, breaking the task down into component actions, and Hierarchical Task Analysis (HTA), identifying tasks and subtasks, categorizing them, and checking the accuracy of the model.[4] Actions in task decomposition can be usefully organized by categories, such as purpose, cues, objects, method, and options.[5] Putting the actions that constitute a task into a hierarchy ordinarily results in the familiar tree diagram or other forms of flowcharting, which can then be verified by walk-through tests by those familiar with the task. A simpler yet less thorough version of task analysis can be completed using sticky notes to identify and organize basic task actions, similar to the process of constructing affinity diagrams.[6]

1. Crystal, Abe, and Beth Ellington. "Task Analysis and Human-Computer Interaction: Approaches, Techniques and Levels of Analysis." *Proceedings of the Tenth Americas Conference on Information Systems,* 2004.

2. Hackos, JoAnn, and Janice Redish. *User and Task Analysis for Interface Design.* New York: Wiley, 1998.

3. Kuniavsky, Mike. *Observing the User Experience: A Practitioner's Guide to User Research.* San Francisco, CA: Morgan Kaufmann, 2003.

4. See note 3 above.

5. Kirwan, B., and L. K. Ainsworth. *A Guide to Task Analysis.* London; Washington, D.C.: Taylor and Francis, 1992.

6. See note 3 above.

Behavioral	Quantitative	Innovative	Exploratory	Participatory
Attitudinal	Qualitative	Adapted	Generative	**Observational**
		Traditional	Evaluative	Self reporting
				Expert review
				Design process

A task analysis grid visualizing stakeholder scenarios and prioritized tasks. Each column starts out with a scenario, describes a task, and is followed by all the sub-tasks necessary to complete the task. The sub-tasks are color-coded and prioritized.

Courtesy of Todd   *Zaki Warfel, Principal Designer, messagefirst | design*

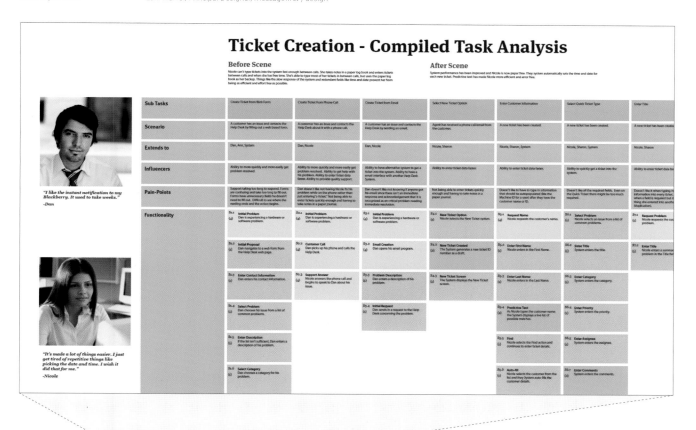

See also *20. Contextual Inquiry • 33. Ergonomic Analysis • 57. Observation*

85 Territory Maps

Territory maps are visual artifacts that represent the shared focus of the design team for anticipated design activities, including the identification of suggested stakeholders.[1]

The process of creating a territory map draws on the existing preconceptions and knowledge of design team members, with the contributions of each person recognized in a shared vision, visually expressed in a diagram. The simplicity of the visual diagram is deceptively powerful, representing an acknowledgement of individual perspectives in a consensus artifact around which the focus of design activities can be fostered and maintained. In this sense, the territory map is a boundary object, serving a critical role in building team dynamic and cohesiveness for collaborative work in design. The territory map need not force individual members to convert to the perspectives of others, but rather serves as an artifact of shared language for effective (and necessary) communication, thereby mediating the design conversation.

The territory map combines a speculative vision of the future as agreed upon by the team, including the key people who may be involved in the design landscape about to be explored. The territory map is therefore constructed early in the design process, during planning, scoping, and definition. This early creation is important in setting the stage for both team consensus and dialogue, and design focus. The model can also help drive ideas for project research.

While territory maps may be drafted in a single collaborative gathering of team members, a more common recommendation is for each member to consider their contributions first on their own, and then bring them together as a group. For example, each member takes time to consider the trends, themes, and ideas, and a list of people or stakeholders they deem important to the topic, along with anecdotal stories to provide context for their choices. These choices and stories are brought to the team as the building blocks of the territory map. From here the various perspectives can begin to be expressed in words and visuals, gradually crafting a diagram representing both individual and shared aspects of the design territory and future vision.

1. Pew, Richard, and Anne Mavor (Eds.). *Human-System Integration in the System Development Process: A New Look.* Committee on Human-System Design Support for Changing Technology. Washington, D.C.: National Academies Press, 2007.

2. Burke, Paul, Sue Nguyen, Pen-Fan Sun, Shelley Evenson, Jeong Kim, Laura Wright, Nabeel Ahmed, and Arjun Patel. "Writing the BoK: Designing for the Networked Learning Environment of College Students." *Proceedings of the 2005 conference on Designing for User Experience, DUX '05,* 2005.

Behavioral	Quantitative	Innovative	**Exploratory**	Participatory
Attitudinal	**Qualitative**	**Adapted**	Generative	Observational
		Traditional	Evaluative	Self reporting
				Expert review
				Design process

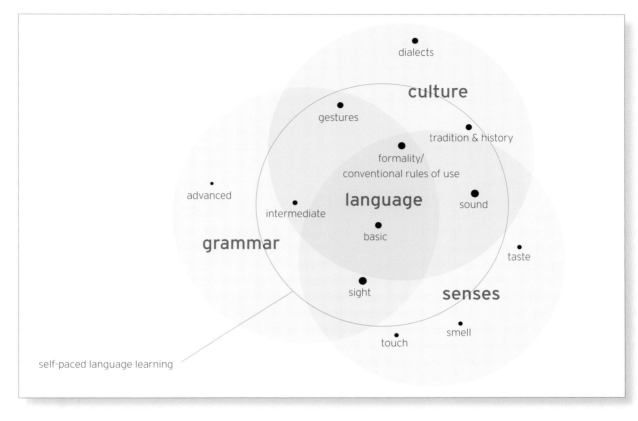

culture

• dialects

• gestures

• tradition & history

formality/
conventional rules of use

• advanced

• intermediate

language

• sound

grammar

• basic

• taste

• sight

senses

• smell

• touch

self-paced language learning

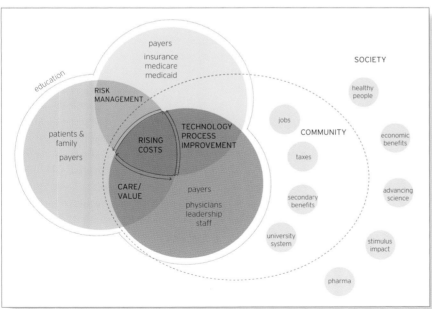

payers
insurance
medicare
medicaid

education

RISK
MANAGEMENT

patients &
family

payers

RISING
COSTS

TECHNOLOGY
PROCESS
IMPROVEMENT

CARE/
VALUE

payers
physicians
leadership
staff

SOCIETY

healthy
people

jobs

COMMUNITY

economic
benefits

taxes

secondary
benefits

advancing
science

university
system

stimulus
impact

pharma

Above: Territory map of the networked learning environments of college students.[2]

Courtesy of Paul Burke, Laura Wright, Nabeel Ahmad, Carnegie Mellon School of Design Masters Program 2005

Left: Territory map of the landscape of healthcare to determine how design solutions can streamline efficiencies.

Courtesy of Christina Payne Earle and Dave Passavant

See also 80. Stakeholder Maps

86 Thematic Networks

Building a thematic network is a step-by-step process that helps to identify, organize, and connect the most common themes in rich, qualitative data.[1]

Researchers have many well-established methods for recording and collecting rich, qualitative data. Equally as important as data collection methods are the methods for analyzing and synthesizing the information into meaningful, actionable design insight. Thematic network analysis provides a methodology that can help researchers work through the challenges of analyzing textual data using a formulaic, step-by-step methodology. The analysis technique serves to not only summarize the main themes constituting a piece of text,[2] but also organizes the information into a weblike illustration that can be used to communicate findings with stakeholders. Thematic networks have three classes of themes:

Basic Themes are text segments derived directly from the textual data, and they represent the most obvious concepts that recur within a text. Because basic themes are simple, they often cannot communicate anything meaningful when they stand on their own.[3] They need to be considered within the context of other basic themes to flesh out a fuller story. As they are combined and begin to illuminate one another, basic themes form organizing themes.

Organizing Themes are a middle-order theme, and they serve to organize basic themes into clusters of similar issues. As an organizing theme takes a group of basic themes under its umbrella, it also seeks to connect to other organizing themes so that together they can form a higher order premise. As separate organizing themes come together, they begin to take on an argument, position, or assertion about a given situation or reality.[4] The macro theme that emerges is the global theme.

Global Themes distill the overarching point of the text into a single statement, and are the most abstracted representations of the textual data. Global themes serve as a summary for the underlying text, and they articulate the deeper meaning and complexity of the data. The global theme can be seen as the heart of the thematic network, and it is through the identification of a global theme that a thematic network can be finalized.

Use thematic networks once the rich, textual data has been collected (e.g., from diary studies, directed storytelling, or interviews), and when you need a step-by-step method to help you tease out the challenges that come with analyzing textual data. The technique can help to systematically break down texts into simpler, manageable clusters of patterns and themes, and then help you to explore relationships between themes so that the most unifying message can be visualized.

1. Although several conceptual foundations influence the thematic networks analysis method, the earliest among the influences are the principles of argumentation theory See:

Toulmin, Stephen. *The Uses of Argument*. Cambridge: Cambridge University Press, 1958.

2. For a step-by-step guide for creating a thematic network. see:

Attride-Stirling, Jennifer. "Thematic Networks: An Analytic Tool for Qualitative Research." *Qualitative Research* 1, no. 3 (2001): 385-405.

3. See note 2 above.

4. See note 2 above.

Further Reading

Lee, Raymond M., and Nigel Fielding (Eds.). "Qualitative Data Analysis: Representations of a Technology: A Comment on Coffey, Holbrook and Atkinson." *Sociological Research Online* 1, no. 4 (1996).

Behavioral	Quantitative	Innovative	**Exploratory**	Participatory
Attitudinal	**Qualitative**	**Adapted**	Generative	Observational
		Traditional	Evaluative	Self reporting
				Expert review
				Design process

Participant Discussion Points

- children's basic needs must be met
- food as building blocks of health
- nutrition is essential
- beneficial
- psychological
- pressure
- motherly urge to nourish
- mutual mother/child well being
- bonding

- sense of accomplishment
- intrinsic motivation
- pleasure
- satisfaction
- peace of mind
- good mom/bad mom
- cooking is more time away from kids
- gender inequity in the home
- frustration

- domestic chores
- exhaustion
- obligation/duty
- guarantee of food quality
- work/life balance
- shopping decisions
- daily dinner decisions

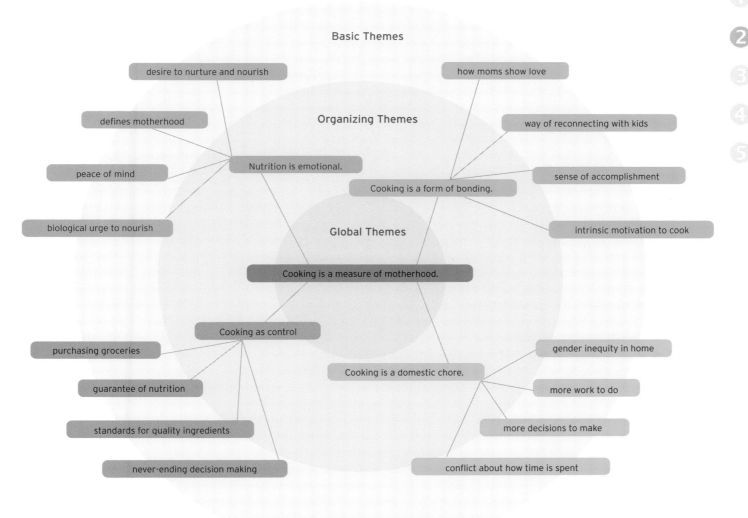

Basic Themes

Organizing Themes

Global Themes

desire to nurture and nourish

defines motherhood

peace of mind

biological urge to nourish

Nutrition is emotional.

how moms show love

way of reconnecting with kids

sense of accomplishment

Cooking is a form of bonding.

intrinsic motivation to cook

Cooking is a measure of motherhood.

purchasing groceries

guarantee of nutrition

standards for quality ingredients

never-ending decision making

Cooking as control

Cooking is a domestic chore.

gender inequity in home

more work to do

more decisions to make

conflict about how time is spent

See also 03. Affinity Diagramming • 17. Content Analysis • 39. Exploratory Research

87 Think-aloud Protocol

Think-aloud protocol is a method that requires participants to verbalize what they are doing and thinking as they complete a task, revealing aspects of an interface that delight, confuse, and frustrate.[1]

Think-aloud protocol is among the most common evaluative methods in the usability community. The protocol is straightforward—it asks people to articulate what they are thinking, doing, or feeling as they complete a set of tasks that align with their realistic day-to-day goals. As a cornerstone method of the usability profession, it affords researchers with a tried-and-true approach not only to see the process of task completion unfold, but also to identify the aspects of a digital or physical product that delight, confuse, and frustrate people so that they can be corrected or improved. There are two common experimental procedures for the think-aloud protocol:

Concurrent Think-aloud is the most common way to conduct the method. The participant works through tasks while articulating what he or she is doing, thinking, and feeling. Depending on a myriad of factors ranging from the participant's personality to task complexity, evaluators may have to repeatedly remind participants to verbalize what they are thinking as they work through a task. The focus of the test should be on *what* is happening, as opposed to *why*; people are reasonably able to speak about and complete a task at the same time without impacting the outcome of a task.[2]

Retrospective Think-aloud begins by asking participants to complete a task in silence (while their activity is recorded with video and/or a screen-capture device). Upon task completion, participants are invited to retrospectively comment on their processes as they watch a replay of their experience with a product or prototype. Retrospective think-alouds can provide additional insight into participant reasoning, intentions, and strategy.[3]

When planning a think-aloud session, rather than setting out to evaluate the usability of an entire product, focus efforts on evaluating aspects that can be tested independently—for instance, site navigation, or a single web form. Although the method is commonly conducted on either low- or high-fidelity prototypes, it can also be used to evaluate products already in the public domain such as competitor products or physical artifacts that require assembly (tents or children's toys), syncing (GPS or MP3 devices), or customization (smartphones or body analysis and weight scales). Video and audio recordings can then be referred back to as testimony of how tasks are actually completed, as opposed to how the organization assumes they should be completed—a necessary shift when embracing a human-centered design philosophy.

1. The think-aloud protocol was adapted for use in the Human Computer Interaction community and documented by Clayton Lewis, an IBM researcher in *Task-Centered User Interface Design: A Practical Introduction*. The purpose of the protocol is to help researchers understand what aspects of the interface people are processing as they attempt to complete a specific task. Also see:

Newell, Albert, and Herbert A. Simon. *Human Problem Solving*. Englewood Cliffs, N.J.: Prentice Hall, 1972.

2. Ericsson, Anders, and Herbert A. Simon. *Protocol Analysis: Verbal Reports as Data*, Revised ed. Cambridge, MA: MIT Press, 1993.

3. Guan, Zhiwei, Shirley Lee, Elisabeth Cuddihy, and Judith Ramey. "The Validity of Stimulated Retrospective Think-Aloud Method as Measured by Eye Tracking." *CHI 2006 Conference Proceedings*, 2006.

Further Reading

Dumas, Joseph S., and Janice C. Redish. *A Practical Guide to Usability Testing*. Exeter, England; Portland, OR: Intellect LTD, 1999.

Lewis, Clayton, and John Reiman. *Task-Centered User Interface Design: A Practical Introduction*. Boulder, CO: University of Boulder, Department of Computer Science, 1993.

Nielsen, Jakob. *Usability Engineering*. San Francisco, CA: Morgan Kaufmann, 1993.

Behavioral	Quantitative	Innovative	Exploratory	Participatory
Attitudinal	Qualitative	Adapted	Generative	Observational
		Traditional	Evaluative	Self reporting
				Expert review
				Design process

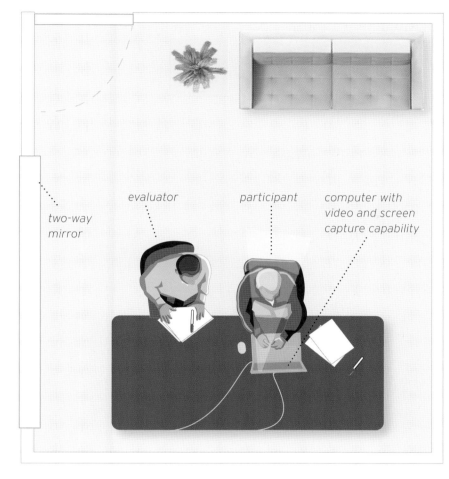

two-way
mirror

evaluator

participant

computer with
video and screen
capture capability

CONDUCTING A THINK-ALOUD

Evaluators should ask participants to verbalize anything that they think, feel, do, or look at while processing the interface—essentially, to "think aloud" as they complete tasks. Evaluators can either ask that participants express their problem-solving approaches out loud as they go about the tasks (concurrent think aloud), or to complete the test in silence, and then review a video with the evaluator and describe their approach after the tasks are completed (retrospective think aloud). Think-alouds can be conducted on a range of low-fidelity to high-fidelity prototypes.

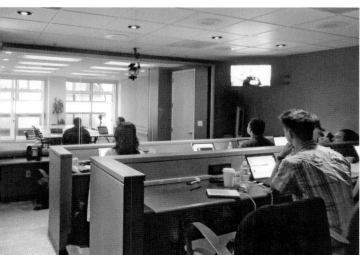

Courtesy of Eugene Eric Kim / Blue Oxen Associates

Courtesy of Kim Dowd

See also *29. Desirability Testing • 66. Prototyping • 94. Usability Testing*

88 Time-aware Research

Intercepting people at the precise moment they choose to complete a task provides keen insight into how they accomplish self-directed goals.

Time-aware research is a moderated, remote testing method that allows researchers to engage with a real person in real time, just as he or she is about to complete a task of interest to the research team. Whereas traditional usability testing methods require participants to travel to a location and then complete a task or set of tasks that are selected by researchers ahead of time, time-aware research happens "just in time" for the research team to observe a task of interest.

The main benefit of using the time-aware research method is its "live recruiting" of participants. Live recruiting intercepts potential participants at the moment that they set out to complete a self-directed task.[1] Also, time-aware research enables the usability test to occur within the context of an individual's native environment, or his or her "technological ecosystem."[2] During a traditional usability test, outside influences are factored out as part of the controlled lab setting. But with time-aware research, if the participant has to access information on other websites, search for information in an email, check his or her calendar, or contact a family member in order to complete the process on your site, that more realistic and less controlled process can be observed in real time with screen-sharing software. The rich user data that accompanies time-aware research tests cannot be duplicated in a lab, and potentially, the results of the research session more closely reflect actual user behavior.

The data collected from time-aware research is similar to the data that is collected during lab-based usability tests, and can be reported similarly. Inform your team members and stakeholders by creating three- to four-minute highlight videos, or a usability report, complete with insight into how the participants' technological ecosystem provides further perspective into user behavior.[3]

For time-aware research to be worth your time and money, aim to recruit around six qualified participants per hour. You can assume that around 1.5% to 2% of visitors who see the screener will complete it, and only a little over half of those will consent to being contacted. Of those, around 65% will be able to participate.[4] Given these estimates, if you enjoy the benefits of having 10,000 unique visitors per day, time-aware research can provide a steady stream of well-vetted recruits. Otherwise, if time-aware research is just one method in your company's ongoing usability strategy, or if you have time in your research schedule, it can still be a powerful addition to your research toolbox.

1. Bolt, Nate, and Tony Tulathimutte. *Remote Research: Real Users, Real Time, Real Research*. Brooklyn, NY: Rosenfeld Media, 2010.

2. See note 1 above.

3. See note 1 above.

4. See note 1 above.

Behavioral	Quantitative	**Innovative**	Exploratory	Participatory
Attitudinal	**Qualitative**	Adapted	Generative	**Observational**
		Traditional	**Evaluative**	**Self reporting**
				Expert review
				Design process

HOW "LIVE RECRUITING" WORKS USING TIME-AWARE RESEARCH

The first step is for the research team to identify an area of their site that they want to improve or better understand. Once identified, web forms and modal pop-up windows (known as the "recruiting screener") can be added to the flow of events of those sections. The purpose of the recruiting screener is to intercept end users as they begin self-directed tasks, and prompt them to sign up for the study. Once a participant qualifies for the research session, and provides the necessary consent to participate, the research session can begin right away.

See also 37. Experience Sampling Method • 69. Remote Moderated Research • 94. Usability Testing

89 Touchstone Tours

The guided tour is designed as a conversation that uses artifacts and the environment as touchstones for questions and insights.

The touchstone tour, or guided tour, is a contextual, empathic method that efficiently immerses the designer in a participant's world, to understand how he or she organizes information and systems through the use of space and cognitive artifacts. The participant is typically at ease in his or her own surroundings, and often enthusiastic about sharing his or her space and objects with an interested researcher. The conversation can be gently guided, but should be flexible enough to allow fluid departures based on highlights selected by the tour guide, and attentive observations by the researcher.

Touchstone tours can be of large environmental spaces, homes, or individual rooms, micro or mobile environments such as backpacks and purses, or even conducted in the digital realm, with the participant guiding the researcher through personal methods of computer desktop and file organization on electronic devices.

Touchstone tours should be thoroughly documented with video, photos, or sketches, and an accompanying transcript of the conversation. Video is ideal for capturing comprehensive and simultaneous visual and audio information, but may be labor-intensive for review and analysis. Photos provide an excellent record that can be easily sorted and annotated and sent to others for discussion and analysis. Sketches are a good method of recording when photos are not possible, and for documenting space layout or furniture arrangements. In all cases, careful notes or audio should be maintained to provide transcripts of the participant's descriptive language.

The outcome of touchstone tours may suggest general design implications, but it is largely an exploratory method for designers to establish baseline familiarity with a territory in early phase research.

Further Reading

For a discussion of cognitive artifacts used in the organization of workplaces, see:

Norman, Donald. "A Place for Everything, and Everything in its Place." *Things That Make Us Smart: Defending Human Attributes in the Age of the Machine.* New York: Basic Books, 1994: 155-168.

Behavioral	Quantitative	Innovative	Exploratory	Participatory
Attitudinal	Qualitative	Adapted	Generative	Observational
		Traditional	Evaluative	Self reporting
				Expert review
				Design process

A touchstone tour guided by a university prototyping shop supervisor highlights specialized tools and processes used in teaching and demonstration, for a design project investigating how to help bring knowledge professionals closer to the master and apprentice relationship.

Courtesy of Max Snyder

See also 04. *Artifact Analysis* • 20. *Contextual Inquiry* • 62. *Personal Inventories*

90 Triading

Triading is an interviewing technique that reveals deep-seated attitudes, perceptions, and feelings toward brands, products, and services.

Triading is a powerful interviewing technique that can be used to elicit constructs that people create in order to make sense of the world around them. George Kelly pioneered the method as a step in the *Repertory Grid* elicitation process, and its foundations are grounded in his *Personal Construct Theory.*[1] The Repertory Grid technique was designed specifically to extract participants' personal constructs while at the same time minimizing researcher bias and influence during interviews.

The process of triading first requires that either the researcher or the participant select six to ten concrete and related brands, products, or services from a particular domain. These examples—which are the stimuli of the study—should represent a range of options representative of the domain. Ideally, participants should be familiar with each of the examples prior to the session, as the purpose of the study is to elicit what is important and meaningful to them.

Once the six to ten examples/stimuli from the domain are selected, the researcher simply asks the participant to pick three of the examples (a triad) for discussion, and then asks the participant to explain how they feel two of the three examples differ from the third. In doing so, a construct that applies to all three examples—and that has meaning to the participant—is revealed. This process can be repeated as many times as necessary, each time with a new triad, and the goal is to elicit as many constructs about the domain that are important to the participant.

When this process is repeated with many participants, a wealth of data emerges about the domain, and it is expected that the constructs identified and ratings will vary from person to person. The diverse results are often both surprising and unrelated,[2] revealing insight that the design team could not have presumed to know prior to the research.

At first pass, the triading steps outlined above can seem overly simplistic, but structuring interviews this way provides researchers with a rigorous and reliable framework to capture people's deep-rooted sentiments and perceptions.[3] Triading can be effectively used when analyzing competitors and their products, and also when comparing different interface design options.[4] Ultimately, triading is a powerful interviewing technique that helps research and design teams to understand how products and services fit into people's existing personal constructs of the world.

1. George Kelly's personal construct theory posits that humans devise subjective classifications—personal constructs—in order to make sense of the world around us. To do this, we devise continuums, by which we rate and judge similar stimuli. The continuums provide us with a means to predict outcomes, and make meaning of new stimuli as it is introduced and tests our existing constructs. See George Kelly's two-volume opus:

Kelly, George. *The Psychology of Personal Constructs (Volumes 1 and 2).* New York: Norton, 1955.

2. Karapanos, Evangelos, Jean-Bernard Martens, and Marc Hassenzahl. "Accounting for Diversity in Subjective Judgments." *Proceedings of CHI 2009,* 2009.

3. Fransella, Fay, Richard Bell, and Don Bannister. *A Manual for Repertory Grid Technique.* Chichester, UK: Wiley, 2003.

Alexander, P. M., and J. J. Van Loggerenberg. "The Repertory Grid: 'Discovering' a 50-year-old Research Technique." *Proceedings to SAICSIT 2005,* 2005.

4. Hawley, Michael. "The Repertory Grid: Eliciting User Experience Comparisons in the Customer's Voice," 2007, www.uxmatters.com.

Behavioral	Quantitative	Innovative	**Exploratory**	Participatory
Attitudinal	**Qualitative**	Adapted	Generative	Observational
		Traditional	Evaluative	**Self reporting**
				Expert review
				Design process

Triading asks: "How do two of these examples differ from the third?"

91 Triangulation

Triangulation is the convergence of multiple methods on the same research question, to corroborate evidence from several different angles.[1]

The primary reason for triangulation is to ensure accuracy of information, by combining sources and mitigating the weaknesses of any single method or source. When collected using various means, data can be compared to confirm whether the same results are being obtained, regardless of method. This will either increase confidence in the results, or suggest a challenge to the design inquiry. The approach can also be used merely to collect more robust information than might be obtained using a single method. Depending on the variety of methods used, triangulation can result in a rich depth of information contributing to the inquiry from multiple data sets and formats.[2]

The most common occurrence of triangulation is to combine observational methods with self-report methods such as questionnaires or interviews. For example, self-reported behaviors could be compared to observations of actual behaviors. Often observations serve to verify self-reports. However, in cases where participants falsely portray their behaviors to align with policies, social norms, or research expectations, observations may reveal contrary evidence. Similarly, following the maxim "actions speak louder than words," self-reported attitudes or opinions may also be contradicted by behaviors. Other forms of triangulation may involve physiological recordings such as heart rate, pupil dilation, or Galvanic Skin Response (GSR) measures in combination with traditional interviews, questionnaires, and observations, comparing physical evidence with self-reports or visible behaviors.

Triangulation can be effective when comparing larger sets of data collection with more focused research using a select number of participants. For instance, it is common to pair a large survey with in-depth interviews, observations, or participatory design activities held with a small subset of the survey population, or similar constituents. Results of in-depth companion studies can provide supporting or contradictory evidence to support or challenge findings, or merely enrich the abstraction of survey results with more humane, anecdotal information collected through personal research interactions. The combination may also result in a healthy mix of quantitative and qualitative data, mutually informative to the same inquiry.

The triangulation of methods can be separated by time, or converged simultaneously. For example, in usability testing, concurrent recordings are typically made of keystroke/mouse or other input operations, facial expressions, and verbalized actions expressed through a think-aloud protocol.

1. "Once a proposition has been confirmed by two or more independent measurement processes, the uncertainty of its interpretation is greatly reduced. The most persuasive evidence comes through a triangulation of measurement processes." From:

Webb, E. J., D. T. Campbell, R. D. Schwartz, and L. Sechrest. *Unobtrusive Measures: Nonreactive Research in the Social Sciences.* Chicago, IL: Rand McNally, 1966. Revised ed., Thousand Oaks, CA: Sage Publications, 2000: 3.

2. Although methodological triangulation is most common, Denzin (2006) describes four different forms:

- *Data triangulation*, data gathered across a variety of times, situations, people.
- *Investigator triangulation*, multiple researchers to gather and interpret data.
- *Theoretical triangulation*, multiple theoretical positions in interpreting data.
- *Methodological triangulation*, multiple methods for gathering data.

From *Sociological Methods: A Sourcebook*, Edited by N. Denzin. New Brunswick, NJ: Aldine Transaction, 2006.

3. Darnell, Michael J. "How Do People Really Interact With TV? Naturalistic Observations of Digital TV and Digital Video Recorder Users." *ACM Computers in Entertainment* 5, no. 2. (August 2007).

Behavioral	Quantitative	Innovative	Exploratory	Participatory
Attitudinal	Qualitative	Adapted	Generative	Observational
		Traditional	Evaluative	Self reporting
				Expert review
				Design Process

1   OBSERVATION DATA:
    VIDEO CAPTURE

2   BEHAVIORAL DATA:
    RECORDED TV INTERACTIONS

3   SELF-REPORT DATA:
    INTERVIEWS

In a study of television watching conducted by Microsoft, cameras were set up in family living rooms to capture human behaviors, while a video feed recorded actual TV interactions such as channel surfing and ad skipping. These "naturalistic observations" were then used as memory triggers and evidence for review and analysis with participants during interviews, converging the methods to correlate behaviors, with TV content (ads, shows, promos) and events in the environment (conversations, phone calls).[3]

Courtesy of Mike Darnell, Microsoft Corporation.

92 Unobtrusive Measures

Unobtrusive methods are used to acquire information without direct contact with participants, through nonreactive physical traces, archives, and observations.

Unobtrusive and trace measures were proposed in the late 1960s in response to the inherent bias evident in self-report and direct-contact methods such as surveys and interviews.[1] The method uses physical evidence from events that have already occurred, archival records, and nonintrusive observations. The measures are designed to be flexible and creative, promoting the use of unusual data sources. They should be critically triangulated with other methods, not used in isolation.

Physical traces are measures made possible through physical evidence of use. Traces are characterized as *erosion measures*, evident through wear patterns or other subtractive factors, or *accretion measures*, evident as some form of deposit. The erosion of floors or grass can be used as an indication of preferred pedestrian traffic patterns; depth of the wear pattern may further suggest how well traveled the pathway is. Examples of accretion measures include litter, graffiti, makeshift signage to account for poor or absent directions, product modifications made by users suggesting shortcomings of a design, or fingerprints on an interface to indicate amount and patterns of use.

Archives are considered unobtrusive measures because as preexisting documents or records, they may be accessed for information without direct contact with participants. Archives of interest may include, for example, actuarial or court documents (births, marriages, divorces, deaths), mass media (newspapers, obituaries, magazines, websites), and sales, industrial, or institutional records. (receipts, library borrowing records, shipping records).

Observation can be an unobtrusive measure when the person being observed does not know he or she is being watched and the researcher has had no input in the structure of the situation, or when the researcher is viewing an event that was previously recorded.

Unobtrusive measures by their very nature involve sleuthing for clues without participant knowledge or informed consent. While most examples of this form of data collection are based on publicly accessible behaviors or records, the researcher needs to be cognizant of ethical boundaries. A limitation of the method may be a lack of details about who has contributed to the data being collected. However, as an informal method triangulated with other means of research, unobtrusive measures are an excellent source of design information.

Digital media has greatly expanded the possibilities for use of unobtrusive measures in research. Digital footprints provide trace indicators of technology use and qualities of social interaction and communication. For example, wireless network locations and the interesting names given to them can be collected and mapped using simple travel with cell phones or laptops.

1. Webb, E. J., D. T. Campbell, R. D. Schwartz, and L. Sechrest. *Unobtrusive Measures: Nonreactive Research in the Social Sciences.* Chicago, IL: Rand McNally, 1966. Revised edition, Thousand Oaks, CA: Sage Publications, 2000.

2. Kim, Miso, and Anne Iasella SanGiovanni. *Visualizing Pittsburgh Graffiti: Using Information Design to Create Awareness Between Community Members and Graffiti Writers* (unpublished Master's thesis). Carnegie Mellon University School of Design, 2004.

Behavioral	Quantitative	Innovative	Exploratory	Participatory
Attitudinal	**Qualitative**	**Adapted**	Generative	**Observational**
		Traditional	Evaluative	Self reporting
				Expert review
				Design process

Right: Unobtrusive trace erosion measures are wear-patterns, here seen in the "desire line" evident as a preferred pathway, and the location of new pavement informed by a previously worn path.

Courtesy of Ana Paula Alencar Rocha / yayaomo.tumblr

Above: Unobtrusive accretion trace measures include deposits such as graffiti and litter. For example, trace measures of graffiti were paired with other research methods for a project using information design and interactive tools to create awareness of the divergent viewpoints held by graffiti writers and community members.[2]

Photo by Cheryl L. G. Riedel, courtesy of Miso Kim

Above: Unobtrusive trace measures often provide evidence of needed design change, here indicated by temporary signage clarifying a misunderstood interface.

See also 04. Artifact Analysis • 42. Fly-on-the-Wall Observation • 74. Secondary Research

93 Usability Report

The usability report is informed by empirical evidence, helping teams decide whether a product is usable enough to release, or needs revision and further testing with more participants.

Usability reports have come a long way from the long-winded documents that still may come to mind for many non-usability professionals. Today's usability findings are often communicated interactively through the use of video, audio, online access to the protocol and discussion guides, and profiles of participants (including their demographics and psychographics) for the ongoing benefit of project stakeholders and the development team. The goal of a report, regardless of its format and delivery, is to clearly outline which parts of the user interface should be fixed or improved.

In an effort to facilitate the quick turnaround of the most findings, it is now common practice for the entire team to observe the usability tests as they occur, and discuss observations in the debriefing meetings that immediately follow the sessions, and then summarize decisions in emails, informal presentations, or interactive information repositories that includes the following:

Executive summary. Describe the most salient and serious usability problems first. If the report is meant to serve different audiences, provide a section tailored to the concerns of each group.

Total number of problems found. For each problem detected, it is important to include information regarding the frequency, impact, and persistence of usability problems.[1] Embedded videos, screenshots or interactive prototypes with callouts, and participant quotations should be included to anchor the problem to actual events.

The list of problems that will be fixed. It is tempting to fix the "low-hanging fruit," or the simplest issues, first. But the main objective is to identify, prioritize, and fix the most severe and persistent.

Reports on positive findings. The number of problems detected should be counter-balanced with a similar number of observed interactions that showed good usability. This tactic avoids depressing or insulting the team, and keeps them motivated to fix what is wrong.

Detailed task and scenario descriptions. Include all necessary information that shows tasks and scenarios are robust and representative enough to effectively get at a range of usability error types.

The time required to pull together the different parts of a report may vary depending on the number of tests, the number of tasks in each test, and the sophistication required of the report. When most of the people on an interdisciplinary team observe the sessions, the report can serve as an agreement on outcomes, instead of a static document that requires further decision-making. Over time, research findings should reveal trends in how your designs evolve based on feedback.

1. For recommendations on how to determine the severity ratings of usability problems, see www.useit.com.

Further Reading

Barnum, Carol. *Usability Testing Essentials: Ready, Set...Test!* San Francisco, CA: Morgan Kaufmann, 2010.

Molich, Rolf, Nigel Bevan, Ian Curson, Scott Butler, Erika Kindlund, Dana Miller, and Jurek Kirakowski. "Comparative Evaluation of Usability Tests." *CHI '99 Proceedings*, 1999.

Rubin, Jeffrey, and Dana Chisnell. *Handbook of Usability Testing: How to Plan, Design, and Conduct Effective Tests*. New York: Wiley, 2008.

Tullis, Tom, and Bill Albert. *Measuring the User Experience: Collecting, Analyzing, and Presenting Usability Metrics* (Interactive Technologies). San Francisco, CA: Morgan Kaufmann, 2008.

"The effectiveness of a report is inversely proportional to the thickness of its binding."
–Todd Wilkens, Adaptive Path

Behavioral	Quantitative	Innovative	Exploratory	Participatory
Attitudinal	Qualitative	Adapted	Generative	Observational
		Traditional	Evaluative	Self reporting
				Expert review
				Design process

EVOLUTION OF USABILITY REPORTS

Over the last two decades, opinions about the best way to deliver usability test results have evolved. Findings that were originally delivered in static, text-heavy reports quickly evolved into slide deck presentations, and from there, into prototypes that allowed stakeholders to "click through" tasks presented to participants.

Today's usability professionals continue to find ways to leverage technology to deliver interactive experiences—and User Insight, a user research firm in Atlanta, is at the forefront of evolving usability testing and reporting practices. Their proprietary platform called "Voice" aggregates all research documents and information—from discussion guides, participant information, research calendars, and testing artifacts—into a secure online repository for stakeholders to access at any time. By consolidating all research-related information in one place, User Insight can track how designs have evolved, how feedback has changed, and how the user experience has improved as a result of conducting usability tests and user research.

Courtesy of User Insight

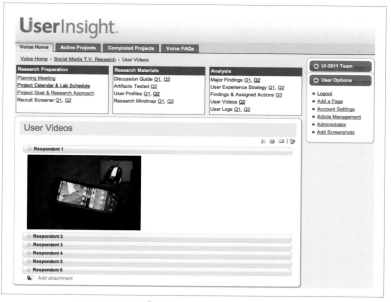

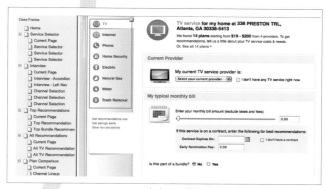

User Insight's *Voice* Delivery Platform

Interactive, clickable prototypes

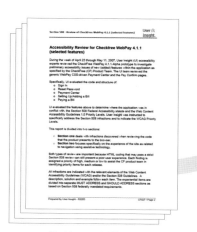

Static usability reports

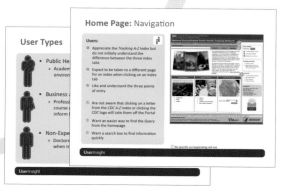

Slide deck presentations with callouts

Design Phase: ① ② ③ ④ ⑤

See also 69. Remote Moderated Research • 87. Think-aloud Protocol • 93. Usability Report

94 Usability Testing

Usability testing focuses on people and their tasks, and seeks empirical evidence about how to improve the usability of an interface.[1]

Usability testing is an evaluative method that allows teams to observe an individual's experience with a digital application as he or she walks through the steps of a given task (or set of tasks). The method is designed to help teams identify the parts of an interface that most regularly frustrate and confuse people so that they can be prioritized, fixed, and retested prior to launch.

Tests are designed around tasks and scenarios that represent typical end-user goals. It is common practice that everyone on the interdisciplinary team works together to identify usability testing tasks and scenarios. *Tasks* should be specific, concrete, and reflect actual goals of the target audience. *Scenarios* contextualize the task, and are written to provide extra information necessary to complete the task. Tasks and scenarios should neither influence the participant to solve a problem a certain way, nor seek to justify product requirements (which often reflect system or developer goals).

Usability tests typically follow the format of the Think-aloud Protocol technique. Some of the errors that observers and evaluators should try to detect include any instance where the participant:[2]

1. understands the task but can't complete it within a reasonable amount of time;

2. understands the goal, but has to try different approaches to complete the task;

3. gives up or resigns from the process;

4. completes a task, but not the task that was specified;

5. expresses surprise or delight;

6. expresses frustration, confusion, or blames themselves for not being able to complete the task;

7. asserts that something is wrong or doesn't make sense; or

8. makes a suggestion for the interface or the flow of events.

As usability tests reveal problems, the team will realize that how they evaluate and use the interface is different from how typical end users do.[3] Also, just as the number of participants in the test directly impacts the number of problems that are detected,[4] so do the number of evaluators—the more evaluators, the more problems will be detected.[5]

Aside from experiment validity, empiricism, and avoiding bias, the key to successful usability testing is to require the attendance of developers and project stakeholders at research events. Many teams are making the usability test observation session the only opportunity to see and weigh in on prototypes prior to launch. With this approach, you are guaranteed to have observers participate in the empirical testing process where they can observe and weigh in on usability problems firsthand.

1. Gould, John D., and Clayton Lewis. "Designing for Usability: Key Principles and What Designers Think." *Communications of the ACM* 28, no. 3 (1985): 300-311.

2. Jacobsen, Niels Ebbe, and Bonnie E. John. "The Evaluator Effect in Usability Studies: Problem Detection and Severity Judgments." *Proceeding of the Human Factors and Ergonomics Society 42nd Annual Meeting*, 1998.

3. Mack, Robert, Clayton H. Lewis, and John M. Carroll. "Learning to Use Word Processors: Problems and Prospects." *ACM Transactions on Information Systems* 1, no. 3 (1983): 254-271.

4. Virzi, Robert A. "Refining the Test Phase of Usability Evaluation: How Many Subjects is Enough?" *Human Factors* 34, no. 4 (1992): 457-468.

5. See note 2 above.

Further Reading

Barnum, Carol. *Usability Testing Essentials: Ready, Set...Test!* San Francisco, CA: Morgan Kaufmann, 2010.

Krug, Steve. *Don't Make Me Think, 2nd ed.* Berkeley, CA: New Riders Press, 2006.

Krug, Steve. *Rocket Surgery Made Easy.* Berkeley, CA: New Riders Press, 2010.

Behavioral	Quantitative	Innovative	Exploratory	Participatory
Attitudinal	Qualitative	Adapted	Generative	Observational
		Traditional	Evaluative	Self reporting
				Expert review
				Design process

Protocol design & pretest

Recruiting

Think-aloud protocol

Courtesy of John Welsh

Observation room

Courtesy of Nate Bolt, CEO, Bolt | Peters User Experience

Unlike attitudinal studies, behavioral experiments such as usability tests can be used with fewer participants to isolate enough problems to help teams confidently decide whether an interface needs to be revised, or is ready for release. When the testing process is included early in the process, over several rounds of testing the team will gain confidence in the usability of the interface as fewer problems are identified.

Design Phase: ① ② ③ ④ ⑤

See also 34. Evaluative Research • 81. Stakeholder Walkthrough • 87. Think-aloud Protocol

95 User Journey Maps

A user journey map is a visualization of the experiences people have when interacting with a product or service, so that each moment can be individually evaluated and improved.

A user journey map tells a story about an individual's actions, feelings, perceptions, and frame of mind—including the positive, negative, and neutral moments—as he or she interacts with a multi-channel product or service over a period of time. By documenting the series of events and interactions that a person experiences, the user journey map can shift an organization's focus from an operational, system-centered view to the larger context in which products and services are used in the real world. It also helps teams pinpoint distinct moments that elicit strong emotional reactions and are ripe for redesign and improvement. By creating discussions around which interactions are working optimally, which are insignificant, and which are failing altogether, the user journey map helps teams develop a shared vision about ways to more effectively augment existing user behavior within their actual contexts of use.

Solid user journey maps are usually created alongside, or immediately following, *personas* and *scenarios* documents. All three deliverables should be heavily informed by direct contact with the customers who use the product or service. Rich, qualitative data that is a result of primary research is the only way to be sure to craft deep, compelling narratives that reflect people's actual needs, feelings, and perceptions that occur before, during, and after product interactions. Each map should represent a journey specific to a persona, as well as include a description of the persona. For the benefit of the internal team, the map should also articulate the event it illustrates: this can be either an entire relationship life cycle, or can be limited to a specific scenario. The map should be an honest representation of an experience, and include moments of indecision, confusion, frustration, as well as delight and closure. Multiple maps will need to be created for multiple personas, as each persona will have different tasks and goals, and will experience different breakdowns and successes on their journey.

The early versions of the document can then serve as a springboard for discussion on the team. Print out an early version of the map on large-format paper, pin it up on a board, and hold a review session where everybody can get up close to the document and mark it up with questions, ideas, and suggestions for improvement. The hands-on, inclusive design activity that brings all decision makers together can go a long way in ensuring that the user journey map becomes a living document for the organization.

Further Reading

McInness, Andrew. "Assess The Effectiveness of Your Customer Journey Map." Forrester Research, 2010.

Browne, Jonathan. "Executive Q&A: Design Personas and Customer Journey Maps." Forrester Research, 2011.

Behavioral	Quantitative	Innovative	Exploratory	Participatory
Attitudinal	Qualitative	Adapted	Generative	Observational
		Traditional	Evaluative	Self reporting
				Expert review
				Design process

USER JOURNEY MAPS: A POP CASE STUDY

In 2010, POP, a Seattle-based digital agency, was engaged by Symetra Financial to craft a multi-year digital strategy centered on the Symetra.com website. Symetra's products—employee benefits, annuities, and life insurance—are somewhat intangible and are often perceived as complex. Due to the nature of the products, as well as regulatory requirements of the insurance industry, each product may have several similar variations available to different clients and demographics in different states.

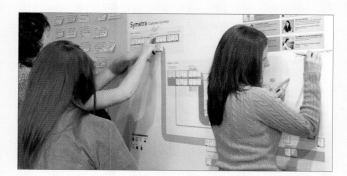

Symetra.com reflected this complexity, and it encouraged customers and sales representatives to rely heavily on person-to-person business consultation. Getting the right information to the right people, and presenting it in way that is clear, concise and builds trust was a tremendous challenge for Symetra.com.

POP conducted 35 phone interviews with Symetra customers and sales representatives as part of the project's research phase. Interviews resulted in the creation of six personas and journeys that reflected the diversity of Symetra's user base and online and offline behaviors. Through these deliverables, POP and Symetra were able to identify the types of content, features, and functionality that would effectively support each persona and provide greater workflow efficiencies via the refreshed website.

Courtesy of Symetra Financial

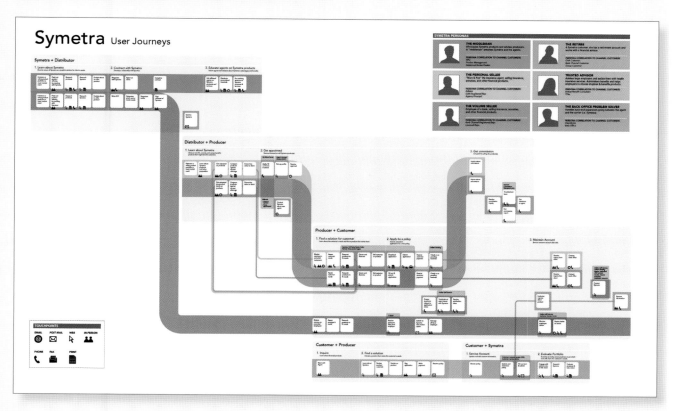

See also 25. Customer Experience Audit • 63. Personas • 73. Scenarios

96 Value Opportunity Analysis

Value opportunity analysis maps the extent to which a product's aspirational qualities align to people's idealized lifestyle or fantasy version of themselves.[1]

When the virtues associated with a product are meaningfully aligned with their values, customers are happy to pay a higher price for the perceived improvement that the product makes to their quality of life. Many of today's products, services, and systems are intentionally designed with aspirational qualities that help people connect to an idealized lifestyle. The connection between a product's attributes and the perceived improvement in one's lifestyle is derived from how we have come to define "value," and help us decide what products meet our definition of excellence.

A technique that can be used to identify the aspirational attributes in a product or service is the Value Opportunity Analysis (VOA). A VOA provides you with a list of value-based criteria, or value opportunities, that can help design teams consider the degree to which a product connects with an audience. The seven value opportunities (and their attributes) are:[2]

1. Emotion: *adventure, independence, security, sensuality, confidence, power*

2. Aesthetics: *visual, auditory, tactile, olfactory, taste*

3. Identity: *point in time, sense of place, personality*

4. Impact: *social, environmental*

5. Ergonomics: *comfort, safety, ease of use*

6. Core Technology: *reliable, enabling*

7. Quality: *craftsmanship, durability*

The VOA can be used to help the team consider the results from multiple angles:[3]

- **Competitive Review.** One of the best uses for the VOA is that it can be used to measure how your product stacks up to a competitor's product in terms of perceived value to the audience.

- **Market Analysis.** Use VOAs to assess the products in your category that are wild successes. Then, assess the failed products. What can you learn from them? Make recommendations that help you build off others' past successes, and avoid repeating the missteps.

- **Multiple Personas.** VOAs can be applied to a product from the points of view of several personas. The analysis can help you identify whether different user needs are being met.

A VOA exercise provides an opportunity for the team to come together to do the ratings, and it will often generate great discussion among members. However, it is critical that the design team and stakeholders who attend the exercise work from a place of deep understanding and empathy, grounded firmly in research, of what the user values and desires.

1. John Cagan and Craig Vogel introduce the value opportunity analysis for identifying product opportunities in their book *Creating Breakthrough Products*, Prentice Hall, 2002.

2. See note 1 above.

3. See note 1 above.

4. See note 1 above.

Behavioral	Quantitative	Innovative	Exploratory	Participatory
Attitudinal	Qualitative	Adapted	Generative	Observational
		Traditional	Evaluative	Self reporting
				Expert review
				Design process

198   Universal Methods of Design

To apply a VOA to a product, first list each value opportunity and its attributes in a column, and then rate each on a subjective scale of low, medium, and high. Depending on your product or service, you may find that some values may not apply to your product; in this situation, simply indicate that there is a "low" measure of success. No rating would indicate failure, or a mindful decision to not pursue the value attribute.[4] The example below shows a value opportunity analysis for child backpack carriers for hiking.

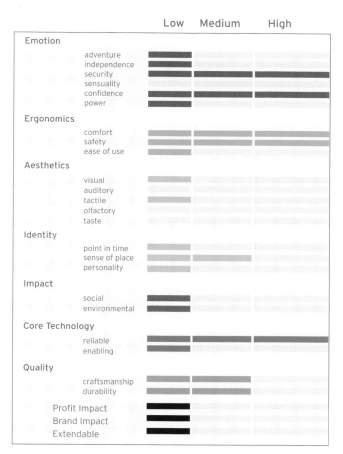

Traditional child backpack carrier for hiking VOA.

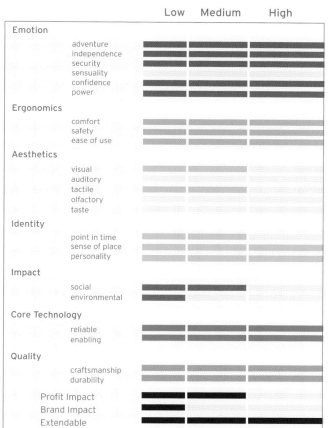

State-of-the-art child backpack carrier for hiking VOA.

See also 15. Competitive Testing • 29. Desirability Testing • 54. The Love Letter & the Breakup Letter

97 Web Analytics

Web analytics are a gateway for your organization to become deeply invested in what your customers are doing online, and why.

The Web Analytics Association defines web analytics as the "measurement, collection, analysis, and reporting of Internet data for the purposes of understanding and optimizing web usage."[1]

In theory, this definition rings true, but in practice, the truth for many organizations is that it's very difficult to gather the right analytics data and know what to do with all of it. The first steps to a successful web analytics discipline in your company are described as follows:[2]

First, you have to articulate what you want out of the data. Clearly, this is easier said than done, but expressing your goals and your clarity of intent for what you want to measure (and gaining consensus on them) should be done early in the process. Knowing where you want to go can help you to better structure your content, analyze your campaigns, segment your visitors, and measure your commerce and process tools.

Once you've determined the information you want to collect and optimized the way it is collected, it's time to translate all of the data into a report people will want to read. Keep reports short, avoid analytics jargon, and focus on visualizing as much data as you can.[3]

One reason why analytics projects fail within an organization is that reports aren't openly shared and their findings are not effectively communicated. Once you have reports, the focus must shift to the regular reporting and distribution of reports to internal stakeholders.

The next critical step is implementing and acting on the knowledge. All too often, either the reports are reviewed for information regarding "what just happened" as opposed to "what can I do now" and no actions are taken; or too many changes are implemented at once and there is no way to track which changes had an impact. When deciding on what changes to make, focus on the micro, not the macro. Small course corrections can have a big impact.

Finally, track the results of the small efforts, share the results, and refine as needed. Document what works well, and what doesn't work well, and avoid trying the same thing over and over again.

Whether analytics data is analyzed alone or combined with methods like *eyetracking*, *usability tests*, *A/B tests*, or *site search analytics*, web analytics can paint a broader, more realistic picture of what people are doing when visiting your site.

1. Web Analytics Association WAA

2. Peterson, Eric. *Web Analytics Demystified*, 2004, http://www.webanalyticsdemystified .com

3. Burby, Jason. *Three Reasons Analytics Fail Companies*, 2004, http://www.clickz.com

Further Reading

Kaushik, Avinash. *Web Analytics: An Hour a Day*. Indianapolis, IN: Sybex, 2007.

Kaushik, Avinash. *Web Analytics 2.0: The Art of Online Accountability and Science of Customer Centricity*. Indianapolis, IN: Sybex, 2009.

Peterson, Eric. *Web Site Measurement Hacks: Tips & Tools to Help Optimize Your Online Business*. Sebastopol, CA: O'Reilly, 2005.

Sterne, Jim. *Web Metrics: Proven Methods for Measuring Web Site Success*. New York: Wiley, 2002.

The Portland, Oregon, firm Webtrends made the first commercially available web analytics program in 1995. Also in 1995, Dr. Stephen Turner from Cambridge, UK, created *Analog*, a free log file analyzer.

Behavioral	Quantitative	Innovative	Exploratory	Participatory
Attitudinal	Qualitative	Adapted	Generative	Observational
		Traditional	Evaluative	Self reporting
				Expert review
				Design process

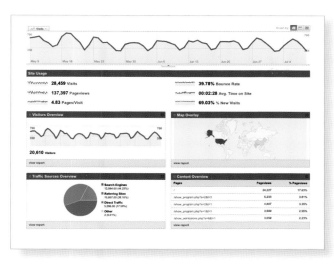

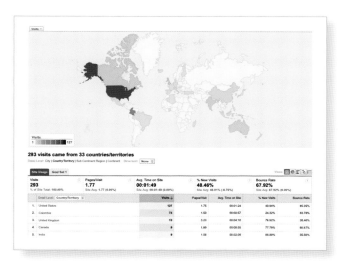

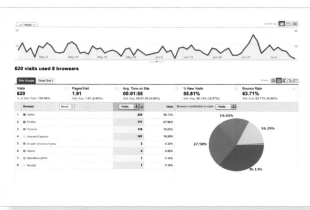

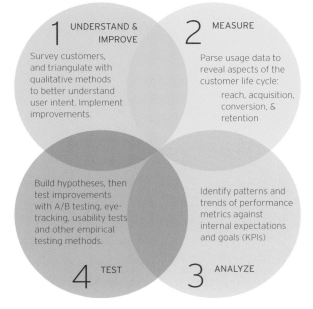

Courtesy of Carnegie Mellon University School of Design

The best web analysts will understand your business and the web in equal measures, and use tools such as Google Analytics, above, to make recommendations for corrective measures. They can help you decide the best way to segment your data including by source (or referrer), by behavior (by what users are doing), and outcome (what goals were met).

1 UNDERSTAND & IMPROVE
Survey customers, and triangulate with qualitative methods to better understand user intent. Implement improvements.

2 MEASURE
Parse usage data to reveal aspects of the customer life cycle: reach, acquisition, conversion, & retention

4 TEST
Build hypotheses, then test improvements with A/B testing, eye-tracking, usability tests and other empirical testing methods.

3 ANALYZE
Identify patterns and trends of performance metrics against internal expectations and goals (KPIs)

See also 01. A/B Testing • 51. Key Performance Indicators • 78. Site Search Analytics

Design Phase:

98 Weighted Matrix

Once your team has generated multiple design concepts, a weighted matrix can help identify and prioritize the most promising opportunities.[1]

The team has done the heavy lifting required of them in the early phases of the design process, and all of the work has inspired a range of promising early design ideas. Sketches and early prototypes are generating lively discussions among team members about which concepts are most likely to connect with the user, and fill the product opportunity gaps in the marketplace.

However, there are times when the sheer number of design options created early in the process can create uncertainty among team members (and for those new to the design process, can even cause a bit of distress). Enter the weighted matrix, which can be used as a method to help you manage a growing number of potential design ideas. The use of this analysis technique creates a forum for shared decision making, and can help overcome the common biases on multidisciplinary teams. The conversations it generates among team members can be equally as useful as its results.

The concept behind the weighted matrix is simple but powerful: essentially, the matrix ranks potential design opportunities against key success criteria. The "criteria" of the weighted matrix represents the primary measures of product success rated on a scale, as defined by the product team and organizational stakeholders. A listing of "opportunities" represents the design ideas that elicit the most serious interest from the team. Together, the matrix can be used to bring the number of ideas down to a more manageable number of about a dozen.[2]

Once there is agreement on the recommended list that comes out of the weighted matrix exercise, it's time for another creative "deep dive," that is now refocused on these agreed-upon design ideas. Results of a weighted matrix shouldn't be used definitively, as the process of narrowing down the list of potential design ideas is still very subjective and qualitative.[3] Its power, however, is in the way it provides a structured process for conversations to happen on the team, and shifting decision-making to a process that is grounded in success criteria, not personal opinions.

1. John Cagan and Craig Vogel introduce the weighted matrix for identifying product opportunities in their book, *Creating Breakthrough Products*, Prentice Hall, 2002.

2. See note 1 above.

3. See note 1 above.

Behavioral   Quantitative   Innovative   Exploratory   Participatory
Attitudinal   Qualitative   Adapted   Generative   Observational
   Traditional   Evaluative   Self reporting
   Expert review
   Design process

BUSINESS CRITERA	WEIGHT	Cargo Organizers	Non-car Accessories	Travel Accessories	Mobilizing Medical Devices	Child Transport
Within Our Companies' Expertise	3	2	3	3	2	2
User Experience	3	2	2	1	3	3
Potential Market Size	2	2	2	3	1	2
Potential for Market Differentiation	2	1	1	2	2	3
Industry Recognition	1	1	1	2	3	3
TOTALS		19	22	24	24	(28)

Ideas that *align* with the brand of a leading cargo and rack system manufacturer

BUSINESS CRITERA	WEIGHT	Work Benches	Garage Storage	Rugged Mobility Devices
Within Our Companies' Expertise	3	3	3	2
User Experience	3	2	3	2
Potential Market Size	2	1	3	1
Potential for Market Differentiation	2	1	2	2
Industry Recognition	1	1	2	3
TOTALS		20	(30)	21

Ideas that *extend* the brand of a leading cargo and rack system manufacturer

WHEN TO USE A WEIGHTED MATRIX

Once there are enough potential ideas generated, there comes a time to focus on the few that hold the most promise. A weighted matrix provides a way to manage potential design options by evaluating each design opportunity against business criteria (as opposed to personal preferences).

See also 26. Design Charette • 49. KJ Technique • 58. Parallel Prototyping

99 Wizard of Oz

In the Wizard of Oz technique, a researcher (the "wizard") simulates system responses from behind the scenes, while a participant engages with a system that appears to be real.

The Wizard of Oz (WOz) technique is a method in which participants are led to believe they are interacting with a working prototype of a system, but in reality, a researcher is acting as a proxy for the system from behind the scenes. Unseen by the participant, the researcher (i.e., the "wizard") is able to intercept and shape the interaction between the participant and the "system," without having an actual system up and running. The goal of the method is to allow the user to experience a proposed product or interface before costly prototypes are built. It also provides a framework to gauge participants' openness and willingness to new ways of doing things, and to explore and discover boundary conditions for innovative and disruptive technologies.[1]

The research session setup requires that the participant be in one location, and the researcher who plays the "wizard" in another. To aid in the process of preparing an appropriate, timely system response, the researcher must be able to observe participant activity (either through video or screen-sharing software). In the early design phases, the wizard will simulate the majority of the behaviors of the system, and the insights gathered can guide and inform the design toward forma-tive ends. As iterative improvements are made to the interface, less and less intervention from the researcher/wizard is required—usually just enough to keep the process moving and bridge the gap between what the current implementation actually provides, and the envisioned system.[2]

During the process, the wizard can take on different roles and simulate different behaviors, includ-ing: the *controller* who simulates system intelligence, the *supervisor* who course-corrects and overrides decisions that the system or participant makes, and the *moderator* who simulates sensory data and makes the envisioned experience feel complete.[3] However, the believability of the simula-tions hinge on the wizard's consistent behaviors with respect to timing, patterns, and system logic.[4]

Consider using the WOz technique anytime you need to gauge how people will feel about—and how they might perform while using—a proposed solution before investing time and money in an actual prototype. WOz is especially useful when designing digital applications and solutions that do not already have established design patterns (e.g., augmented reality systems, and ubiquitous comput-ing applications). The method is a flexible, iterative technique that can be used to guide and lead design efforts (formative) in the exploratory, conceptual phases of a project as well as toward the latter phases, when conclusive, measurable (summative) ends are more appropriate.

1. John F. "Jeff" Kelly from the IBM Thomas J. Watson Research Center originally coined the "OZ Paradigm" in 1980, to describe the methodology he developed while completing his dissertation at The Johns Hopkins University. As it gained popularity in the fields of Human Factors, Experimental Psychology, and Usability Engineering, the name of the method changed to reflect the 1939 MGM movie *The Wizard of Oz*, in which an ordinary man hides behind a curtain, and uses technology to convince everyone he is an omnipotent wizard. See:

Kelly, John F. "An Iterative Design Methodology for User-Friendly Natural Language Office Information Applications." *ACM Transactions on Office Information Systems* 2, no. 1 (1984): 26-41.

2. See note 1 above.

Dow, Steven, Blair MacIntyre, Jaemin Lee, Christopher Oezbek, Jay David Bolter, and Maribeth Gandy. "Wizard of Oz Support Throughout an Iterative Design Process." *Pervasive Computing* (October-December 2005): 18-26.

3. See note 2 above

4. See note 1 above.

5. Patel, Seema, et. al. "A Guided Performance Interface for Augmenting Social Experiences with an Interactive Animatronic Character" *Proceedings of 2006 American Association for Artificial Intelligence*, 2006.

Further Reading

Buxton, Bill. *Sketching User Interfaces: Getting the Right Design and the Design Right.* San Francisco, CA: Morgan Kaufmann, 2007.

Gould, John D., John Conti, and Todd Hov-anyecz. "Composing Letters with a Simulated Listening Typewriter." *Communications of the ACM* 26, no. 4 (1983): 295-308.

Behavioral	Quantitative	Innovative	Exploratory	Participatory
Attitudinal	Qualitative	Adapted	Generative	Observational
		Traditional	Evaluative	Self reporting
				Expert review
				Design process

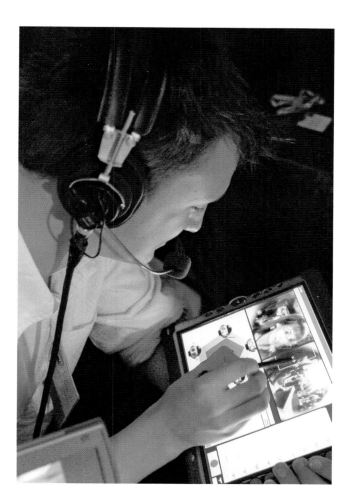

Quasi's Guided Performace Interface

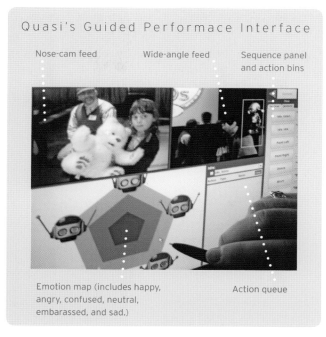

Nose-cam feed   Wide-angle feed   Sequence panel
                                            and action bins

Emotion map (includes happy,   Action queue
angry, confused, neutral,
embarassed, and sad.)

Thousands of people have had compelling interactions with the animatronic character Quasi the Robot without knowing that behind the scenes, a human actor controls the robot through a Guided Performance Interface (GPI). The interface allows non-technologists to guide Quasi's performance, and engage and captivate people (especially children) for prolonged periods of time. Quasi is an exciting example of robotics that combines artificial intelligence and human teleoperation into a believable, engaging, and delightful experience.[5]

Photos by Peter Stepniewicz, courtesy of Interbots, LLC

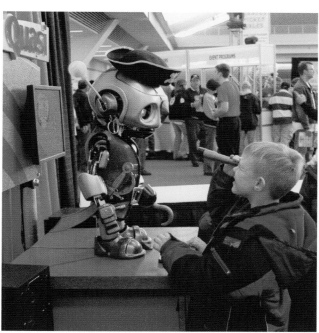

See also 36. Experience Prototyping • 68. Rapid Iterative Testing & Evaluation • 79. Speed Dating

100 Word Clouds

Word clouds are a method of information visualization that organizes text-based content into interesting spatial arrangements.[1]

Word clouds are "colorful word collages"[2] that show the most frequently used words or word pairs in just about any text-based source document. In a word cloud, words are assigned different font sizes based on word frequency—usually, the bigger the word, the more frequently it occurs in the source document. As a visual summary of the textual data, the word cloud serves a function akin to a table of contents for a book—it provides the reader with enough information to form a general impression of what the content is about, before the reader actually engages in a deep read of the content itself.[3]

Word clouds are visually engaging because of the various dimensions that they employ: typeface, font size, font color (or color palette), the number of words included in a cloud, word proximity, and word orientation. With so much visual variation, there is a sense of "discovery" that the image can impart as the reader processes it. However, the characteristics that make word clouds visually compelling are the same attributes that make it easy for readers to develop misleading impressions of the underlying data. These disparities can distort the actual message in the textual data, and there is a chance that salient information could be misinterpreted or missed altogether.

The decision to use word clouds has to strike a balance between the desire to create an engaging visual with the need to accurately represent rich, qualitative data. Word clouds should be qualified with the following information: A) where the data came from and details about the methods through which it was collected; B) what the typefaces, colors, sizes, overall shape mean (if anything); and C) disclosure of whether there has been any data scrubbing or segmenting.

Once properly qualified, word clouds can serve as helpful, *communicative artifacts*[4] for design teams. They can be used when archiving transcripts; the visual markers of each cloud create a *gestalt* unique to each transcript and can facilitate in its recall. During a presentation of research findings, word clouds can also be a lighthearted way to engage stakeholders and invite discussion about the *gist* of the transcripts before delving into more rigorous analysis techniques and findings. As with all visual representations of research data, the goal of using word clouds should be to clarify and highlight what is there, and avoid introducing misleading or misrepresenting information.[5] When used with care, word clouds can serve as a gateway to understanding deep, rich qualitative, text-based data.

1. Word clouds are adapted from tag clouds, which have been traditionally used on social bookmarking sites for both navigation and visualization of common and popular terms. Word clouds decouple navigation from the visual representation of words, and are being used to explore options of typography, white space, color, and arrangement based on a large set of text-based data. Websites http://www.wordle.net and http://www-958.ibm.com provide the ability to create word clouds, and other text-based data visualizations. See:

Feinberg, Jonathan. "Wordle" in *Beautiful Visualization: Looking at Data through the Eyes of Experts*. Beijing; Sebastopol, CA: O'Reilly, 2010.

2. See note 1 above.

3. Rivadeneira, A. W., Daniel Gruen, Michael Muller, and David Millen. "Getting our Head in the Clouds: Toward Evaluation Studies of Tagclouds." *Proceedings of CHI*, 2007.

4. See note 1 above.

5. See note 3 above.

Further Reading

Arnheim, Rudolf. *Visual Thinking*. Berkeley, CA: University of California Press, 1969

Donath, Judith S. "A Semantic Approach to Visualizing Online Conversations." *Communications of the ACM* 45, no. 4 (2002): 45-49.

Behavioral	Quantitative	Innovative	Exploratory	Participatory
Attitudinal	Qualitative	Adapted	Generative	Observational
		Traditional	Evaluative	Self reporting
				Expert review
				Design process

From interviews of mothers with picky eaters.

From interviews of fathers with picky eaters.

When interview transcripts are segmented based on meaningful criteria, the word cloud that is subsequently generated can reveal potentially insightful and surprising themes. Shown here are word clouds generated from interviews with parents of picky eaters segmented by mothers and fathers, and a combined transcript. As with all text-based, qualitative research data, more rigorous content analysis should occur so as to avoid misrepresenting the underlying text-based data.

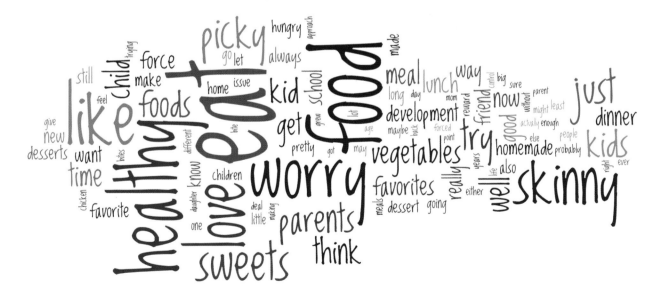

Combined transcripts of all parents with picky eaters.

See also *17. Content Analysis* • *39. Exploratory Research* • *48. Interviews*

Acknowledgments

The countless contributors that made this book possible are noted throughout these pages, on attributions for images and case studies, in captions and citations. However, this only tells half the story. Our debt of gratitude is extended beyond these words to our many colleagues, students, and friends who so willingly gave of their time, efforts, and materials, particularly in the form of case studies and project images to help us tell compelling stories of design research through concrete, realistic, visual examples. The companies represented here are outstanding, but the individuals responsible for making corporate contributions materialize for us are true angels. The faculty, students, and alumni of the School of Design and the Human Computer Interaction Institute at Carnegie Mellon deserve special recognition, for their incredible dedication to the quality of their work, which they so enthusiastically shared with us for this project.

Remarkably, the balance of our deepest thanks for contributions goes not to people we knew we could count on, but to strangers we imposed upon after being captivated by their work in papers and books, at conferences, and online, meeting only virtually through websites, twitter, flickr, email, phone, and skype calls. That these people were so willing to contribute to a book merely described to them, by authors they did not know, is a testament not only to the strength of the design community, but to the shared motivation to see good research actively promoted and published in our field. And to those from well outside the design community whom we tapped for contributions, we hope that you feel welcomed and recognized by the good company you keep in this book, and that your presence among us incites your own personal curiosity about what we do in design.

Our thanks to the crew at Rockport, who despite our steep learning curve in the publishing process, were ultimately patient with us and saw this project through to the beautiful result we envisioned, but could only realize with their support.

And finally, one person we simply must mention by name is Will Lidwell, co-author of *Universal Principles of Design,* our favorite book and inspiration for our own. Thank you Will, for your enthusiastic support of our idea, and for being our advocate when introducing us to Rockport.

About the Authors

Bruce Hanington is an associate professor, director of graduate studies, and former program chair of industrial design in the School of Design at Carnegie Mellon University in Pittsburgh, Pennsylvania. He has dedicated his teaching and research to methods and practices for human centered design, with an emphasis on design ethnography, participatory design, and the meaning of form in context. He has consulted on design projects with GE Appliance and Johnson & Johnson, and his work has been published in *Design Issues, The Design Journal,* and *Interactions,* with chapters in *Designing Inclusive Futures* and *Design and Emotion: The Experience of Everyday Things.*

Bella Martin is a design practitioner and independent user experience consultant. After contributing to award-winning design projects for Microsoft Research, the U.S. Postal Service, GlaxoSmithKline and Allstate Financial, she now invests much of her time consulting for organizations who are new to the methods of user-centered research, but eager to give their users a voice in the design process. Bella holds a Master of Design in Communication Planning and Information Design from Carnegie Mellon University, where she first began her ongoing work in visualizing user-centered research methods. She lives in Atlanta, Georgia.